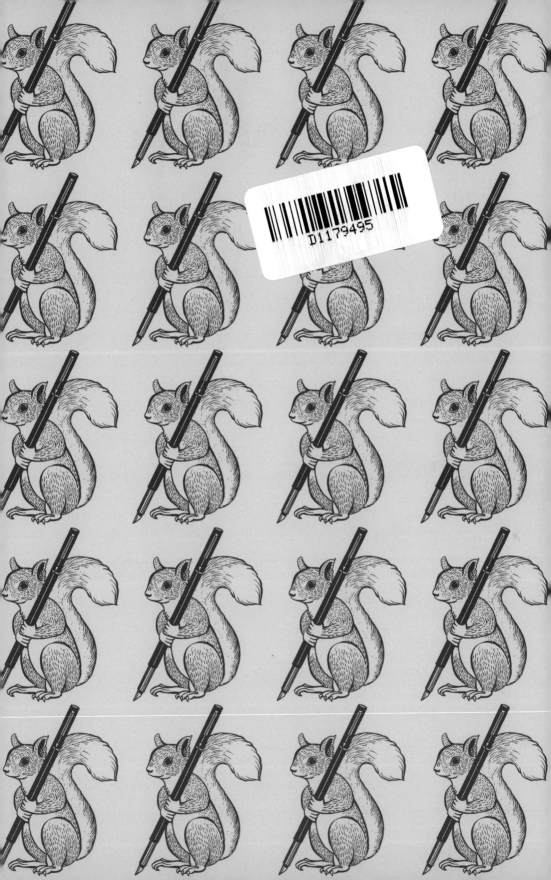

ALASDAIR GRAY

PORTRAIT
OF LANARK
AUTHOR IN
MEDIAS RES
CIRCA 1967

Man is the lie that forces & eats its self
& the result is squatter.

ALASDAIR GRAY

Critical Appreciations and a Bibliography

Edited by Phil Moores

THE BRITISH LIBRARY
Boston Spa & London   2002

First published by the British Library in May 2002

© The British Library 2002
© Alasdair Gray 2002
© Jonathan Coe 2002

Illustrations: © Alasdair Gray 2002

ISBN 0 7123 1129 7 (trade edition)
ISBN 0 7123 1134 3 (signed edition)

Series Editor: AE Cunningham

Printed in Great Britain by St Edmundsbury Press

For Kate

CONTENTS

EDITOR'S PREFACE

PHIL MOORES

THIS IS NOT AN AGE OF GREAT WRITERS; THIS IS NOT AN AGE OF great anything. We do not seem to like 'great' people in general; they set a standard too difficult to live up to, and comparisons are demoralising. It is much easier to focus on their faults than that which sets them apart. Nowadays we are happier with celebrities rather than heroes, and the contents of their homes are more interesting than the content of their minds. The whole thing probably started when Lytton Strachey duffed up Florence Nightingale. The rich, famous, gifted and driven have to be within reach, so that we can say: 'I could have done that, I just never bothered'. But Alasdair Gray *is* someone special; in Will Self's words, 'a creative polymath with an integrated politico-philosophic vision'.

Gray's influence upon British writing in general, and Scottish writing in particular, is significant. In an age of small-scale novels of manners, he is writing huge state-of-the-nation addresses that deal with love, politics, war, death, childhood, religion and disease, sometimes all at once. We need writers who can embrace such grand themes – the 'great American novel', but produced on our own doorstep. Books such as *1982, Janine* display his ability to link relationships on a personal level with politics at large, without hectoring or pontificating – a rare trait in twentieth-century writing. We should also praise writers who assume that their readers are taking an active intellectual part in the process, grown-ups well capable of knowing that they are reading a book rather than living somebody's life through the written word. The ease with which Gray plays with the form of the book and the novel, while never experimenting for the mere sake of it, is impressive: typographical games, mock erratum slips, an index of plagiarisms and professorial notation all engage the reader in an interchange, sometimes playful, sometimes dramatic, but without ever distancing them from the emotional story they are being told. Writers *should* take such risks, but few do. Perhaps the biggest risk of all, however, is to portray aspects of oneself and one's own psyche of which one is not completely proud. There is obviously a great deal of Gray in many of his main characters, so it is easy to take this too far and view them as entire self-portraits. Gray must know that his readers might do this, but does not shy away from sometimes giving these characters shameful attributes.

The British Library's *Critical Appreciations* series offers the opportunity for scholarly (but not densely academic) appreciations of living authors, keenly appreciated by those who know them but perhaps not known widely enough. It seemed an appropriate forum for a book such as this. Many of the contributions are written by friends of Alasdair Gray. This is a reflection both of the degree to which he has been part of Scottish literary life and of the high regard in which he is held by his fellow writers and artists. If their essays, spiced with personal recollection, kindle a desire to read or re-read the work of Alasdair Gray, this book will have achieved its purpose. There is no doubt that the great critical works that will ultimately place Gray in what is left of a literary canon will appear in due course. In the meantime, this book offers approachable well-written essays that will be of great interest to all those who take pleasure in his work, together with a fine selection of his art. This volume benefits from Gray's book design skills and his auto-biographical contribution, but he has had no editorial role.

So what is the reader offered in this collection? Kevin Williamson (founding editor of Scottish publisher Rebel Inc) and novelists Jonathan Coe and Will Self, write about the influence of Alasdair Gray. **Will Self** writes an introduction unlike any of the other contributions, in which he puts his case for Gray as one of Britain's most important living writers. **Jonathan Coe** provides a very personal view of his discovery of *1982, Janine* amidst what he saw as a desert of modern literary fiction and how it encouraged him to write. **Kevin Williamson** looks at Scotland in the early 1980s, places *Lanark* and *1982, Janine* in a personal context and makes links between the explosion of 'Scot-lit' in the 1990s with the work produced by the likes of Gray, James Kelman and Liz Lochhead ten years earlier. S. B. Kelly and Elspeth King make detailed studies of two neglected areas of Alasdair Gray's output: his poetry and his artwork. **Stuart Kelly** takes the *Old Negatives* and *16 Occasional Poems* collections and takes you through them poem by poem, drawing a narrative of growth and development through the poems that can take you back to the fiction with a fresh eye. **Elspeth King** has employed Gray as both Official Artist Recorder for Glasgow's People's Palace and to paint a ceiling mural for the Abbots Hall museum and is also one of his close friends, she brings great warmth to her essay upon Gray's artworks, making a case that his success as a writer has led to him being unfairly regarded as a dabbler in the world of art, rather than the fine artist he is in his own right. **Angus Calder** has worked with Gray upon *The Book of Prefaces* and is an authority on Scotland's cultural history, he is therefore well-placed to write upon the unusually benign and well-meaning small-n nationalism that pervades all of Gray's non-fiction. Professors Philip Hobsbaum and Stephen Bernstein offer exemplary academic readings of Gray's fiction. **Philip Hobsbaum** looks at one distinctive aspect of Gray's writing: the easy way that he makes the common-place magical and the fantastical common-place. **Stephen Bernstein** studies Gray's 'minor' novels and makes an interesting distinction between these books and the major works (*Lanark, 1982, Janine* and *Poor Things*): namely that the minor novels involve the main character ruining their life by 'doing to others as they've been done to themselves'. In addition to these original essays, **Alasdair Gray** has contributed an annotated up-to-date CV of his life and works and an interview he did with Kathy Acker in 1986, which taken together give an insight into Gray's influences, biography and methods of working.

Before beginning work on this volume, my path had only crossed the once with Alasdair's. He came to Leeds to sign copies of *Poor Things*.

After the readings, I plucked up the courage to ask him about the references within *Lanark*'s index of plagiarisms to many chapters that weren't actually in the book. He told the audience how he had not wanted his friends to feel left out, so created non-existent plagiarisms just for them. I had taken a rucksack full of books for him to sign and, while making small-talk as he wrote, I happened to mention Flann O'Brien. Alasdair was straight to his feet, leaning against a handy bookcase and doing his best impersonation of a man who was more than half a bicycle (read *The Third Policeman* and all will be explained).

A year or so later, I sent him some pages from a novel rejected by every agent and publisher who saw it. I regretted doing it as soon as I put it in the pillar-box, but in times of weakness we do peculiar things. Three weeks later, I got the following reply:

> Dear Mr Moores,
>
> Thank you for your letter and enclosure of the 4 July 1995. I am sorry to tell you that I am a selfishly greedy old fart who is too interested in his own work to be useful to other writers and other people. Please tell this to anyone you know who is interested. Please also accept the copyright of this letter as a gift, in case you wish to reproduce it elsewhere.
>
> Yours faithfully
>
> Alasdair Gray

Any editor setting out on a work such as this worries that he may not find enough contributors willing and able to undertake the task. In this instance, nearly everyone I approached agreed to be involved. I should not really have expected otherwise. It is the effect Alasdair Gray has on those who know him – witness the pantheon of literary and academic stars who worked for and with him to finish *The Book of Prefaces*. He has, it seems, a great many friends. And this, I feel, is of far more importance to him than any number of books such as this, or wrestling at the top of the bestseller charts with J. K. Rowling and Stephen King. Perhaps that is the most admirable thing about him of all.

March 2002
Yorkshire

INTRODUCTION

WILL SELF

A LETTER ARRIVES FROM PHIL MOORES WHOSE ADDRESS IS listed as follows: British Library, Boston Spa, Wetherby, West Yorkshire. He encloses a selection of essays about the work of the Scottish novelist, artist, poet and politico-philosophic *éminence grise*, Alasdair Gray. You are holding this book in your hand so you know what those essays are, but picture to yourself (and let it be a Gray illustration, all firm, flowing pen-and-ink lines, precise adumbration, colour – if at all – in smooth, monochrome blocks), my own investigation of these enclosures.

> **Detail 1:** I sit, islanded in light from a globular steel reading lamp of fifties vintage. Around me on the purple-black floorboards are sheaves of paper, my brow is furrowed, my chin is tripled, my fingers play a chord upon my cheek.

> **Detail 2:** I go to my spare bedroom and retrieve the copy of Gray's novel *Something Leather*, that the author gave me himself. (At that time, the early nineties, Gray carried a small rucksack full of his own titles, which he offered for sale at readings. Mine is inscribed: 'To Will Self, in memory of our outing to Cardiff'. We went to

1

Wales by train from London, with an American performance poet called Peter Plate. My wife tells me that Plate usually likes to pack a gun, but alas, in Cardiff this was not possible. The hotel was glutinously rendered and fusty in the extreme. There may well have been diamond patterned mullions. After the three of us had given a reading – of which I remember little, saving that a Welsh poet gave me a copy of his self-published collection *The Stuff of Love*, good title that – Plate, Gray and I retired to the hotel and drank a lot of whisky. The bar was tiny, the hotelier obese. Either Gray, Plate and I carried the hotelier to bed, or Gray, the hotelier and I carried Plate to bed, or there was some further variation of this, or, just possibly, we all dossed down together on the floor of the bar. At any rate, we were all also up bright and early the following morning, Gray his usual self, shy, gentle, yet strident and immensely talkative. Mm.), and begin to reread it.

Detail 3: In the hallway, where the larger hardbacks are kept, I retrieve my copy of Gray's *The Book of Prefaces*, sent to me by Gray's erstwhile English publisher, Liz Calder (for reasons of Scottishness and Loyalty, Gray has been subject to publishing books alternately with Calder's house, Bloomsbury, and Canongate. Liz Calder worships Gray as if he is a small, bespectacled, grey bearded deity. It could be that Gray is the God in Liz's narrative. God is in all Gray's narratives. Somewhere.)

Detail 4: In mine and my wife's bedroom I face a wall of books and intone 'I wonder where that copy of *Lan*—' but then see it.

Detail 5: I have retreated, together with books and papers, to my study at the top of the house, where I write this introduction ('introduction' in the loosest sense, what could be more otiose than to gloss a collection of critical essays with one more?) on a flat screen monitor I bought a month ago in the Tottenham Court Road. (Toby, who used to 'do' my computers for me, said that it was pointless replacing the old monitor when it packed in, and that I should upgrade the whole system. Contrarily, I decided to downgrade Toby instead.) Gray does not type himself.

All these vignettes of me-writing-the-introduction are linked together by tendrils of vines, or stalks of thistles, or organs of the body, or lobes of the brain, or are poised in conch shells and skulls, alembics and crucibles, mortars and other vessels of that sort.

Moores feels that: 'It's sad that there is still a gap for this book for a writer/artist of Alasdair's importance: perhaps it's because he's Scottish, perhaps because he wasn't young enough to grab the media's attention like others of the 80s "Granta Young Novelists", but whatever the reason his profile is still too low. Perhaps this book will help (but probably not).' Hmm. Such pessimism and cynicism in one so young (and I envision Moores as young, although the British Library is not where you would expect to find anyone who was not – at least psychically – a valetudinarian.) Personally, I find it very easy to imagine Gray as a svelte, highly photogenic, metropolitan novelist. In the mid-nineties, when I went often up to Orkney to write, on a couple of occasions, when I was passing through Glasgow, I took Gray and his wife Morag MacAlpine out to dinner at the Ubiquitous Chip, a restaurant where Gray himself – some years before – had done murals on the walls of the staircase leading to the lavatories. Gray would strike attitudes over his Troon-landed cod, reminding me of no one much besides Anthony Blanche in Waugh's *Brideshead Revisited*. Anyway, who gives a fuck about his profile? Literary art is not a competition of any kind at all, what could it be like to win? Suffice to say, Gray is in my estimation a great writer, perhaps the greatest living in this archipelago today. Others agree. I've only just now looked up *Lanark*, his *magnum opus*, on the Amazon.com website (this dumb, digital, obsolete computer multi-tasks, as do Gray's analogue fictions), the sales were respectable, the reader reviews fulsome. One said: 'I owe my life to this book. In 1984 I was marooned in the Roehampton Limb-fitting Centre, the victim of a bizarre hit-and-run accident, whereby an out of control invalid carriage ran me over several times. The specialists all concurred that I would never walk again, even with the most advanced prostheses they had on offer. After reading *Lanark* by Alasdair Gray, such was my Apprehension of a New Jerusalem, arrived at by the author's Fulsome Humanity, tempered by the Judiciousness of his Despair, and the Percipience of his Neo-Marxist Critique of the Established Authorities, that seemingly in response to one of the novel's own Fantastical Conceits, I found myself growing, in a matter of days, two superb, reptilian nether limbs. These have not only served me better than my own human legs as a form of locomotion, they have also made me a Sexual Commodity much in demand on the burgeoning fetish scene of the South West London suburbs.' Any encomium I could add to this would be worse than pathetic. Gray's friends and collaborators are represented in this collection, as are his fans. Some essays deal with Gray's fiction, some with his political writing, others with his exegetical labours, and others still with his visual art. I have attempted, through this fantastical schema – part reverie, part parody, part fantasy – to suggest to you quite how important I view Gray to be. In Scotland, where the fruits of the Enlightenment are still to be found rotting on the concrete floors of deracinated orchards, Gray represents quite as much of a phenomenon as he does to those of us south of the border. However, to the Scottish, Gray is at least imaginable, whereas to the English he is barely conceivable. A creative polymath with an integrated politico-philosophic vision is not something to be sought in the native land of the hypocrite. Although, that being noted, much documentation concerning Gray's work now reposes in Wetherby, and you have this fine volume in your hand. Treasure it. Grip it tightly.

Will Self
London 2001

ARCADIA AND APOCALYPSE
The Garden of Eden and the
Triumph of Death

Anywhere people are at ease with each other is heavenly, especially
in a natural setting. Wherever they compete destructively is hell.[1]

PHILIP HOBSBAUM

THE WORK OF ALASDAIR GRAY HAS SOMETIMES BEEN SINGLED
out for its eccentricity. William Boyd called him 'redoubtably modernist'
but also said that 'he was in the line of idiosyncratic visionary writing'.[2]
Frank Delaney associated him with 'the natural anarchy of the Scots'.[3]
David Harris wrote of Gray's 'prodigious gift for the grotesque'.[4]
Hermione Lee declared 'Full-blooded post-modernism is mostly European
and American, and it's interesting to see an ambitious native version of
it'.[5] There is something in such statements.

Gray's aspirations, however, are those of the good craftsmen who
constitute his family background. In his *Saltire Self-Portrait*, he declared
'while writing or painting I forgot myself so completely that I did not
want to be any different'.[6] He also said 'My family and schooling made
art seem the only way to join mental adventure, physical safety and
social approval'.[7] The individual manner in which such attitudes are
expressed in Gray's novels and stories may be attributable to peculiar
circumstances rather than a peculiar personality. The question of

literary style, however, is a complicating factor. This will be determined, if at all, as we proceed.

One has to say, first, that the novels, even more than the stories, are ego-bound. Dickens has *David Copperfield* and D. H. Lawrence has *Sons and Lovers*, but, in one guise or another, Gray is always his own hero, and personal experience is his raw material. Few novelists have been able to get away with such self-absorption.

One reason why this is possible to Gray is that he grew up in a city – Glasgow – that was passing through a rapid process of transformation. He also has an aetiology – that of an asthmatic, with the usual complications – which of necessity gave rise to dramatic events. A third reason is his remarkable command over language. He has the gift of making the ordinary circumstance fascinating, and to make what is fascinating appear credible.

The hero of *Lanark*, Thaw, is an *alter ego*: an art student, impoverished, lonely and sexually frustrated, who seeks company among the prostitutes. He picks up a woman in the centre of town and they go in a taxi to a block of buildings where she takes him up to her attic flat. It is cosy and reassuring after the loneliness of the streets. However, as they begin intercourse, she notices that something is wrong:

> 'What's that?'
> Thaw was breathing hard and didn't answer. She said, 'Stop! What's that?'
> 'Nothing,'
> 'You call that nothing?'
> 'It's eczema, it isn't infectious, look—'
> 'No you don't! Stop! Stop it!'
> She got up and started to dress, saying 'I cannae afford to take chances.'[8]

This is from what may be termed the realistic part of *Lanark*, Gray's major novel and the one that made his name. There is a degree of detail here – 'Thaw was breathing hard', 'I cannae afford ...' – that suggests authenticity. Thaw's embarrassment is almost too shocking to bear, but the woman's plight is seen and understood. A touching moment comes when she refuses even a token payment for the time she has spent with him.

The apparently realistic inner two sections are flanked, fore and aft, by two that may be termed science fiction, or even allegory. These modes may seem to differ on the surface but are, in fact, linked thematically. In the mythical city of Unthank, it is not only the protagonist that is afflicted.

Escaping from a party, a further *alter ego* called Lanark follows Rima, a girl he already knows, through murk and clammy fog. She takes him to her home, which is up a steep wooden stair. It consists of a small room, with not much in the shape of furniture. There are, however, a few personal touches, such as crayon sketches on the wall, a carved clock with no hands, a stringless guitar on a chest of drawers, and a teddy bear sitting on a mattress that does duty for a bed. The place soon warms up, and Lanark begins to feel comfortable and to gain confidence:

> He touched her shoulders.
> 'Let me undress you?'
> She allowed this. As he unfastened her brassière his hands met a familiar roughness.
> 'You've got dragonhide! Your shoulderblades are covered!'
> 'Does that excite you?'
> 'I have it too!'[9]

Unlike Thaw's encounter with the prostitute, this disfigurement proves to be a bond between Lanark and Rima. In this section of the novel, people with dragonhide eventually turn into dragons. The process has a kind of beauty. Lanark's arm, the part of his body that is affected, grows in size and is admired. A small boy tells him 'You could murder someone with that'.[10] Considered by itself, and not as a disease, the glossy dark green hide of the arm, with its steel blade claws, looks quite healthy.

Lanark lands up in an Institute that is full of patients with varying degrees of dragonhide. He becomes a doctor and is confronted with a creature well on the way to dragonhood. It may once have been Rima, but is now transformed.

> The observation lens had not prepared him for the cramped smallness of the chamber and the solid vastness of the monster. The tabletop was a few inches above the floor and from the crest on the silver head to the bronze hooves on the silver feet the patient was nearly eight feet long.[11]

It is quite heraldic, with the stylised glamour of an escutcheon. Eventually, if not cured, the patient will disintegrate – go nova. However, in the present case, there is a crack, then a clang, as the head falls off. There is another clang as the thorax splits and falls apart, covering the floor with fragments like ornate scrap metal. Within the now fragmented carapace crouches a weeping girl, and this indeed proves to be Rima. That, it seems, represents a cure.

Though the events may seem fantastic, they are recounted in the same careful prose that characterises the 'realistic' sections of the book. As with Defoe and with Borges, the power of Alasdair Gray lies in the nature of the details recorded, and not in any extravagance of writing. Fine style, and even bomphiologia, can occur in Gray's work, but only by way of special effect. Yet his most prosaic details seem extraordinary, mainly because of the meticulousness with which they are described. That, in its turn, comes from the astonishing truthfulness – the authenticity – of the narrative.

There is a recurrent pattern – a pattern rather than a theme – that binds the various episodes of *Lanark*, and indeed other works, together. The protagonist tends to be lonely, depressed, seeming to himself unattractive, often wandering in bad weather. He is in search of solace, and appears to find it: whether in the spurious comfort of a whore's bedroom, the personal details marking a student's flatlet, or the prestige of being accorded the title – it is no more than that – of 'doctor'. Just when this protagonist is beginning to get comfortable, the appearance of relief is whisked abruptly away, and he finds himself exposed to censure, humiliation, or worse. This often involves details hardly any writer would be willing to recount, lest the downfall be attributed to his own experience and he finds an audience of readers added to those characters in the book who are repelled, sneering or indignant. The texture of Gray's work has a feeling quite distinct from that of any other author.

Near the end of *Lanark* there is an episode that could, as bare plot, come out of any of a thousand books. It recounts the ramble of a father and son into the countryside. The physical details are, at first, uncomfortable. The protagonist finds himself knee-deep in a cold, quick little burn. He is tugging some of the stones out and flinging them on to the bank, and the ache in his back and shoulders suggests that he has been doing this for some time before he extricates himself.

However, the presence of his ten-year-old son has been an alleviant. They are building a dam together, and conversing amicably as they build.

> 'I don't believe in God, you know,' said Alexander.
> Lanark blinked sideways and watched him wrenching clods from the bank. He said, 'Oh?'
> 'He doesn't exist. Grampa told me.'
> 'Which grampa? Everyone has two.'
> 'The one who fought in France in the first war. Give me a lot of that moss.'
> Without sitting up Lanark plucked handfuls from a dank mossy cushion nearby and chucked them lazily over. Alexander said, 'The first world war was the most interesting, I think, even though it had no Hitler or atomic bombs. You see, it mostly happened in one place, and it killed more soldiers than the second war.'
> 'Wars are only interesting because they show how stupid we can be.'
> 'Say that sort of thing as much as you like,' said Alexander amiably, 'but it won't change me.'[12]

If this is not in fact drawn from experience, it feels as though it was, what with the inconsequential dialogue and the interrupted rhythms. Father and son chat as they work, agreeing to disagree.

However, Alexander *does* change. The two stroll on, they wend uphill, the father carries the son when he is tired and beginning to complain, then puts him down and they take separate paths for a while, they reach a high point, they find a dead seagull and bury it. All seems so comforting and normal.

Then it is taken away. What has occurred may have been a dream. At any rate, it has gone:

> Something cold stung his cheeks. He opened his eyes and saw the sky dark with torn, onrushing clouds. He was alone with nothing at his feet but a scatter of stones with old bones and feathers between them. He said 'Sandy?' and looked around. There was nothing human on the moor. The light was fading from two or three sunset streaks in the clouds to the west. The heather was crested with sleet; the wind whipped more of it into his face.
> 'Sandy!' he screamed, starting to run. 'Sandy! Sandy! *Alexander!*'[13]

It is consummately done, without a hint of sentimentality. 'He was alone … There was nothing human on the moor …'. Gray has few rivals in the representation of despair, and the power comes from the simulation of companionship by which such representation is preceded and the realisation of aloneness with which it is infused.

Whether illusion or despair is in question, Gray does not deal in clichés, verbal or conceptual. Because most writers are in the habit of so indulging themselves – one has only to look at the best-sellers of yesteryear – his work has the effect of being original. It is true that the novels other than *Lanark* are uneven. Yet most of them show this approach: the exact notation of what actually happens rather than what might be deemed to have happened. They are the careful narration of authentic experience.

Many a writer in middle age has occasion to lament the passing of a friend. Those very words are a cliché, but that is not how mourning presents itself in *1982, Janine*. The novel consists of an interior monologue attributed to an engineer occupying a hotel room and drinking himself into oblivion. This circumstance gives Gray the opportunity to experiment with various flashbacks.

The most effective of these concerns a character found also in *Lanark*. There, he occurs as Aitken Drummond:

> Aitken Drummond was not a member of the group. He was over six feet tall and usually wore green tram conductor's trousers, a red muffler and an army greatcoat. His dark skin, great arched nose, small glittering eyes, curling black hair and pointed beard were so like the popular notion of the Devil that on first sight everyone felt they had known him intimately for years.[14]

In *1982, Janine*, he is called Alan:

> I can remember none of these things without his great head in its Harpo Marx cloud of curly hair, though black not blonde, and his Groucho Marx face but with a goatee beard improving the slightly weak chin. Nobody who saw him knew if he was strikingly handsome or strikingly ugly. He had a sallow-skinned Arabic-Italian-Jewish look. I think his father was Jewish. His mother was Irish. 'Not Catholic Irish but tinker Irish,' was how he described her and he certainly dressed like a tinker. […] I remember various long woollen scarves, an army tunic with marks on the sleeves where the stripes of a sergeant had been unstitched.[15]

There are differences, of course. Drummond wears green tram conductor's trousers while Alan's trousers are part of an evening dress-suit. However, in recollection, the two characters, each from a different book, seem to conflate. He marches side by side with his friend, the protagonist – Thaw in *Lanark*, Jock in *1982, Janine* – seeing the passers-by in the distance staring at his towering height, his great head, his arms folded on his chest.

There is characteristic dialogue, with a smartness redolent of Conan Doyle's Sherlock Holmes stories, yet retaining an individual cadence.

> 'I have to be careful in case my mother's at home. If she dislikes someone she's liable to retire to her bedroom and burn a pheasant's tail feather.'
> 'What does that do?'
> 'I shudder to think.'[16]

> 'This man is magic. Describe anything you want done and he will do it quietly, expertly, and – if you arouse his blood a little – quickly [...].'
> I said firmly, 'I know nothing about stage lighting.'
> 'Good,' cried Alan, 'you will teach yourself to do it properly. You know my methods. Apply them, and soon lovely girls like Helen here will be flitting around you in all kinds of fascinating undress.'[17]

The verbal surface alludes to Sherlock Holmes; however, the import is startlingly different. By such techniques, the character is tangibly put before us but only after we are definitely told he is dead: 'I once knew a man who was not a coward, not an instrument. He died'; 'damn damn damn damn him for dying, that bastard should never have died.'[18]

With all this, the character is built up – his skills, his humour, his sexual success – until the reader is quite prepared to accept at face value what seems to be an unexpected rencontre between Alan and the protagonist.

> It was a sunny summer in Glasgow, the streets quieter than usual. Perhaps it was the start of the fair fortnight. I walked along St George's Road and saw Alan strolling toward me round the curve of Charing Cross Mansions, arms folded on chest, great face surveying the white clouds. I was filled with delighted relief and laughter, I ran to him crying, 'You're not dead! You're not dead!'
> He smiled and said, 'Of course not, that was all just a joke.'
> And suddenly I grew terribly angry with him for making such a cruel joke. And then I awoke, unluckily.[19]

The circumstantial detail persuades the reader into acceptance. There is the relative quietness of the streets, with the inhabitants of Glasgow away on holiday at Blackpool or in Benidorm. There is the architectural curve of Charing Cross Mansions as seen from the city end of St George's Road. And there is Alan – he of the arched nose, great height, deliberate walk. Yet he is of an order of being different from the other entities. He is dead.

The solid description serves only to lead us up to the unexpected betrayal; that withdrawal of happiness that is the hallmark of Alasdair Gray. Consider the force of that word 'unluckily'. His dreams have the immediacy of here and now, but they are there to be broken. In an interview with Christopher Swan, Gray described his theme as 'the garden of Eden and the triumph of death'.[20] This is, perhaps, the shrewdest remark ever to have been made about his work. In *Something Leather*, after much sado-masochistic experience, Senga finds fulfilment in an unfraught relationship with the previously unawakened June. In *Poor Things*, the mediocre practitioner McCandless, in some ways a surrogate of Thaw and Jock, worships at the shrine of the malformed genius, 'God'.

Yet is 'God', God? His appearance, if not intimidating, is certainly strange.

> His big face, stout body and thick limbs gave him a dwarfish look [but] as he passed other people you saw he was a whole head taller than most.[...] He had the wide hopeful eyes, snub nose and mournful mouth of an anxious infant.[21]

There is a striking *coup d'oeil* when McCandless sees in the distance a two-year-old child with a tiny puppy. As this vision nears, it turns out to be 'God', alias Godwin Baxter, with a huge Newfoundland dog.[22] Thus the claims of verisimilitude and fancy are simultaneously satisfied by means of an almost laborious specificity, as often happens in the prose of Gray's master, Robert Louis Stevenson.

Godwin Baxter appears to have conducted a brain transplant from a foetus to the drowned body of its own mother. The result he calls Bella. Her sexual appetites are inordinate and when she announces her intention to marry McCandless, at whom she has recently thrown herself, the reaction of 'God' is suitably cosmic:

The only part of Baxter which moved was his mouth. It slowly and silently opened into a round hole bigger than the original size of his head then grew larger still until his head vanished behind it. His body seemed to support a black, expanding, tooth-fringed cavity in the scarlet sunset behind him. When the scream came the whole sky seemed screaming. I had clapped my hands to my ears before this happened so did not faint as Bella did, but the single high-pitched note sounded everywhere and pierced the brain like a dental drill piercing a tooth without anaesthetic. I lost most of my senses during that scream.[23]

History repeats itself: the first time as tragedy, the second as farce. Here we have significant parallels with *Lanark* and, indeed, with other such trios throughout Gray's work. The grotesque but masterful 'God' does duty for Drummond/Alan. The 'steady and predictable' McCandless is an inexact simulacrum for Lanark/Thaw. The Bella persona, who may also be Victoria, has something of the inconsistency and waywardness of Rima.

In spite of the past terror and the lady's present elopement with another, McCandless manages to live happily in conjunction with Godwin Baxter, brilliant son of a brilliant father, the surgeon Sir Colin. As McCandless puts it in his careful prose, which has antecedents as far back as the eighteenth century, 'If hard rewarding work, interesting, undemanding friendship, and a comfortable home are the best grounds for happiness then the following months were perhaps the pleasantest I have known'.[24] True, Bella is away, travelling in Europe with her seducer whom she gradually drives into insanity. But she sends informative letters back, and the pairing of males is often a recipe for happiness in the work of Alasdair Gray, women being a disturbing intrusion.

In any case, Bella finally returns, and she is due to be married to McCandless on Christmas Day at Lansdowne United Presbyterian Church on Great Western Road. As narrated in the painstaking language of McCandless, the nave is empty, for the happy couple had invited no one and had not advertised the occasion at all. Empty, that is, but for a row of five men in the front pews. Nobody knows who they are, yet McCandless has a premonition that he is in a bad dream from which he must struggle to awake. One of these men objects to the wedding taking place. His grounds at first seem formally absurd. He alleges that the so-called Bella Baxter is in reality Victoria, Lady Blessington, née Hattersley. An improbable background is provided by this first speaker, who claims to be her husband, and by four witnesses: the lady's father, her doctor, the husband's lawyer, and a private detective who has been hired to track her down following her disappearance from her husband's home.

By now, the weight of evidence is beginning to make this background look all too probable. It has some points of reference to the early life of Joan Ure, a friend of Alasdair Gray, whose story he told in a joint production, *Lean Tales*.[25] Certainly it seems bleak enough. Once again, the magic carpet has been withdrawn from beneath the feet of the protagonist, in this case, Dr McCandless. There ensues a good deal of drama, told mostly by means of dialogue. It expresses conflict rather than misery, turning on the question of whether Bella is a runaway wife or the drowned corpse of that wife invigorated by the brain of the foetus that was developing within her. The episode ends with the suicide of her alleged husband and the delayed marriage of Bella, if that is who she is, and McCandless.

The real suffering comes with the death of McCandless's friend, Godwin Baxter. This is told in the accents of Dr Watson lamenting Sherlock Holmes, a little less grammatically than in Conan Doyle's story, 'The Final Problem': 'It is with a heavy heart that I describe the last days of he who I will always consider the wisest and the best of men'. Grotesque, as McCandless sees him in life, Godwin is also grotesque in death. A failure in emotional equilibrium consequent upon the marriage of McCandless to Bella has resulted in damage to nerves and alimentary canal. It is impossible for 'God' to continue living with dignity. Swallowing down a glass of wine, his laughter swells up to a peal so huge that his heart stops and, as McCandless relates:

> [I] discovered his neck was broken and that *rigor mortis* had instantly ensued. Rather than break his joints in order to lay him out flat I ordered a cubical coffin four and a half feet wide, with a shelf inside on which he was placed, sitting. He sits like that to the present day, under the floor of the mausoleum Sir Colin acquired in the Necropolis overlooking Glasgow Cathedral and Royal Infirmary.[26]

Matter-of-fact as these references to Godwin Baxter may seem, they are punctured in a letter addressed to posterity by his wife. She explains herself as a plain sensible woman and not the Lucrezia Borgia or La Belle Dame Sans Merci described by McCandless. Godwin is not the monster McCandless makes him out to be but 'a big sad-looking man [...] so careful and alert [...] that [...] all women felt safe and at peace with him'.[27]

And Bella herself is not a transplant but a woman fleeing from her father and husband and seeking sanctuary with this Good Doctor.

The whole book turns on questions of identity, and finds them irresoluble. This, as much as the theme of Paradise Withdrawn, is a besetting problem in the work of Alasdair Gray. Compared with his novels, the various commentators have tended to ignore his stories. Yet it is in these smaller forms that one finds his most exquisite craftsman-ship. *Unlikely Stories, Mostly* is a retrospective collection rather than a new book. As Stephen Bernstein says in his pioneer monograph, *Alasdair Gray*, during the lengthy composition of *Lanark* (1953-76) the author had been steadily writing short stories.[28] Yet Bernstein chooses not to discuss these works, even though the best of them have the weight and presence of a novella. Truly, they contain material of considerable range and complexity and exhibit extraordinary variety of mode and technique. In any serious reckoning, they would be regarded as being among the most far-reaching and indeed prophetic utterances of our time.

The protagonist of 'Five Letters from an Eastern Empire' appears to have been chosen from birth to be reared and educated in order to write a great poem in praise of the Emperor. The reality is prefigured by a sentence in an account of Gray's failure to fulfil the conditions of the Bellahouston Travelling Scholarship in conjunction with the Director of the Glasgow School of Art. This is reproduced in Gray's composite production, *Lean Tales*: 'The excellence of this plan, approved by Mr Bliss, is not lessened by the fact that I eventually spent two days in Spain and saw nothing of interest.'[29]

The story itself depends on the manipulation of a time sequence. The poet, Bohu, after much preparation, is told that his city is destroyed together with all its inhabitants, including his father and mother, in order that the Emperor may order the building of a new one. We have already seen the Emperor. He is a puppet manipulated by 'headmasters'.

Struck with the wickedness of this proceeding, Bohu writes a poem denouncing the injustice of the Emperor, and dies. The Emperor's Headmaster of Literature approves the poem and alters its title by removing a single syllable, so that, thus revised, the poem now means the opposite of what the poet intended. It is now called 'To the Emperor's Justice'. Armed with this justification, posted in every public place, the Emperor is able to accomplish that which had previously not been an established fact but only a threat: he is able to accomplish the destruction of the city. The depth of the irony may be seen if one considers that, of the four letters Bohu writes to his parents, the third and fourth are written in the belief that they are already dead. But they in fact die only when he has written his poem and after he himself has died. His denunciation of the Emperor for tyranny is published as an ode in praise of tyranny, even though the final act of that tyranny had not taken place when the poem was written.

The style of this remarkable work, as the epigraph from *Rasselas* may suggest to us, is adapted from Dr Johnson. However, behind that style lurks the utterance of Swift, whose work the author of *Rasselas* disliked. It is well within Gray's power to modulate from one to the other. The Happy Valley described by Johnson is reified in the garden surrounding the palace where the poet is supposed to do his composing:

> We stood near the thick hedge of cypress, holly and yew trees which hide all but some tiled roofs of the surrounding buildings. Triangular pools, square lawns and the grassy paths of a zig-zag maze are symmetrically placed round the pavilion in the middle. In each corner is a small pinewood with cages of linnets, larks and nightingales in the branches. From one stout branch hangs a trapeze where a servant dressed like a cuckoo sits imitating the call of that bird, which does not sing well in captivity.[30]

There, as an ominous reference to the likely arrest of the poet's faculties, Gray has accentuated the custodial element endemic in this bower. That is suggested by the geometrical disposition of the facilities, the confinement of the birds to cages, and a general atmosphere of regimentation.

The style transmutes into the darker imagining associated with Swift when the respective pagodas of justice are evoked. The pagoda of revocable justice is where gifts are conferred that can afterwards be taken back, such as homes, wives, salaries and pensions. The pagoda of irrevocable justice is where disobedient people have things removed that cannot be returned, such as eardrums, eyes, limbs and heads. This latter foreshadows the fate accorded to the rival poet, Tohu, whose work has not found favour at court. That fate is retailed formally, in the shape of a scroll of the sort used for public pronouncements:

> The emperor asked his famous poets Bohu and Tohu to celebrate the destruction of the old capital. Bohu said no. He is still an honoured guest in the evergreen garden, happy and respected by all who know him. Tohu said yes and wrote a very bad poem. You may read the worst bits below. Tohu's tongue, right shoulder, arm and hand have now been replaced by wooden ones. The emperor prefers a frank confession of inability to the useless words of the flattering toad-eater.[31]

The Swift of 'A Modest Proposal' emerges from the startling use of the word 'replaced' to express the fiendish brutality that has fatally maimed the hapless Tohu. Many writers find terror in domesticity; the use of a homely word such as this suggests that Gray finds domesticity in terror. 'Replaced' would normally suggest improvement, but this context would seem to be highly abnormal. But then again, if we consider the sadism manifest in the conduct of various dictators ruling certain contemporary republics, perhaps it is not so abnormal as all that. This author, as is the case with Swift, compels us to reassess 'normality'.

A parallel suggests itself. There was an announcement made on the radio during the last days of King George VI that described the terminal phase of that monarch's cancer by saying: 'Structural changes have taken place in the King's lungs.' The irony there was unintentional, but it nonetheless signifies an incongruity akin to the 'replacement' of certain limbs belonging to Tohu. Such announcements of state, and still more its actions, represent a soulless disregard for humanity in favour of competition. His horror at such depersonalisation is one of Gray's key themes.

The dream, of being a favoured poet in the halls and gardens of the Emperor, has become a nightmare. Such hope as was once entertained renders what is left by its withdrawal all the more dreary, not to say despairing. This story was written immediately after Alasdair Gray at last became a senior member of a great university, its Fellow in Creative Writing. He found himself, a would-be imaginative spirit, surrounded by what seemed to be a vast number of professors. It is interesting to note that Bohu's poem is rewritten and ruined by a Headmaster of Literature. Not much energy is required for this defacement to take place. It is the spoiler's art. Without interpreting 'Five Letters from an Eastern Empire' as a wholesale attack on university education, it is warrantable to suggest that the entry of the author into the system was not the intellectual paradise he might have hoped it would be. Much that is destructive has emerged from such a system. We may remember a phrase of Winston Churchill's at the onset of the Second World War: 'a dark age made all the more terrible by the lights of a perverted science'.

Like *Nineteen Eighty-Four*, this novella allows no positive. It is strange, then, to find Anne Varty opining that the reader is left with a sense of 'irreducible human values'.[32] This is as though to adopt, in lieu of *King Lear* as Shakespeare wrote it, the cheerful finale of Nahum Tate's adaptation: 'Truth and virtue shall at last succeed.' That voices precisely the opposite sentiment of the original.

Nothing succeeds in the 'Five Letters'. The only hope one can raise is the fact that the fable seems to have come down to us, just as has that of Orwell's political satire. Someone must have been doing the telling. However, the reader is not, as Ms Varty seems to think, in the position of Bohu's parents. How would they have had access to the rewriting of the poem by the Headmaster of Literature about the Emperor's injustice? At best, readers are in the position of Edgar and Albany at the end of *King Lear* – that of Shakespeare, not the travesty-with-happy-ending provided by Tate – confronted by the Triumph of Death and wondering whether out of that ruin they can construct a viable form of life, let alone a paradise.

Anne Varty has given us the most detailed reading of Gray's shorter fiction so far, and it is disappointing. In extenuation, one might say that Gray can be exhilarating to read but very difficult to analyse. For example, the basis of a story called 'Logopandocy' is the writing of Sir

Thomas Urquhart, the seventeenth century pamphleteer and scholiast, with whose work Varty gives no evidence of being acquainted.

Perhaps the general reader need not traverse those tortuous pages, either. Yet it is true to say that 'Logopandocy' is at one and the same time deeply original and a shameless plagiarism. For example, the anecdote of a young man and young woman who are accused of consorting with succubi is taken verbatim from the fourth book of an almost unreadable pamphlet by Urquhart purporting to discuss a universal language. It discusses almost anything else, in fact, and is called *Logopandecteision*, from which word Gray has Englished his title.

Urquhart is remembered, if at all, as the translator of Rabelais. According to R. D. S. Jack and Roderick Lyall, who edited another pamphlet, *The Jewel*, his linguistic virtuosity causes him to be more adventurous than Rabelais.[33] This is explained by Urquhart himself as a result of French failing to match English in its range of vocabulary. In this same work, *The Jewel*, Urquhart quotes with approval a maxim from Seneca (although he thought it was Aristotle), which Dryden was to translate as 'Great wits are sure to madness near allied'. Certainly, the lunatic exuberance of Urquhart pervades this story drawn from his works, and gives us – what may be the story's main *raison d'être* – a notable and individual sense of character.

The chief works of Urquhart have a degree of local life taken as exhibitions of linguistic virtuosity, but are otherwise quite maddening. There is neither logic nor plot, even though some purport to explain Urquhart's concept of a universal language. What Gray has done is select some of the best passages from these writings and arrange them in such a way as to give the impression of a lively character expressing himself. This leads to extravagance. What is a special effect elsewhere becomes the mode of narration here. It is sheer ventriloquism. In the original, Urquhart is long-winded, repetitive and liable to endless digressions. In 'Logopandocy' he comes over as courageous, humorous, very much able to meet disaster with a cheer, dust himself down, and start all over again.

In his *Logopandecteision*, Urquhart says:

> [...] most strange of all it is that in my Lands should be found of those, who (though they can neither read nor write) will

nevertheless be able to exchange discourse with any, concerning the Nature of the Heathenish deities, and afford pertinent reasons for the variety of sacrifices, and other circumstantial points usual to be performed in the days of old.

I asked them how they came by this knowledge, they told me, that the fathers taught them it, who had it from their progenitors, unto whom (say they) it was derived from their first fore-father, that accompanied my predecessors Alypos, Belistos, Nomostes, Astioremon and Lutork in their aboriginarie acquest of the Land of their Ancestors residence...[34]

The version of this condensed into the prose of Gray runs thus:

Tenandrie: all are descended (as they themselves avouch) from progenitors who accompanied my ancestors Alypos, Belistos, Nomostor, Astioremon and Lutork in their aborignarie acquest of the land, receiving from these such good yeoman leases for the digging and manuring of it that they very suddenly took deep root therein, and bequeathed to their children the hereditary obedience owed to their masters.[35]

Gray postpones and abridges any discussion of how the tenants came by their knowledge. This enables him to speed up and clarify the narrative. Such is the proceeding throughout 'Logopandocy'. It is considerably more concise than its various originals. The impression of loquacity is given, without exposing the modern reader to Urquhart's garrulous tendency towards repetition and tedium.

Urquhart's pamphlets are overtly concerned with such matters as a universal language; the 'jewel' that gives one of these pamphlets its title. However, they continually digress into such matters as Urquhart's misfortunes at the hands of the Presbyterians, the loss of his goods, and the notable persons he has met. One of these is The Admirable Crichton, who has passed into proverb with the help of J. M. Barrie's play of that title. It takes Urquhart something like 12,000 words to retail the life of this hero. Gray manages it in just over 400, mainly by concentrating on what interests him most:

CRICHTON [...] who in one day at the Sorbonne in Paris, from nine in the morning to six at night, did argue in Hebrew, Syriack, Arabick, Greek, Latin, Italian, English, Flemish, Dutch, Spanish, French and Sclavonian, in prose and verse, at his disputants' discretion, thereby resolving the knurriest problems propounded to him by the choicest and most profound philosophers, mathematicians, naturalists, mediciners, surgeons, apothecaries, alchymists, civil law doctors, canon law doctors, grammarians, rhetoricians and logicians in that greatest of all cities which is truly called the Abridgment of the World [...].[36]

In this way, 'Logopandocy' conveys the flurry and excitement of Urquhart without indulging in his verbosity.

Urquhart's own work has no centre save that of his own personality, and that is often obfuscated by the plethora of his writing. Gray gives 'Logopandocy' a centre by providing an entirely apocryphal episode that dominates the whole.

For some time in the 1650s, Urquhart was imprisoned in the tower of Windsor Castle by the Commonwealth forces. Gray produces an encounter there that could have happened but that almost certainly did not. This contributes to the genre known as Imaginary Conversation:

> He entered to me peeringly, having the use of a single eye, and that a failing one, yet I saw it allowed him enough light to admire my figure, and this admiration I was able, in part, to return, for although we are neither of us small men, we both lack that redundant height and girth which gross multitudes think commonplace: his manner also was pleasingly jocund and his voice familiar to my ear, for he pronounced his R, *littera cannina*, the latin dog-letter, extreme hard as we Scots do, a certain sign of a Satyricall Wit.
>
> We furthered our amity by also discovering, beneath radically opposed views of church and state, an equal hatred of Presbyters (*press-biters*, he called them; I did not disclose that the like witticism had occurred to myself).[37]

Although referred to as the Chief Secretary of State and never in fact named, this plainly enough is the great poet Milton. Since Urquhart himself never refers to Milton, Gray draws for much of his description on John Aubrey.[38] It is integrated marvellously into the plasm of writing adapted and imitated from Urquhart. The question of the Universal Language is touched upon, but never explored. Urquhart himself maintained that his papers on the topic were scattered after the Battle of Worcester. Gray avails himself of this precedent. The report of the Imaginary Conversation is interrupted at two crucial points by the ingenious excuse, 'Here a great part of the manuscript has been eaten by mice'.

Historically, Urquhart probably died in 1660, soon after the Restoration. Indeed, he is said to have expired in a fit of relieved laughter induced by this event. However, there is so much that is uncertain about Urquhart's life, especially as regards his travels, that Gray allows a degree of licence to his narrative. 'Logopandocy' has Urquhart voyaging through strange lands, getting lost and recovering himself, hearing strange tongues, having gone past Byzantium, Tartary, Samarkand and other strange places he cannot name, and arriving at what may be the borders of China. The last words of the story read:

> It occurs to me that the first pure language my ancestors shared before Babylon was not of voice but of exactly these smiles and stroaks of the hand. I believe I am come to the edge of the greatest and happiest discovery of my life.[39]

On this note of hope and exploration, so characteristic of the indomitable character Gray has recreated, the story ends. If his Urquhart through all his tribulation has not attained Paradise, at least he seems to expire in anticipation. Nobody can take that away from him!

However, the basis of this art is a profound pessimism. Over and over again there is the sense of an ardent individuality pitted against a remote and impersonal government. The policy of the government in question usually produces dirt, disease, want, warfare. Nothing succeeds in the two 'Axletree' stories, any more than in their most immediate prototype, 'The Great Wall of China', by Franz Kafka: 'If from such appearances any one should draw the conclusion that in reality we have no Emperor, he would not be far from the truth.'

The two stories are best treated as one. The axletree arises out of the business (and busyness) of a prosperous Empire. It is a working-out of the axiom, that a complex entity needs to expand if it is not to collapse. The Emperor gains his idea of expansion from a saint he consults. This saint, who does not have a reputation betokening success, thrashes the Emperor into a dream-state in which he envisages a gigantic tower rising from the hub of his Empire apparently indefinitely into the sky. Only he calls it an axletree, that which connects one entity to another, because a tower is liable to become unstable. This conception has properties both of the Great Wall of China and of the Pyramids. Its immediate purpose, in other words, is not immediately perceptible, but it gives employment to millions, many of whom are buried within its structure. The Emperor knows that he is dying as a result of the severe beating he has sustained at the hands of the saint, and he decrees that the structure will start with the building of a gigantic tomb.

By comparison with other tales in *Unlikely Stories, Mostly* the narration is neutral, a personality only starting to emerge well on in the second part of 'The Axletree'. Then the narrator appears to be some kind of clerk, about the same level of individuation as one finds in Kafka's prototype. This is a technique familiar in Gray, whereby fantastic and even apocalyptic circumstance is told in a circumstantial manner so as to render it credible. The narrator comes into evidence more or less simultaneously with the realisation that the axletree, which has by this time risen almost illimitably from the earth, has in fact a finite barrier. An exploring party reaches the highest summit of all and fires off rockets to test the upper air:

> The chief set the tube to launch a rocket vertically for a quarter of a mile: the colour and length of the fiery tail would show the nature of the air it travelled through. All being ready, he told me to start the water clock, then lit the short fuse. My eyes, of course, were on the clock, which ticked off only four drops before I heard an explosion. Looking up I saw a great shower of sparks. Our rocket had broken at a height of sixty feet. 'A dud,' said the chief, and fired another, which also broke up too soon.
> 'Sir!' I said, staring at the clock. 'It has exploded at exactly the same height.'
> 'Coincidence!' grunted the chief, but checked the third rocket very carefully before firing, and that also broke at the same height. I trembled and the chief was sweating. With great precision he angled the tube and fired the fourth rocket upward along the diagonal of a square. It exploded six drops later. We fired the remaining rockets at the same angle in twenty different directions with same result. Which showed there was a very wide obstruction sixty feet above our heads.[40]

This circumstantial manner is a mode linking Defoe, Marryat and H. G. Wells. It is to be remembered that the Axletree has by now become – as well as very high – vast and complicated. There are various international companies developing diverse areas, and the military are in control at the very top. If we allegorise the matter, this is an Empire that has over-expanded. The presence of the water-clock as a device of measurement suggests the Roman Empire. If so, it stands for all conglomerates at all times. And this super-conglomerate is up against a barrier:

> Three days later I stood with the chief on top of a strong, prefabricated silver pylon, and the sky was a few inches above my upturned face. It was too transparent to be seen directly, but glanced at sideways the lucid blue was rippled by rainbow glimmerings like those golden lines cast by sunlight on sand under shallow water. [...] As gently as possible I stretched out my hand and touched. The sky was cool and silken-smooth with an underlying softness and warmth. I felt it with my whole body. The feeling was not sexual, for it excited no part more than the rest, not even the fingertips touching the slender rippling rainbows. The sway of the tower began diverging from the flow of the ripples, which took on a broken look. Fearing that the loveliness was escaping, my hand pressed instinctively harder and a tide of blood flowed down from the fingertips, staining the arm to the elbow. I stared at it, still pressing hard and feeling no pain until the chief struck my arm down and I fainted.[41]

The feeling was not sexual? By now it is clear that the axletree is not only the simulacrum of an Empire but also of a gigantic phallus. The narrator appears to be part of it, touching and fingering and pressing and producing blood. A poet, who is one of the directors, refers to this 'many-headed, bloodstained cactus of a poisoned and poisoning TOWER'.[42] So the Axletree does not connect. It occludes, aggrandises, absorbs, hoards. It has cut its adherents off from common humanity. The final attempt to erect it further, to thrust it through the sky, results in disaster. The work of two thousand years melts like a sandcastle. In its ruins, the survivors discover a marble block carved in the language of the old Emperor. His name, it appears, was Ozymandias.

One thinks of Shelley's poem, about a shattered mass of statuary in the desert, which bears an inscription that can be read in two distinct ways:

> My name is Ozymandias, king of kings,
> Look on my works, ye mighty, and despair.

Taken conceptually, such works as these of Gray would seem to offer little or no purchase to hope. The basic mood is akin to that of Swift, Kafka, and the character of Rupert Birkin in the earlier chapters of

Lawrence's *Women in Love*. Each and every human institution appears to be targeted and gunned down: arts, science, education, medicine, local and national and international politics. Human relationships are set up only to disintegrate. If no other factor makes for disintegration, then death, striking prematurely, does. And it is usually the brave and the creative who die first.

However, all this is to extrapolate. Though the fact remains that the structure of Gray's fictions affords a bleak view of human possibility, yet, as well as structure – the plot, argument, ethical standpoint of a text – there is texture. In Alasdair Gray, texture tends to be exuberant. Either this is because of the extraordinary nature of the events retailed or it is a result of language verging on, and sometimes for special effects excelling, the manic. Ordinarily, structure and texture can be separated only for the purpose of critical discussion. To confine oneself to structure is to risk discussing the ideas inherent in a text as though they were the text itself. On the other hand, to confine oneself to texture is to risk discussing effects of style out of context, without sufficient reference to the circumstance that brought them about.

In Alasdair Gray, however, there is a kind of conflict between structure and texture which is, on the whole, unusual. The most gloomy incidents may be recounted in a jocose manner. The matter of tragedy may be relayed in the mode of comedy, or even of farce. This is to play one of these major elements – structure – against the other – texture. A complex effect is brought about by traits of style which a 'pure' stylist might consider inappropriate. One should not underestimate the command over language that renders this possible and, further, renders it as literature.

The quotation last cited could be replayed, so to speak, with verbal substitutes for the words used by the author:

> As tenderly as possible, I extended my hand and touched. The sky was chilled and tranquil with an underlying velvety heat. I experienced it with my whole body. The emotion was not sexual for it stimulated no organ more than the rest, not even the fingertips touching the tenuously vibrating rainbows. The movement of the tower began diverging from the stream of the ripples which assumed a degree of fragmentation. Fearing that the beauty was escaping, my hand pushed instinctively harder and a

> flow of blood escaped down the fingertips, soiling the arm to the elbow. I looked at it, still pushing hard and experiencing no pain until the chief forced my arm down and I fainted.

Care has been taken in this adaptation to give equivalents for the words omitted. The quotation still makes sense. Yet much has been lost in recension. The speaker in the original denies any sexual component, but there is no reason to take his word on the matter. Alasdair Gray has used unreliable narrators on several occasions other than this. Be that as it may, any eroticism has now evaporated. In the original, brief as it is, there are three occasions of the use of the word 'feeling' and its derivative: 'I felt it with my whole body', 'the feeling was not sexual', 'feeling no pain'. In the original, this tactile component is ardent, even passionate, and it is linked with unexpected pain. In the revision, the words 'felt' and 'feeling' are substituted, and 'experienced', 'emotion', 'experiencing' stand in their stead. This, however, is to abstract and attenuate. That distinctive erotic charge, 'pleasure just this side of painful fun' as the poet Peter Redgrove phrased it, has become a damp squib.

Further: in the recension there is a consistent degrading of tone: 'I extended my hand', 'no organ more than the rest', 'a degree of fragmentation'. Possibly some other context might rescue such words, but in this context they seem ugly. It is the language of unfeeling prose, of hasty journalism, of that kind of writing prepared to accept the next best thing instead of *le mot juste*. Thus, even though the basic meaning may be held to remain undisturbed, the associations and resonances have been tampered with. The result is that a delicately balanced piece of description loses its internal rhythm and reads like a poor translation of what might have been – in this case, most certainly was – a distinctive original.

The function of this exercise in rewriting is to indicate that extrapolation from the narratives of Alasdair Gray is liable to leave out most of what makes those narratives meaningful. Gray is much more than a purveyor of ideas. He pits his ideas, which frequently give rise to pessimistic attitudes, against something which one can only call joy in life. Even if that joy is withdrawn – as it often is, suddenly and painfully – the trace remains, if only by way of reminiscence and implication.

Therefore the 'eccentricity' and 'modernism' of Gray is something more intricate and rewarding than can be suggested in the reviewers' necessarily extrapolatory prose. The delicacy of perception manifest in the texts discussed here rescues them from the black pessimism which any summary might presume. Though there is no reason to find life enjoyable, find it enjoyable his various narrators succeed in doing. There is more to living than the failure of politics, or even the failure of human relationships. One can find contact in misery, as both Thaw and Lanark do; one can fulfil, if only temporarily as McCandless does, one's dream; one can pause, as Urquhart does after many tribulations, on the brink of a great discovery. There is always a measure of hope. Even if one's fingers are lacerated attempting to caress the sky, the beginning of the caress is there. Death will certainly triumph, but Gray's heroes have had their Eden. At least, they have anticipated Eden. Nobody can take that away from them.

Notes

1. Alasdair Gray, postcard to Philip Hobsbaum, 11 January 2001.
2. William Boyd, *Times Literary Supplement*, 27 February 1981.
3. Frank Delaney, *Sunday Times*, 1 July 1990.
4. David Harris, *Sunday Times*, 18 January 1998.
5. Hermione Lee, *Observer*, 3 March 1981.
6. Alasdair Gray, *Alasdair Gray*, Saltire Self-Portraits, IV (Edinburgh: Saltire Society, 1988), p. 3.
7. Ibid.,p. 14.
8. Alasdair Gray, *Lanark: A Life in Four Books*, rev. edn (Edinburgh: Canongate, 1985), p. 344.
9. Ibid., p. 36.
10. Ibid., p. 41.
11. Ibid., p. 72.
12. Ibid., p. 512.
13. Ibid., p. 517.
14. Ibid., 242.
15. Alasdair Gray, *1982, Janine* (London: Cape, 1984), p. 109.
16. Gray, *Lanark*, p. 255.
17. Gray, *1982, Janine*, p. 115.
18. Ibid., p. 106.
19. Ibid., p. 117.
20. Christopher Swan, 'An Interview with Alasdair Gray', *Fiction Magazine*, 4 (1982). Much of the same interview was later included in the *Saltire Self-Portrait*.
21. Alasdair Gray, *Poor Things* (London: Bloomsbury, 1992), p. 12.
22. Ibid., p. 16.
23. Ibid., p. 52.
24. Ibid., p. 72.
25. Alasdair Gray, 'Portrait of a Playwright', in *Lean Tales* by James Kelman, Agnes Owens and Alasdair Gray (London: Cape, 1985), pp. 247-255.
26. Gray, *Poor Things*, p. 244.
27. Ibid., p. 259.

28. Stephen Bernstein, *Alasdair Gray* (Lewisburg: Bucknell University Press, 1999), p. 19.

29. Alasdair Gray, 'A Report to the Trustees of the Bellahouston Travelling Scholarship', in *Lean Tales*, pp. 185-213.

30. Alasdair Gray, *Unlikely Stories, Mostly* (Edinburgh: Canongate, 1983), p. 91.

31. Ibid., pp. 119-120.

32. Anne Varty, 'How the Laws of Fiction Lie: A Reading of Gray's Shorter Stories', in *The Arts of Alasdair Gray*, ed. by Robert Crawford and Thom Nairn (Edinburgh: Edinburgh University Press, 1991), p. 135.

33. Sir Thomas Urquhart, *The Jewel*, ed. by R. D. S. Jack and R. J. Lyall (Edinburgh: Scottish Academic Press, 1983), p. 12.

34. Sir Thomas Urquhart, *Logopandecteision* (London: Giles Calvert and Richard Tomlins, 1653).

35. Gray, *Unlikely Stories, Mostly*, p. 143.

36. Ibid., p. 148.

37. Ibid., p. 166.

38. Aubrey's first-hand account is reprinted as 'Mr John Milton: Minutes by John Aubrey, 1681' in *The Early Lives of Milton*, ed. by Helen Darbishire (London: Constable, 1932), pp. 1-15.

39. Gray, *Unlikely Stories, Mostly*, p. 194.

40. Ibid., pp. 247-248.

41. Ibid., pp. 251-252.

42. Ibid., p. 259.

ALASDAIR GRAY'S PERSONAL

CURRICULUM VITAE

1897 My father, Alexander, was born in Bridgeton, east Glasgow, by Jean Stevenson, daughter of a coalminer. She had worked as a power-loom weaver before marrying William Gray, industrial blacksmith, Congregational kirk elder and Sunday-school teacher. William's favourite hobby was walking; his political heroes were William Ewart Gladstone and Keir Hardie. Their son Alex left school early, became clerk on a dockyard weighbridge and part-time soldier in the territorial army. When war was declared in 1914 he joined the Black Watch regiment, fought in France, became quarter-master sergeant and suffered a shrapnel wound in the belly in 1917 or 18, for which he received a small pension for the rest of his life. From the end of the first world war to the start of the second he worked a cardboard-cutting machine in a Bridgeton box-making factory, and in his spare time was a keen hill-walker, mountain-climber and worker for non-profit making companies of a social-equalitarian, recreational kind: a short-lived entertainment company called the Co-Optimists, The Ramblers' Federation, Camping Club of Great Britain, Scottish Youth hostel Association and Holiday Fellowship. He did unpaid secretarial work for these, having mastered typing, and for a short time wrote a column in the *Glasgow Herald* about open-air affairs. He enjoyed the works of George Bernard Shaw – had his complete plays in the 1934 edition, also the Everyman edition of Ibsen's plays in Archer's translation. The 1914–18 war made an agnostic of Alex Gray but (as he said) 'not an evangelical agnostic'. He never quarrelled about religion with his parents or anyone else.

1902   My mother Amy was born in Bridgeton by Emma Minnie Needham, daughter of a Northampton barber. Emma's husband, Harry Fleming, was a boot clicker – a kind of foreman in shoe factories – who brought his wife to Glasgow after English employers blacklisted him for his trade union activity. He liked reading to his family and with *Tess of the d'Urbervilles* brought my mother and her sister to tears. Amy became a shop assistant in the store of Campbell, Stewart and MacDonald, a clothing firm. She liked to sing, could accompany herself on the piano, attended opera and joined the Glasgow Orpheus Choir. She also went on rambles with the local branch of the Holiday Fellowship, on one of which she met Alex Gray.

1931   Alex and Amy married and came to live at 11 Findhorn Street, Riddrie, east Glasgow: one of the earliest and best planned housing schemes built under the Wheatley Act, the only equalitarian measure passed by the first Labour government elected in 1924. It lay between Alexandra Park on the west, Cumbernauld Road on the south, the huge double locks of Monkland Canal to the north, which curved to pass under Cumbernauld Road, enclosing Riddrie on the east before skirting the grounds of Barlinnie Jail. This scheme contained most things its inhabitants could need; two small shopping centres with baker, butcher, fishmonger, grocer, barber, newsagent-tobacconist, sweetshop, fish-and-chip shop, chemist; two Protestant churches, one of architectural merit; a Protestant primary school, splendid public library, a bowling green and allotments; also (on the other side of the Cumbernauld Road) two large cinemas, a Catholic church and primary school. The western half of the scheme was three storey tenements, the eastern was semi-detached villas, but many gardens, a tree-lined boulevard, the nearby park and a craggy knoll crowned with big old trees gave it a suburban, even rural feeling compared to Bridgeton, my parents' pre-marital home. Bridgeton was a working-class district that was not a slum, but a place where families of any size lived in two-room flats, the largest room being a kitchen with one cold-water tap, a fire range for all heating and cooking, and a bed recess. The other room was usually much smaller. There were communal lavatories on the communal stair, and municipal bathhouses for those who paid to wash in warm water. Interior lighting was still mostly gas. Alex Gray had lived in such a flat with three half-brothers by his father's first wife, who slept in the smaller room, and a sister he slept with in a hurly bed – a low bed with wheels which was stored under the kitchen recess bed by day and pulled out at night. Alex and Amy's Riddrie flat had three rooms with a fireplace in each, a small kitchen, a lavatory bathroom, hot-water supply from a tank behind the living-room fire, and electrical light. Alex's half-brothers emigrated and his parents died before my birth. Amy's parents came to live two blocks away from her in a semi-detached villa on the Cumbernauld Road.

I have annotated these three entries more than most others because they show why I know that Socialism can improve social life, that the work we like best is not done for money, and that books and art are liberating.

1934 Born on 28 December.

1937 Birth of my sister, Mora Jean Gray.

1938 Attended Riddrie primary school.

1940-42 Evacuated along with mother and sister, the three of us being first billeted on a farmer's family near Auchterarder in Perthshire, where I had my first asthma attack beside a corn-threshing machine. Rooms were later rented above a tailor's shop in Stonehouse, a Lanarkshire mining town. The farm experience was used in the *Lanark* Oracle's Prologue. Stonehouse gave the setting for Jock McLeish's childhood in *1982, Janine.* Meanwhile my dad was working as assistant manager in a hostel for munitions workers in Reading, a job he got through his voluntary work for the Holiday Fellowship, whose chairman had now a high place in the Ministry of Munitions.

1942 Alex Gray was appointed manager of a hostel for munitions workers in Wetherby, a Yorkshire market town. This was a large compound with many one-storey prefabricated dormitory blocks for munitions workers (about 2000 young women) linked by flagged paths to a central block containing offices, canteen, lounge with library and concert hall where films were shown at weekends: there was also a bungalow for the manager and his family, who joined him. My sister and I attended what was called the Church School, in Wetherby itself. While never forgetting that I was a Scot from Glasgow I mostly enjoyed life here, climbing trees, making dens in bushes, damming streams, picking brambles, cycling. I joined the Church of England choir (which was an excellent social club for boys) and sang in an oratorio, *The Crucifixion*. I read voraciously all works with elements of fantasy – *Alice in Wonderland, The Wind in the Willows*, Hawthorne's *Tanglewood Tales*, Kingsley's *The Heroes* and *The Water Babies*, the latter fascinating me by its mixture of genres: I was specially interested in books illustrated by the authors – Kipling's *Just So Stories*, Thackeray's *The Rose and the Ring*, Lofting's Dr Doolittle novels. How I came to write my first poem and the poem itself appear in 'Mr Meikle', the last of *Ten Tales Tall and True*. Having read a prose version of *The Odyssey* for children I wrote a one-scene play about Ulysses in Polyphemus' cave. My father typed it and my schoolteacher let me produce it in the classroom with me as Polyphemus. The only fiction I enjoyed before the age of fourteen was fantastical and mythical, but I also loved popular accounts of astronomy, natural history, archaeology, world history: *The Miracle of Life; Gods, Graves and Scholars; The Story of Mankind* and *The Home of Mankind*, written and illustrated by Hendric Van Loon.

1944 The hostel closed when the war ended, we returned to Findhorn Street and my father, whose only qualification for a professional job was the fact that he had succeeded in one for five years, had no wish to return to cutting cardboard. He became a labourer on a building site, then a site wages clerk with Scottish building firms. In England I had no sense of worry about exams or my future. Back in Glasgow my parents and teachers (the first took care to meet and discuss me with the second) were eager for me to get the mathematic and language skills that would fit me for a professional job via University. I consciously hated then (and still hate) the idea that anyone should suffer boredom and pain now in order to enjoy a better life later, but the ruling educational system was based on this, which may explain why I alternated between eczema and asthma attacks until my mid-twenties. I was urged to concentrate on maths, Latin and chemical formulas, which I could not learn because they were taught as mere memory exercises.

1946   Went to Whitehill Senior Secondary School, where teachers of art and English gave me scope and opportunity. So did Miss Jean Irwin's Saturday morning art class in Kelvingrove Art Gallery and Museum, which I attended during the summer months between the ages of 11 and 17, and saw an Edvard Munch exhibition of all his greatest paintings, which showed a world very like the Glasgow I knew. My father subscribed to the *New Statesman and Nation*, whose literary section was edited by V. S. Pritchett. His leading articles were a completer introduction to the great novelists of Russia, France and Britain than the schoolteachers gave, and from the reviews I gathered that Donne, Hopkins and Eliot were great poets, Melville and Kafka great novelists. These I obtained from Glasgow public library. Dad subscribed to The Readers Book Club, through which I enjoyed:

> *The Essential James Joyce* (*Dubliners* and *Portrait of the Artist as a Young Man*)
> *The Essential Hemingway* (selected stories, *Fiesta* and extracts from other novels)
> *A Voice through a Cloud* by Denton Welsh
> *The Death of the Heart* by Elizabeth Bowen.

These showed how mundane twentieth-century experience could be worked into art. All but Hemingway drew upon diaries. I had begun keeping sporadic diaries of daily existence when twelve, destroying them as I aged enough to reject them as childish, but I think Joyce's *Portrait of the Artist* suggested such notebooks could preserve useful raw materials for a book. But the Readers Union edition of Joyce Cary's *The Horse's Mouth* perhaps influenced me most of all. The artist hero, Gulley Jimson, is a character based (I heard recently) on Stanley Spencer. He is a neglected artist because his only wish is to paint large murals, which are no use to art galleries and dealers. He dies cheerfully painting one in a derelict church that a local authority starts demolishing. The theme of the mural is the Biblical creation. Jimson's artistic vision is informed by the poetry and philosophy of William Blake, which led me to study the Oxford edition of Blake's poetry in Riddrie public library, examine facsimiles of his books in Glasgow's Mitchell library, and decide to master an old testament book as a theme for narrative painting as completely as Blake had mastered the Book of Job. I quickly chose Jonah, first because it is very short, secondly because God is shown there working with and through a cowardly prophet who dislikes God when not actively inspired by him: and also shows God threatening evil to evil-doers, but refraining from hurting them when they repent. I read also the Readers Union edition of *Nineteen Eighty-Four* with Waley's translations of the Chinese classical poetry anthology and comic epic *Monkey*. Other epic allegories brought to me by the BBC Third Programme (a constant treasury of good things) were Goethe's *Faust*, Louis MacNeice's *The Dark Tower* and Wyndham Lewis' *Childermass*, later enlarged to a trilogy. I must stop listing books, plays, films which made me want to show details of my own possible life as part of a panoptic, almost picaresque fantasy.

1952   Mother died. Received prizes and Higher SCE for Art and English. Entered Glasgow Art School as described in the Thaw section of *Lanark*.

1953   On the last day of this year, after closing time outside the State Bar, I met Robert Kitts, a Slade art student come to Glasgow for Hogmanay. We convinced each other that we were geniuses, meeting next day to discuss and share poems and books we were writing. Through Robert (with whom I corresponded) I met London medical students, Mary and her brother Bill Hamilton, who specialised in entomology. Robert Kitts later introduced me to the London of television studios and Kelvin Walker.

1954 Having decided to write a tragic novel about Duncan Thaw, and knowing the start and end, I tried to do so in the art school summer holiday and finished *The War Begins* chapter, and hallucination episode in *The Way Out*.

1954–57 MURAL on **Horrors of War** (Glasgow Crucifixion and Apocalypse with Fall of Star Wormwood) in Scottish–USSR Friendship Society, 8 Belmont Crescent, Hillhead, Glasgow.

1956 *Jonah*, play written for and performed by Glasgow School of Art puppetry department.

1957 Graduated in design and mural painting; received Bellahouston travelling scholarship; used it as described in the *Lean Tales* account 'A Report to the Trustees'.

1958 Began painting a **MURAL** on **The Seven Days of Creation**, Chancel of Greenhead Church of Scotland, Bridgeton, Glasgow, in return for cost of painting materials only, while supporting myself by part-time art teaching in Lanarkshire schools. Also painted a cloudy **Firmament** with stars of David on the ceiling of Belleisle Street Synagogue, Giffnock, Glasgow. (Both buildings were demolished in the seventies.) Became friendly with Archie Hind and Joan Ure.

1960 Took part in public demonstrations against the coming of USA nuclear submarines to the Holy Loch. Painted large canvas, **The Fall of the Star Wormwood** for a CND exhibition **Artists Against the Bomb**, arranged by Church of Scotland clergy in Glasgow and Edinburgh.

1961 Brian Smith, secretary of Scottish CND, leased a soon-to-be-demolished ancient building in West Bow, Edinburgh, and ran it as a CND nightclub called Festival Late, with a staff of helpers paid irregularly out of the door takings. I painted murals in black and gold on the whitewashed walls of the main dance room, and did a variety of cabaret turns (a lecture on how to build your own rhinoceros, and singing melodramatic sentimental and patriotic Victorian ballads). Here I met and quickly married Inge Sørensen, a Danish nurse who left her Edinburgh city hospital job to live with me first in 11 Findhorn Street, shifting shortly after to Hill Street, central Glasgow. **MURAL** illustrating **The Book of Jonah** in private flat, 280 West Princes Street, Hillhead, Glasgow.

1962–63 Became scene painter for Glasgow Pavilion and then Glasgow Citizens' Theatres: designed scenery for pantomime *Dick Whittington*. Completed the Creation mural, Greenhead.

1963–64 Drew social security benefit as unemployed scene painter. Painted. Submitted Book 1 of *Lanark* to Curtis Brown Literary Agency who rejected it. (Published with three other Books as one volume in 1981.) Birth of son.

1964 *Under the Helmet*, 50-minute TV documentary about Gray's work in painting and verse, was networked by BBC; Bob Kitts director, Huw Wheldon producer. Payment for this allowed a start as a self-employed artist and writer, with seven one-man exhibitions at the Edinburgh Traverse Gallery and Glasgow Kelly Gallery in the following years, aided by some lecturing on art appreciation for Glasgow University Extra-Mural Department.

1968 *The Fall of Kelvin Walker*, 50-minute TV play, networked by BBC2. **MURAL, Black and White Earth Mother Phantasmagoria** in stairwell of private house, 10 Kelvin Drive, Hillhead, Glasgow. Before Christmas moved to 39 Kersland Street, West Glasgow. *Quiet People*, 30-minute radio play, BBC Scotland.

1969 Received grant from Scottish Arts Council to make a series of prints illustrating own verses. *Dialogue*, 30-minute radio play, BBC Scotland. **MURAL, Falls of Clyde landscape**, The Tavern,

Kirkfieldbank, Lanarkshire. Left wife and son. Lodged at 11 Turnberry Road.

1970   *The Trial of Thomas Muir*, 30-minute radio play, BBC Scotland.

1971   *The Night Off*, 45-minute radio play, networked by BBC. *Dialogue*, one-act stage play, performed by Stage Company, Gateway Theatre, Edinburgh Festival, with Blocks Play by Cecil Taylor. *Honesty* and *Martin*, 20-minute TV plays, Scottish BBC Schools.

1972   *Today and Yesterday*, series of three 20-minute plays, for Scottish BBC Schools series. *Dialogue*, 30-minute TV play networked by London BBC. *Triangles*, 60-minute TV play networked by Granada. *The Fall of Kelvin Walker* stage version taken on tour by the Stage Company, Scotland.

1972–74 Attended Philip Hobsbaum's writers' group, where I became friendly with Tom Leonard, James Kelman, Chris Boyce, Angela Mullane and others.

1973   *James Watt*, 10-minute TV play for Glasgow Schools service. *The Man Who Knew About Electricity*, 20-minute TV play networked by London BBC magazine Full House. *Homeward Bound* and *The Loss of the Golden Silence*, one-act stage plays produced by Pool Lunch Hour Theatre, Edinburgh. *The Loss of the Golden Silence*, 30-minute radio play, BBC Scotland. **MURAL** on **The Book of Ruth**, Greenbank Church of Scotland, Clarkston. Father died.

1974   **MURAL** on ecological cycles, Exhibition Centre, Palacerigg Nature Reserve, Cumbernauld. **Retrospective Painting Exhibition** in the Collins Gallery, Strathclyde University.

1975   *McGrotty and Ludmilla*, 50-minute radio play networked by London BBC. Designed and illustrated *A Scent of Water*, children's stories by Carl MacDougall. Returned to 39 Kersland Street, first wife and son having left there for England.

1976 *Beloved*, 60-minute TV play networked by Granada. As producer had changed script without consultation, I withdrew my name from the credits, which may have stunted my career as a playwright. From then till 1988 a great part of my income came from subletting rooms to acquaintances. **MURAL: Florid Jungle**, in courtyard of Ubiquitous Chip Restaurant, Ashton Lane, Hillhead, Glasgow. (Painted in return for meals, and later destroyed by damp penetration.)

1977 *Socrates*, 60-minute TV play networked in England by Granada. Employed as Glasgow's official **Artist Recorder** for nine months by curator Elspeth King, painting portraits of contemporaries and streetscapes for the People's Palace Local History Museum.

1977-79 **Writer in Residence**, Glasgow University.

1980-81 **MURAL: Arcadia**, back stairwell of Ubiquitous Chip Restaurant.

1981 *Lanark*, a novel, Canongate, Edinburgh. Received David Niven and Saltire awards, also Scottish Arts Council design award. From this date onwards I lived almost wholly by writing, designing and illustrating books, mainly my own.

1982 *Tickly Mince*, review written in collaboration with Liz Lochhead and Tom Leonard, acted in the Pleasance, Edinburgh, and Tron Theatre, Glasgow.

1983 *The Pie of Damocles*, review in same venues by same writers, with addition of James Kelman. *Beim Zugführer*, translation of 30-minute radio play rejected by the BBC, and broadcast by West Deutsches Rundfunk. *Unlikely Stories, Mostly*, Canongate, Edinburgh, a collection of tales which received Times Literary Supplement and SAC design award. Designed and illustrated *Shoestring Gourmet*, Canongate, Edinburgh, recipe book by Wilma Paterson.

1983–95 Designed 15 original covers for *Chapman* literary magazine.

1983–84 Wrote advertisement and three commentaries to *The Anthology of Prefaces*, for an agent, Fiona Morrison, who got it accepted by Canongate Press three years later.

1983–85 Iain Brown (producer) and Sandy Johnson (director) asked me to work with them on a screen play of *Lanark*. Iain (then of Midnight Movies) bought the film rights, paid me to work with Sandy Johnson on script and story board. The Thaw section was completed.

1984 *1982, Janine*, a novel, Cape, London.

1985 *The Fall of Kelvin Walker*, novella, Canongate, Edinburgh. *Lean Tales*, Cape, London, story collection with James Kelman and Agnes Owens. *Saltire Self Portrait*, Saltire Society, Edinburgh, small autobiographical pamphlet, with interview.

1986 *McGrotty and Ludmilla*, stage play at Tron Theatre, Glasgow. *5 Scottish Artists Show*. Organised and paid for a large *Retrospective Exhibition*, with printed catalogue, of works by self and contemporaries which was shown in Glasgow McLellan Gallery, Talbot Rice Gallery, Edinburgh and Aberdeen Art Gallery.

1987 *The Story of a Recluse*, 50-minute TV play, networked by BBC. Signed contract to write *The Anthology of Prefaces*.

1988 *Old Negatives – Four Verse Sequences*, Cape, London.

1988-90 Was art editor, designer and illustrator (unpaid) for Dog and Bone, a small unprofitable publishing house financed by Angela Mullane, partly so that the typesetter she employed could also work on *The Book of Prefaces* under my direct supervision. We issued two poetry books, two crime fictions, a comic novella, a cookery book and a paranormal study before collapsing.

1989 Decanted to 52 St Vincent Terrace, Glasgow G38. Met Morag McAlpine.

1990 *McGrotty and Ludmilla*, a novella, Dog and Bone, Glasgow. *Something Leather*, a novel, Cape, London. *The Fall of Kelvin Walker*, stage play, Arches Theatre, Glasgow.

1991 Married Morag McAlpine and moved to her home in 2 Marchmont Terrace, Glasgow.

1992 *Why Scots Should Rule Scotland* (political pamphlet published for a general election), Canongate, Edinburgh. *Poor Things*, Victorian historical novel, Bloomsbury, London, received Guardian and Whitbread awards. Sold the film rights to Iain Brown, now of Parallel Pictures Company.

1993 *Ten Tales Tall and True*, short stories, Bloomsbury, London.

1994 *A History Maker*, science-fiction novel, Canongate, Edinburgh. This adapted TV play, planned in 1966, given to Canongate in return for the copyright of the Preface Anthology, which I then sold to Bloomsbury in return for an advance of £1000 a month.

1995-96 **MURAL: The Thistle of Dunfermline's History**, Abbot's House Local History Museum, Maygate, Dunfermline. Commissioned by Elspeth King on behalf of the Carnegie Trust.

1996 *Mavis Belfrage*, novella and short stories, Bloomsbury, London. *Songs of Scotland*, 100 traditional songs chosen by Wilma Paterson, book designed, illustrated and co-edited by Gray, Mainstream, Edinburgh. *Working Legs*, play written for Birds of Paradise Theatre Company for the disabled, taken on tour of Scotland.

1997 *Why Scots Should Rule Scotland*, the 1992 pamphlet extensively rewritten for another general election, Canongate, Edinburgh. *Working Legs: A Play for People without Them*, published as a book by Dog and Bone, Glasgow,

1999-01 **MURAL on Arcadia Theme**: a restoration and enlargement of the stairwell mural in the Ubiquitous Chip Restaurant.

1999 *Introduction* to the books of Jonah, Micah, Nahum published by Canongate, Edinburgh.

2000 *The Book of Prefaces*, published by Bloomsbury, London. *16 Occasional Poems 1990-2000*, published by Morag McAlpine, Glasgow.

2001 *A Short Survey of Classic Scottish Writing*, published by Canongate, Edinburgh. **MURALS**: Restorations of Jonah painting in 280 West Princes Street and ecology mural, Palacerigg former nature reserve (now called Country Park), Cumbernauld. Iain Brown forms *Poor Things Ltd*, a company intending to film the book. I start work as professor of Creative Writing at Glasgow University, sharing the post and salary with James Kelman and Tom Leonard.

2002 Introduction to Carlyle's *Sartor Resartus* for Canongate Classics publication, Edinburgh.

Books by Alasdair Gray Containing Fragments of Autobiography

Lean Tales (The Postscript), Jonathan Cape
5 Scottish Artists Retrospective Show Catalogue, Famedram Press
Alasdair Gray: Saltire Self-Portrait 4, The Saltire Society,
  Edinburgh
McGrotty and Ludmilla (Acknowledgements), Dog and Bone Press
Something Leather (Critic Fuel, an Epilogue), Jonathan Cape
Ten Tales Tall and True (Mr Meikle – An Epilogue), Bloomsbury
Mavis Belfrage with five other tales (Edison's Tractatus),
  Bloomsbury
Sixteen Occasional Poems (Poems 1, 2, 3 and Postscript), Morag
  McAlpine

(They can be ordered from: morag@mcalpine44.freeserve.co.uk)

ALASDAIR GRAY INTERVIEWED BY KATHY ACKER : 1986

A Public Interview at the ICA, London

This interview with Kathy Acker was recorded at the Institute of Contemporary Arts in 1986, when I visited London to publicise The Fall of Kelvin Walker. *The transcription of the recording proved that my words had been, like most impromptu speech, muddled, repetitive, and wrong about dates. My answers here have been corrected, neatened and arranged more logically, some of them shortened and others greatly enlarged. The whole is now, after many revisions, a true account of my working life before the age of 51. Kathy Acker's introduction and questions are unchanged.*

KA: Alasdair Gray is one of my two favourite writers in English-speaking countries (I won't say England). Just very briefly and simplistically, one of the reasons why I admire Alasdair's writings so much is that in a novel such as *Lanark* he does just about everything. He takes what is usually a popular genre or mode – that of fantasy – and turns it into a vehicle for politics, for descriptions of very personal lives in Glasgow and in Scotland, where he ventures into social realism as in the story about Thaw and just does the unexpected. At the same time, he has a structure in which you always are aware of a mind that is rigorous in its method of asking questions so you have all this simultaneous with a feeling mind that explores in every way the heights and depths of the imagination. Such venturing is rare in the novel and rare in the 'British' novel, although I'm not quite sure that he's a 'British' writer. It seems that Alasdair works in genres and that something like *Lanark* takes the vehicle of a fantasy novel. *Kelvin Walker* is a sort of essay on morals, but it disguises itself as a comedy of manners and the reason it is a comedy of manners, or a comedy of errors, is because each character has national characteristics which are played against ideals in what is a very, very funny novel.

What I really want to know is generally how do you make your novels, at what point does the structure appear?

AG: My three novels were written in different ways. At an early age I wanted to write a Great Book, and kept starting, but each time I read what I'd written I saw my words were those of a child. In adolescence I wrote almost nothing but adolescent gush and kept thinking 'this won't do'. My favourite genre in those days was tales beginning realistically, then shifting to a world of wonders through a rabbit hole, magic door or space ship. But when I went to Glasgow Art School in 1952 I had read or was reading Joyce's *Portrait of the Artist*, Joyce Cary's *The Horse's Mouth*, also Orwell's *Nineteen Eighty-Four*, most of Kafka and Waley's translation of *Monkey*, the comic Chinese Buddhist epic.

I now meant to write a realistic story about a Glasgow artist who would be very like me but commit murder and suicide because nobody loved him and he felt that he could never make the great art work he imagined. This was the biggest tragedy an imaginative narcissist like myself could imagine. I regretted that my hero had to be an artistic Young Bloke – too many books about those – but it was easiest. I had more information on the person I was and would like to be than I had on anybody else, which was depressing. It is a pity that writers write so often about being artists. The best kind of writer doesn't need to do that but I had to do it. But at the same time I was scribbling notes or passages for a Kafkaesque novel set in a modern vision of hell. Then when nineteen or twenty I read Tillyard's book *The English Epic and its*

Background. He began by discussing the great poems of Homer and Virgil, but said many works of prose were planned as epics: Herodotus's *Histories,* for example, *Bunyan's Holy War,* and Gibbon's *Decline and Fall.* He thought that the Scottish novels of Walter Scott, read together, amounted to a Scottish Epic. I remember thinking, 'Aha! Then my great novel must be an Epic!' For an Epic could contain everything I enjoyed in other books: the struggle of someone I could identify with, wide social scope, summings-up of the past, prophetic views of the future, and comic or fantastic escapes into supernatural worlds which were parodies or allegories of my own.

I now planned to put my descent to the underworld in the centre of my *Portrait of the Artist as a Young Man.* At a queer kind of drunken party my hero would meet an elderly gent (like me now) who would tell him a lengthy fantasy which would be enjoyable in itself: but when the readers returned to the realistic tale, and reached the end where the central character kills himself, they would see that his future would be the one described in the fantasy, and that the person he had met was the ghost of his later self. Between 1954 and 1978 I worked at different times on both tales, and the fabulous *Lanark* part became so much bigger than the realistic *Thaw* part that I decided to put the realism inside the fable. I think this 'Change of Life' happened when I was thirty-five.

KA: When did you start writing?

AG: I was probably nineteen, in 1954, when I decided I knew enough about my first novel to start writing that and found I was not mistaken. During a summer holiday from art school I wrote the first chapter of the Thaw section almost exactly as it is now, apart from adjectives and adverbs which I later cut out. I finished it twenty-four years later but I didn't spend twenty-four years writing it. I was doing lots of other things. There may have been a year or two in which I didn't write any of it at all, but I usually thought of it when standing at bus-stops – it was something to do with my head. I wanted the book to describe some of the worst and best things that can happen to a man, and sometimes thought, 'Maybe I will never experience enough to properly describe some of the worst and best things. What if I never marry? What if I never have a child?' Et cetera. But these things happened, so *Lanark* contains some convincing realities, and was printed in 1981.

The *1982, Janine* novel wasn't intended, because I only meant to write one novel and one book of short stories; but when writing what I thought my last short story it began to swell. It was based on a thought I had had in the early 1960s when I was a lecturer in Art Appreciation for the extra-mural department of Glasgow University. I often went by train to places like Dumfries, had my hotel accommodation paid for, and went to a hall where I spoke to people about Van Gogh and Gauguin. Afterwards in the hotel, not being conversational with people I don't know already or haven't been introduced to, I often sat in a corner of the bar parlour hearing folk talk about their work as farmers or as auctioneers or salesmen. I thought, 'Aha! They don't know who I am because I'm not talking. Little do they know who this is. Actually I don't know either – I might be anybody. But I hope I'm more important than they think.' I then imagined – I suppose I was conceiving myself at a distance – I imagined a man with a smug sense of being potentially greater than everybody, a sense he maintained by being nobody, by being alcoholic and REFUSING TO THINK ABOUT HIS LIFE. I had no idea of this man's sex life or working life because these things didn't interest even him. All that interested him was his potential, which the world would never notice. Later that evening I lay in bed and imagined him lying in bed foreseeing himself next morning on a station platform waiting for a train, and nobody else on the platform would know that for him just standing waiting for a train was a balancing act equivalent to a tightrope-walker on a high wire: only *he* would recognise the miraculous strength and self-control it took for him to stand still and seem ordinary while waiting for a train. I thought – I didn't like this man but felt I could put him into an interesting short monologue.

When I began writing it fifteen or sixteen years later, however, the monologue swelled up by taking in matters I had never intended to use in a book, for I agree with James Joyce when he says that great art should not move, that only improper arts (propaganda and pornography) move us, but true art arrests us in the face of eternal beauty, or truth, or something like that. But this particular story started discoursing of improper things: sex fantasies I had meant to die without letting anybody know happen in this head sometimes, and political diatribes. Anyway, it kept getting bigger and bigger until I had to divide it into chapters, and with every chapter I wrote I felt that the next would be the last. At the start I never thought he would try to kill himself, but by the tenth chapter I found him so obnoxious and he was so obnoxious to himself that I thought, 'He is going to kill himself and quite right too.' So I rewrote an earlier part, planted a bottle of pills on him that he could resort to and then I thought … next chapter he's done for. When I came to describe him actually taking the pills I thought, 'What happens now?' What usually happens when people try to take an overdose of pills? They usually sick them up. But what after that? Must he then, in the interests of realism, return to his dreary, alcoholic, prosperous job – his life-in-death? And I thought, 'I've made him a miserable bugger and put him through a load of pain, even though he's put others through it as well. Couldn't I give him a little light at the end of the tunnel? That would be a change.' So I made a novel I had not foreseen.

KA: Just let me interrupt for a second. Is it true you really agree with Joyce about things not moving, because your books are full of sexual fantasies and political wonderings?

AG: My excuse is that I put these things into a personal voice. In *Coriolanus*, Shakespeare has put a tremendous, strong, right-wing justification of elitist government into the mouth of one of his characters, one of his more decent aristocrats who realises that in order to manage the plebs you have to pretend to be one of them, *even though you're not.* You mustn't just bully and disdain them. He tells the parable of the belly, and explains it in a very clear right-wing speech which is probably what Shakespeare and most of his audience believed was a justification of aristocratic government. That political speech is artistically proper because it is uttered by a forceful character in a believable place at an interesting moment of social tension. I hope the things that happen inside my man's head are sound art for a similar reason. And I tried to make my man as different from me as possible, I did not want another bloody artist as a central character so I made him small and neat where I'm rotund and messy. I made him a scientist, a technician, somebody whose inventive skills were not aesthetic but practical. I had him start manhood with his best moment of sexual and social fulfilment, and his pleasure and possibilities from then onward taper to nearly nothing – my life has travelled the opposite way. But by making him wholly opposite I produced a negative self-portrait.

KA: Have you ever worked with a woman as a main character?

AG: Only in some plays, but always she's been seen in relation to a man. I haven't the insight to imagine how a woman is to herself.

KA: So how was *Kelvin Walker* constructed? Did that start with any political idea?

AG: It started as a television play broadcast nineteen years ago. The idea came from a time when I sometimes wrote and performed little cabaret turns, at first for art-school shows and then for CND concerts, so I always had my eyes open for an odd situation which could be caricatured. The oddest situation occurred to me when a television producer in London was in a position to make films about anyone who he liked and decided to make them about obscure friends who he felt OUGHT to be famous. So he made one about me. I was living on social security at the time and got a telegram saying 'PHONE BBC. REVERSE CHARGES.' I did so and Bob said, 'I want you to meet Huw Wheldon at quarter to twelve on Thursday morning at Shepherds Bush, to discuss this film about you.' I said, 'No, on Thursday I have to sign on at my Labour Exchange at ten past nine.' Bob said, 'Ah, but you can take a taxi to the airport,' and I said, 'I cannot afford to take a taxi,' and he said, 'We'll book one. It will collect you at your Labour Exchange and when you get to Heathrow look for a man with a sign saying Herz Cars and he will drive you to Shepherds Bush.' I enjoyed the huge social derangement of being made to feel rich and famous, neither of which was the case. It became easy to fantasise about a young Scot in sixties London. One thing about being Scottish in London in those days was a sense of removed pressure, the freedom of feeling that because no Londoner understood me, I might, with a bit of push, become (here it comes again) anybody. In most communities people's potentials are limited by their relations' and neighbours' knowledge of them. I did not fantasise about abandoning my wife and son – that would have been too personal. I fantasised about a young Scot who arrives in mid-sixties London with a gigantic euphoria caused by one fact – his father isn't near him. His father – like many men of strong faith – uses his faith to crush people under him, especially his children. But faith isn't an issue in England and Kelvin cannot be much embarrassed by anything people say or do to him there because his Dad is the only thing he really dreads. I wrote an imaginary interview between this youth and a businessman he fails to impress – I conceived it as a cabaret turn, and then imagined another scene for him in a Soho café in which he greets a girl with the words, 'Do you mind if I engage you in conversation?' And suddenly the scenes suggested other ones, became an evolving play, a play about an outsider (outsiders were popular in the late fifties and sixties) Making It To The Top by dint of nothing but glibness. But when he reached the top I began to think, 'What a nasty person he is'. He was only likeable as somebody with nothing going for him trying to climb to the top of the ladder. Of course, when a success he becomes as exploitive and greedy as the people he's joined. So I thought, 'I want to knock him down. Aha! Bring his father back. That'll cut him down to size.'

KA: In your other novels you make a point of listing the influences which helped to produce them. Were you influenced directly by anybody's writing in *Kelvin Walker*?

AG: I remember that in writing *The Fall of Kelvin Walker* I was influenced by a play by Donleavy called, I think, *Fairy Tales of New York*. It was printed in some small, international American literary magazine in the late fifties. I remember a scene where a young chap, in an interview with a businessman, talks his way into quite a top-level job simply because he's got a way with words. The young man is slightly naive and the great big businessman is also naive, but he doesn't know it. As for the main form of the plot, it is very much like Synge's *Playboy of the Western World*, though I didn't notice that either when writing it. But as Leavis says, 'Probably most inspiration is unconscious reminiscence'.

KA: How does your artwork fit in with your writing?

AG: I don't think it does before the writing stops and I design the resulting book. When I came off the Labour Exchange as a result of getting the Kelvin Walker play taken, I couldn't support myself by writing for radio or television, because I only got a commission once or twice a year, or less. But I got occasional portrait and mural commissions, and so with the two I was able to do both. Nobody strongly encouraged me to concentrate on either. I couldn't have lived by just one of them.

KA: Has it been hard for you to make a living as a writer? Has it been possible?

AG: It wasn't possible at first. The only paying job I was fit for after art school was schoolteaching. I luckily married a lady who preferred her husband at home even though it meant not bringing much money in. A respectable Scottish wife would have probably kept me teaching for years by being nice to me. I would come back from a day of teaching in a state every teacher knows, tired out and only able to talk in short phrases of single-syllable words for a couple of hours afterwards. Of course my wife, who had been feeling lonely a lot of the day, would say things and I would say, 'Hmm, yes,' and she would say, 'Why aren't you talking to me?' and I would think, 'I'm working like this for you and you won't even give me peace to recover from it.' And at last I told her that aloud and she said, 'Well if you're doing it for me then you had better stop because I don't like the result.' So after two years I got work as a scene painter, and when I lost that job I lived on the dole and by art for a while. My wife disliked many things about me but she never complained about our poverty. I was lucky in what other people thought a miserable marriage. It wasn't really. Then after my wife and I parted, I came to rent a big tenement flat and sublet rooms to friends. That helped. For the last two years I've had hardly any money worries.

KA: But didn't it gnaw at your writing at all, any economic concerns?

AG: The worst time was 1969 when I wrote about the horrid city of Unthank in *Lanark*, book one. I stopped writing, saw the domestic situation I was in and thought, 'I don't want to face this world, let's get back to the hellish one I'm imagining'. The truth was worse than the fiction, and drove me to it.

KA: Did you feel that you were alone or did you feel that you were supported by a community of artists?

AG: The only professional writer I knew before the age of thirty-five was Archie Hind, the author of the novel *The Dear Green Place*, which came out in the late 1960s. He and I knew each other, but you can't have a community of just two. The community which supported me was an aunt I could always run to for a meal and friends I could borrow a fiver from, Archie and his wife Eleanor and some painter friends. And around 1972 or 73 I came to know Liz Lochhead, Tom Leonard and Jim Kelman, who live near me in Glasgow. We baby-sat for each other, read and criticised each other's work. No doubt we were, or are, a mutual admiration club, but we HAVE made admirable things. Through a writing class run by Philip Hobsbaum, I met other writers and poets, one a journalist, one a lawyer who became very helpful friends indeed.

Question from the audience: Do you write about people who you like? Who are your favourite characters among those that you've written about?

AG: From the point of view of personally liking, there's a girl called Jill in *The Fall of Kelvin Walker* whom I like very much. She's a not very clever, slightly upper-class English woman, but her instincts are all decent. I think she's the nicest person I've written about. She was copied from a nice person. I'm prejudicial toward some characters, but identify with all of them. I don't need to like them because I don't need to like myself. I find myself interesting, not likeable, but that doesn't bother me. I've a VAST toleration for myself. Sorry, it's impossible for somebody to talk about themselves in public without mentally wanking.

Question from the audience: What is your next book going to be about?

AG: I don't think I'm going to write more fiction. I'm fifty-one. Almost certainly I'm going to get more complacent the more money divorces me from real suffering. (Thinks … Thank God.) I'm pretty sure that I'm not going to write any more fictional works.

KA: Why?

AG: I don't think I have any ideas, even though *1982, Janine* came from a short story that grew very big. It was an idea that I had for many years before I started it. I feel, however, that every fiction book I've written has been very different from the other and if I wrote another one it would be very like one of the four I've done already. In fact, I would bore myself if I … any other idea I would have would be very boring to develop.

Question from the audience: Your writing seems to me to contain a lot of anger. Do you agree?

AG: You might be right, but not while I'm at work. When writing about strong emotion I feel outside it, which is essential to describing a thing well. The main excitement of authorship is stopping the work being a bore. I keep wanting to surprise myself by a new development and thinking, 'Aha! Good heavens, could he do that? Or might this happen? Yes, of course it could!' That process excites me. But I don't feel anger, misery or lust when describing them, just satisfaction when the job goes well.

If I start talking about the things I don't like in contemporary social and political society, my voice goes up and I become intense, become repetitive and realise that a tape-recording is unwinding from my mouth and I have heard it before. I try not to get angry because as soon as you start yelling at people they naturally start doing it back AND nobody learns. No ideas are communicated.

Question from the audience: Your books use a lot of eccentric typography. How did that start?

AG: My typographical mucking about started in the epilogue to *Lanark*, which is especially addressed to critics of the novel's pretensions. I wanted it to contain every academic device starting with footnotes, then remembered early Bibles used to have marginal notes and thought let's have that, that's not usually done, hence my index of plagiarisms.

My next book, *Unlikely Stories, Mostly*, contained 'Logopandocy', a story about words, which I doubt if one in twenty readers can be bothered with. I put in many illustrations, hoping that when folk came to stories that bored them, they would find it entertaining to look at and hop over and try elsewhere. 'Logopandocy' pretends to be written by Thomas Urquhart, an actual Scottish knight, who translated Rabelais into English, had many linguistic theories about the origin of language, and was so mad keen on words that he invented them and multiplied them in a way that was common in the seventeenth century – it wasn't regarded as bad practice. I had the notion of his diary becoming partly a double entry ledger with his profits on one side, losses on the other. Then I got the idea that while brooding on his losses Urquhart grows angry and intense, so the alphabetic letters and words in the column of injustices done him get larger and larger and start to squeeze in the column listing good things. I don't type myself, but I have friends who do so I drew a plan of the way I wanted it typed, and got it typed that way to show to the printer it was possible.

Then in *1982, Janine* I had a man talking inside his head, talking and remembering and fantasising in many different voices, one of them the voice of his God who interrupts him in brackets, questioning the assumptions by which the character moves, saying 'Why?', 'How?' and 'You weren't happy'. I came to imagine my man taking pills and falling into a fever in which the voices crowding his mind become simultaneous. On one margin the voice of his body complains of the feverish temperature he's condemned it to, while in the middle his deranged libido fantasises and alternates with his deranged conscience denouncing him for having such fantasies. On the other margin, in very small print, the voice of God tries to tell him something important, tell him he has missed the point of living in a voice he can hardly hear, because it is not thunderously denouncing, to correct him in gentle, sensible words which become a quotation from that great e e cummings poem which starts

> pity that busy monster man unkind not

and ends with

> say there's a hell of a good universe next door,
> let's go.

Because the world our humanity has built would be a wonderfully good one if we could change our mind a bit and do things more fairly. But before my man can be fair to others he must be fairer to himself. He doesn't realise that the job he's doing is bad, and killing him, and that he doesn't need it. He needs a whole nervous breakdown to tell him that. I thought that typographically enacted, this climax would be exciting, would surprise folk, especially when followed by some blank pages to convey sleep – perfect peace for a while. I like surprising, but there has to be a good reason. If you don't surprise with something sensible, you'll soon be forgotten. But I won't use typographical tricks again. Another version would look second hand, second rate.

KA: In all your novels, God comes in and you seem to identify with him, sometimes he is the voice of reason ….

AG: Yes, God usually arrives in some form or other, but the God changes depending on who believes in him. The God in *Kelvin Walker* is just an exaggerated form of himself. I tend to approve of the Jewish notion that it's wrong to think of God as having any character, as it will always be an idealised, and therefore idolised, form of the thinker. This process is described in *The Ruling Class* – I forget who wrote it, but it's a great film. The hero is an English Earl who discovers he is God when he notices that while praying he is talking to himself. Absolutely logical. And insane. But I will toy with insanity and say, 'God is the character of the universe minus myself,' and like many others I feel God – feel in harmony with the infinite and the eternal – in rare moments of highly privileged smugness. Quite a lot of leisured people feel that among lakes and mountains. They don't always call it 'God' or 'The Eternal' or 'The at-oneness' because that kind of language is not English, but however it's conceived, all the definitions of God have a sort of truth. God is one of the most popular characters in fiction. You've got to believe in even the rotten forms of him, just as you've got to believe in Iago or Mr Pickwick.

KA: It seems to me that the voice of God in your stories is always the voice of reason.

AG: I think that if you have a God you'd better keep it reasonable. But I suppose some people need unreasonable Gods to get out of a situation that their reason is insufficient to embrace.

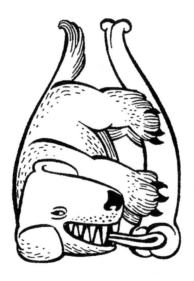

1994, JANINE

JONATHAN COE

IN 1984 I WAS A TWENTY-THREE YEAR OLD POSTGRADUATE student at Warwick University, writing – or, for the most part, failing to write – a doctoral thesis on Henry Fielding. In those days, however enlightened your teachers at school and university, the task of reading 'English' literature was still interpreted literally. After several years of studying the poetry, drama and fiction that (in those days at least) made up the canon, I could be forgiven for thinking that nobody north of Wordsworth's Cumbria had ever put pen to paper. Not even Burns got a look-in, as far as I remember. So when I found Alasdair Gray's *1982, Janine*, I approached it through the mist of a complete ignorance of Scottish writing.

Furthermore, like most people then and now, I knew almost nothing about contemporary literature, and cared less. If I wanted to read something for pleasure, I would usually buy some classic English novel in an affordable Penguin edition. That seemed a reasonable guarantee of quality. Having an interest in comedy, I had once read a Kingsley Amis novel on a friend's recommendation, but it hadn't impressed or amused me. I couldn't really see how it was possible to write a novel like *Lucky Jim* more than thirty years after *Ulysses* had appeared, or in the same decade that *The Unnamable* was published. It seemed roughly as pointless as composing a Gilbert and Sullivan operetta in the era of Stockhausen and Cage. And spending time on reading such a book seemed an equal act of perverseness.

If I read contemporary fiction at all, I gravitated towards what people called 'experimental' writing. I had dipped my toe into Robbe-Grillet, and Pinget, and possibly even Christine Brooke-Rose, but had withdrawn it again quickly and with a sharp intake of breath, finding the waters chilly and unwelcoming. Someone had instilled at the back of my mind a quaint notion that novels should have an emotional as well as a cerebral impact, that they should contain characters with whom the reader was made to sympathise, that they should carry the reader, buoyed up by curiosity, on a propulsive narrative journey. None of the experimental writers I read seemed to do any of these things (although I still couldn't see, personally, why they should be incompatible with modernist methods).

These feelings put me at odds with my fellow students and tutors, many of whom believed that, where contemporary fiction was concerned, something exciting was in the air. This was in the early 1980s, remember. A display of public rivalry between Anthony Burgess and William Golding had considerably raised the profile of the Booker Prize. The English literary magazine *Granta* had just published its first list of The Best Twenty Young British Novelists. This campaign had caught the imagination of the media, and the moody, chiselled faces of some of these Young Turks gazed out of the pages of the style magazines. People were telling me that I *had* to read Martin Amis' *Money* and Graham Swift's *Waterland* and McEwan's *The Comfort of Strangers* and Barnes' *Before She Met Me*.

All of which I did. And yet ….

And yet I would still rather have been reading *Tom Jones*. And still I hadn't found anyone who was doing for the novel of the late twentieth century what Fielding had done for his era, or Sterne for his. A tall order, I realise, but isn't the reader of fiction, with millions of titles to choose from, entitled to make tall orders?

I remained, all the same, a perpetually hopeful browser of the university bookshop. This was in the days before I had penetrated the London literary world, with its codes and coteries, its gossip and its inside information, so like all such hopeful browsers, I was groping in the dark, and whether or not I bothered to pluck a book down from the shelves depended upon four things: the title, the jacket illustration, the publisher's blurb and (occasionally) whether there was a persuasive quotation anywhere on the cover. In this way, I was lucky enough to discover, at around the same time, another novel that was to have a formative influence: *Christie Malry's Own Double-Entry*, by B. S. Johnson. An endorsement by Samuel Beckett ('a most gifted writer') seemed to point to something out of the ordinary, and for once I found what I was looking for: a subversive, involving, politically engaged novel that at the same time had an intelligent self-reflexiveness, a willingness to interrogate its own formal procedures. Johnson died too early to have discovered Alasdair Gray's work; I don't know if Gray is familiar with Johnson's. They have much in common.

And then, shortly after making this discovery – or perhaps it was shortly before – my eye was caught by a copy of *1982, Janine* in the Penguin paperback edition. I can remember now the exact position on the shelf that it occupied in the university bookshop, and turning the volume over in my hands I came, first of all, upon the following words:

> This already dated novel is set inside the head of an ageing, divorced, alcoholic, insomniac supervisor of security installations who is tippling in the bedroom of a small Scottish hotel. Though full of depressing memories and propaganda for the Conservative party it is mainly a sado-masochistic fetishistic fantasy. Even the arrival of God in the later chapters fails to elevate the tone. Every stylistic excess and moral defect which critics conspired to ignore in the author's first books, *Lanark* and *Unlikely Stories, Mostly*, is to be found here in concentrated form.

If I were ever to give a masterclass in blurb writing, I think this would be my set text. Not only does it tell you everything you need to know about the book, it also, more importantly, defines the author's own attitude towards it: mordant, ironic, self-deprecating. I bought the novel and took it back to my hall of residence, quietly confident that it was going to change my life.

1982, Janine is strong meat. I don't refer primarily to the Sadeian fantasies; what disturbed me more, given the rarefied air of political puritanism that I (and most other people on campus) breathed in those days, was its sustained willingness to inhabit the Tory mindset. For a while – knowing nothing about Alasdair Gray – I thought that the book must actually have been written by a Tory. Even in my state of hopeless political and literary naïvety I had worked out that great writers (Céline, for instance) could have objectionable political opinions, and it gave me a wicked thrill to think that I was reading something written by a *bona fide* supporter of the party whose every credo I had come to fear and despise. But gradually I came to see that *1982, Janine* is a socialist novel of the best and most satisfying kind: it makes out an unanswerable case (unanswerable while you are reading it, at any rate) for Conservatism as a state of absolute spiritual bankruptcy. Jock McLeish's Conservatism is something he has to cure himself of, every bit as much as his alcoholism and his S&M fantasising, if he is to become a human being again at the end of the book.

Of course I loved the playfulness of *1982, Janine*: the brilliantly-designed typography in Chapter 11 to signify Jock's descent into alcoholic delirium (B. S. Johnson was using similar devices in *Travelling People*, but Gray takes it further and does it better), the joky page headings in every margin, the enigmatic chapter summaries ('An empty future, a colourful present, a fucked nation and more forgotten history are introduced by a dream, two old socialists and an exciseman'). But what impressed me most was the ease and the lack of embarrassment with which this playfulness took its place alongside a profound seriousness. A similar claim was being made for some of the writers on the Granta list, and yet to me, at that time, Martin Barnes, Julian McEwan *et al* seemed somehow too suave, too urbane to – well, to *let themselves go*, if you like, in the way that Gray did so exhilaratingly. On the one hand I couldn't imagine them taking his extreme formal risks; and on the other, there was a nakedness, a raw vulnerability and above all an element of plain speaking about *1982, Janine* that seemed to represent the absolute antithesis of metropolitan cool:

> Are there many people without illness or disability who sit at home in the evening with clenched fists, continually changing the channel of a television set and wishing they had the courage to roll over the parapet of a high bridge? I bet there are millions of us.[1]

As I made my way through the novel, sentences like this – simple statements of obvious but unspeakable truth – kept hitting me like a sharp slap in the face administered kindly to someone in a swoon.

I was later to realise that this is the characteristic Alasdair Gray mode: he gets the reader into a state of fantastic high spirits, largely by means of the bubbling inventiveness with which the books are presented, the sense of being – as far as the formal peripherals are concerned – in thoroughly genial if eccentric company, and then proceeds to douse us thoroughly with a bracing bucketful of his radical good sense. The effect is something like getting overheated in a sauna and then plunging immediately into a cold pool with a delicious mixture of horror and relief. To take two random examples from *1982, Janine*:

> he [Jock's Dad] certainly prepared me for LIFE – which is a spark of delight buried under routines disciplines possessions plans and compromises which are meant to protect it, help it grow, make it useful to other people, and which eventually smother and kill it.[2]

Or:

> A smart Tory does not believe this is, or can be, a pleasant world for most folk. He knows that anyone with five pounds in an account has inadvertently invested half of it in practices which would make him vomit if he could see them.[3]

The apogee of this mode is reached a few years later in *Poor Things*, with the chapter in which the naïve Bella Baxter has all the idealism crushed out of her during a series of conversations with the brutally cynical Harry Astley. Astley systematically demolishes the foundations of her optimism with a series of pithy life-lessons under headings such as History, Freedom and The Benefits of War. He even disillusions her about sex by telling her that in England 'wives are treated as the public ornaments and private pleasure parks of wealthy landowners, industrialists and professional men'.[4]

I have always found the sex in *1982, Janine*, incidentally, among the most boring ever committed to paper. This might be intentional (Jock himself is clearly bored witless by his own fantasies at the end of the book – this is one of the reasons he decides to abandon them) or it may simply prove that we all have different fetishes and what excites one person's sexual imagination may leave another's flaccid and indifferent.

None of the sexual material in the novel strikes me as dodgy, however (it all takes place in somebody's head, after all), except for the way Jock McLeish once or twice uses the word 'rape' to describe occasions when women (Helen, Sontag, the editor) have engaged him in loveless sex and then abandoned him. Calling this 'rape' seems at the very least to be arguable, but it in no way detracts from the novel's central insight: its recognition that many people, in moments of unhappiness, use sexual fantasies in the same way they use alcohol, to ward off unpleasant memories and to lull themselves into an uneasy sleep.

Anyway, it's only the fantasy sex that is boring. The 'real' sex, the sex that is supposed at some point to have taken place outside Jock McLeish's head, is described with a plainness and honesty and lack of sensationalism that makes it deeply sympathetic and compelling, if entirely unerotic. Jock's first description of sex with the editor has always haunted me:

> We had to be drunk first. Each knew what the other wanted but was terrified all the same, terrified of not giving pleasure, terrified of not receiving it.[5]

Again, this seemed to run against the grain of much that I'd read in contemporary fiction, where the dominant methods were either to affect an ironic swagger and bravado about sex, or to exploit male sexual timidity and awkwardness for largely comic effect. Gray's clear-sighted recognition that terror might have a large part to play in a new sexual encounter impressed and astonished me: it seemed a magnificent achievement to battle your way towards such statements – to *earn* the right to include them, I suppose – by setting them within a framework so complex and playful and alert to the novel's myriad formal possibilities.

And on a larger scale, this is what Gray has brought off both in *1982, Janine* and *Lanark*. The strongest sections of both books, in my opinion, are the lengthy social realist passages that lie at their centres: the Duncan Thaw *bildungsroman* that makes up Books One and Two of *Lanark*, and the Edinburgh Festival episode that occupies almost a third of *1982, Janine*. The pleasures that readers derive from these sections are deeply traditional: rich characterisations, involving narratives, emotional engagement, and so on. But the novels in which they are lodged are anything but old-fashioned. Somehow, in these books – and later on in *Poor Things*, the third of his masterpieces – Alasdair Gray found a way of reconciling all the strongest virtues of classic fiction with a thoroughly self-questioning and (damn! just when I thought we'd managed to avoid the word) postmodern sensibility. This was what excited me so much back in 1984, this was what I had not yet found in the work of Graham Barnes and Martin McEwan, this was what made me realise that contemporary fiction could still be a vivid and vital way of interpreting the world, and so this (indirectly and some would say trivially) was what revived my flagging impetus to continue writing fiction myself.

So there you have it.

On a final, even more personal note, I should add that *1982, Janine* inspired me in other ways, too. Three years later I got a job in the proofreading department of a large London law firm. I found myself working opposite a rather beautiful young Australian woman who I might never have asked on a date if her name had not been Janine, and if I had not been so obsessed with Alasdair Gray's novel. Reader, I married her. Later I wrote a novel called *What a Carve Up!* and dedicated it to '1994, Janine', phrasing the dedication so that it referred to my wife, to the year of publication and also to the novel that had so excited me ten years earlier. I sent a copy of the novel to Alasdair Gray and a few days later received his reply, on the back of a postcard depicting 'The Artist and His Wife' by Peter Severin Krøyer:

> I'm glad to see a reference to a book I wrote, in the dedication to Janine at the start of It's a Carve Up [sic] – delighted to know my book was a good influence. But now the happiness of more than 2 lives depends on you. If you ever get divorced I'll cut my throat.
> Sincerely
> Alasdair Gray.

Ever since then, we have felt obliged to stay together through thick and thin, for literature's sake if no other.

Notes

1. Alasdair Gray, *1982, Janine* (London: Cape, 1984), p. 72.
2. Ibid.,p. 96.
3. Ibid., p. 137.
4. Alasdair Gray, *Poor Things* (London: Bloomsbury, 1992), p. 155.
5. Gray, *1982, Janine*, p. 58.

'AN EQUAL ACCEPTANCE OF LARKS AND CANCER'
The Poetry and Poetics of Alasdair Gray

S. B. KELLY

TO SAY THAT ALASDAIR GRAY'S POETRY IS UNLIKE ANYTHING else in contemporary Scottish poetry tells us very little. *Everything* that Gray does – poetry, prose, plays, paintings or polemics – is unlike anything else in contemporary Scottish culture. His very idiosyncrasy is the hallmark and lodestone of his talent. That said, it must be admitted that Gray's poetry is less well known, and consequently there has been less critical engagement with his poetic output. In the course of this essay, I will present a close reading of Gray's two major poetic texts, *Old Negatives* (1989) and *Sixteen Occasional Poems* (2000), that will hopefully offer a key to the nature, or technique, of his poetry and a commentary on its underlying concerns.

Firstly, however, we should address the question of why Gray's poetry has not enjoyed the public acclaim of his novels. The answer to this seems less connected with the merits of his poetry than with the differing contexts of reception between prose and poetry. Scottish literature in the second half of the twentieth century suffered from an unfortunate false dichotomy of writers into either 'poets' or 'novelists'. Many of the writers depicted in Sandy Moffat's painting *Poet's Pub* wrote little or no prose fiction, and many were antipathetic to the genre. As Norman McCaig said: 'Write prose if you want to, but do it in a darkened room and wash your hands afterwards' – a comment that always puts me in mind of Gray's *1982, Janine*. The debate on the relevant virtues of prose and poetry had rumbled on in like vein since the early eighteenth century; with accusations of populism frequently levelled against prose fiction; and, indeed, the relative scale of publication reinforcing the idea of the select audience for poetry and the mass audience for prose. This urge for categorisation leads to sound-bite identification: Anthony Burgess referred to Gray as 'the most important Scottish novelist since Sir Walter Scott', conveniently sidelining the fact that both also wrote poetry.[1]

One must not be too hard on Burgess, because the 'culture of categorisation' was exacerbated by the bibliographical problems of poetry publication. For Burgess to have known about Gray's poetic oeuvre would have required him to keep an eye on magazine publication: Gray's work appeared in *Lines Review*, *Glasgow Review*, *Clanjamfrie* and later in *Chapman* and *Prospice*, among others. To reconstruct a literary reputation from magazine publication needs an archaeological turn of mind. As Thom Nairn correctly observes in 'The Necessity of Dragons', *Old Negatives*, when published in 1989, was the cumulation of thirty years of writing poetry.[2]

Without wishing to state the obvious, *Old Negatives* is a book. The book has always had a totemic, material existence in Gray's work; from the postmodernist erratum slip to the coded messages beneath the dust-cover. *The Book of Prefaces* is a hymn to the book. Moreover, *Old Negatives* has an internal logic, even a narrative, that cannot be fully comprehended through sampling the work in magazines. This is not to say that the poems do not stand as intact entities in their own right; rather that they reinforce each other and set up dialectic conflicts between each other. *Old Negatives* is divided into four verse sequences that add up into a collection; with *Occasional Poems* as a fifth epode to the quartet.

In a Cold Room 1952-57

Old Negatives is a book about love, and in the tradition of the Metaphysical poets, this love encompasses both the erotic and the theological. The opening poem, 'Time and Place', on a first reading situates the reader in a world not dissimilar to many of Philip Larkin's poems: nocturnal locations, jazz music, and a narrator in some way excluded from the sociability and hedonism.[3] There are, however, indications of something different going on. The narrator passes through a 'dark arch' into candlelight, eerily reminiscent of an ecclesiastical building. The dancers stamp their feet to a beating drum, connoting some ritualistic element to the proceedings. As the other revellers depart to mattresses and couches – not beds – the narrator awaits 'that hint of revelation'. 'Revelation' perfectly encapsulates that nexus of erotic and theological imagery that underpins the first section; at once conveying a sense of titillation, of disrobing, and yet carrying the dark undertones of the Book of Revelation, and the Apocalypse. 'Predicting', the second poem, fast-forwards to the next morning. If a revelation has occurred, the reader is not yet privy to it. Picking up from the word 'dregs' in the previous piece, the opening stresses the expended: cinders, gnawed bones, empty streets. These melancholy meditations alter mid-way through the poem, when the narrator confesses to a 'remote hope':

> *when* these couples find they cannot sleep
> a girl I know *will* yawn and rub her eyes. *(my italics)*

The confident predictive tone, which seems to imply some guilt or distance between the lovers, is, however, undercut. 'Perhaps' the girl will 'talk with me'.

The next poem, 'Loneliness', appears to cast the narrator as an arch-Romantic, afflicted with the 'soul's proper loneliness'. The reader is brought up sharp by the last line – 'and a heart crippled by its weight of lust', rhymed with the previous line for maximum finality. Gray has lured the reader into figuring the narrator as an excluded, pining character, and the sudden admission of physical need and physical desire further complicates the narrator's voice. 'Mistaken' brings these disparate self-images together. The poem flirts with both the form and the register of the sonnet, beginning 'Let me be honest and condemn my love'. The argument of the first stanza introduces an important concept to the sequence as a whole: that love leaves an absence in the narrator. The second stanza, through subtle, syncopated rhymes, evokes an idyllic vision of companionship in the face of inevitable mortality, but is written in the conditional, stressing all the while that love is not such a blissful dwam. In the final part of the poem, the strength of Gray's voice reaches its crescendo. Love is not sympathy but 'must be felt hard in the lower part'. The line's brusque, Anglo-Saxon monosyllables and spondaic rhythm ram home the point. The conclusion –

> you make as little heat in me
> as I can make in you

– is a stark confession of mutual sexual failure. Moreover, it introduces another of Gray's favourite concepts; the idea of the body as machine. The body becomes a 'generator', an engine. Throughout *Old Negatives*, machines and flesh are presented as alternative versions of the human condition in the face of utter absence, void.

'Mistaken' and the subsequent poem, 'The Experiment', are intrinsically linked in terms of the development of the sequence. 'The Experiment' opens with a variation on the 'prophecy' line in 'Predicting' – 'When will these couples find they cannot sleep?' – only this time it is answered.

> When the moon sinks and the cat mews for its milk
> When the pressed nostril is sated with coupled skin.

The first line, with its murmuring alliteration, might be taken to mean that the waking is an inevitable and everyday occurrence, except that the second condition implies an element of disgust, especially through alternating plosive 'p' sounds with hissing 's' alliteration. The first line of 'The Experiment' is placed on the page to align with the last line of 'Mistaken', further emphasising the connection between the sleeplessness and a form of sexual ennui or incapacity. 'Sleep' becomes ambiguous, simultaneously suggesting 'When will these couples discover that they cannot sleep (together)' and 'When will these couples be unable to sleep (peacefully)?' The final two lines of the poem introduce a radical new register and volte-face:

Good. That leaves time for a small experiment:
THE UNION OF TWO VOIDS IN A COLD ROOM.

The conditions have not been met. The couple will be together, although it is now described in a manner utterly without warmth. The 'Good' is particularly sinister, changing the caustic, self-pitying prophetic voice into an omnipresent and interfering deity. The capitalisation should not be mistaken for declamation: in Gray's work it has a carved quality, a quiet, if insistent rhetoric. The line features the title of the subsection 'in a cold room', with its clinical feel, and introduces the 'void'. Void is particularly apt, connoting a vacuum but retaining the legal sense of ineffectual, or ineligible. The page layout confronts the reader with two voids, two empty white spaces engulfing the poems. It is rare, even unique, to see the techniques of Concrete Poetry so fully deployed in the service of Confessional Poetry.

The actual experiments are detailed in the next poems, 'The Unit' and 'The Split'. The spare and taut poems give way to more expansive, and more humorous, work. The voice, glimpsed at the end of 'The Experiment', is more fully developed into a pseudo-scientific jargon, a mock-serious lecture on the physics of sexual attraction. Gray utilises bathos to great effect here:

> Now, taking careful aim,
> it starts to travel inwards in a spiral accelerating rapidly until
> look out! Wham! It's struck her! They're together!
> No they're not.
> Veronica sidestepped at the last moment.

The obvious comedy and exuberance can blind the reader to the technical skill with which this scene is constructed. The long, second line of the quotation, through short vowel assonances mimics its subjects, and the breathless, quirky rhythms of line three set up the contradiction perfectly. The poems do, nonetheless, have a serious edge. The body is described as 'an envelope enclosed by a void/and enclosing a void', a bubble in nothingness. The horror of these lines is in part due to the factual basis: humans are a torus around an emptiness (the stomach); although Gray extends the metaphor into metaphysical absence. It is against such a nihilistic universe that love is foregrounded.

This ironic, almost playful, tone disappears in the central section of *In a Cold Room*. The typeface reverts to the italicised capitals. The observant reader will find a typically Gravian paradox about this part of the sequence. In the contents, it is entitled 'Cries of Unceilinged Blood' whilst on the running head this becomes 'Statements by an Unceilinged Blood'. The changing title begs a question: are these 'cries', and therefore, the product of a mind in pain; or 'statements', thus supposedly incontrovertible facts about the Universe? Is this section a subjective or objective description? The poems themselves provide little help – the tone changes from biblical parody of authority, as in *'IN THE BEGINNING WAS THE CAVITY.'* to plangent repetition *'ALONE ALONE COLD COLD COLD AND ALONE'*. The strength of these poems is not in that they propound a consistent theology of nothingness, but that they allow the reader space in which to construct and challenge the meaning. The body, and the Universe, is presented metaphorically as a machine, *'A RACKETY SLIPSHOD THING OF GUT AND NERVE'*, yet, at the same time, as some vital, if malevolent force, *'A CANCER IN THE CLAY'*.

In the concluding section of *In a Cold Room*, the dialectics that have informed the progress of the poem are laid bare. 'Accept, Reject' switches between the capital italic voice, preaching opposition to pain, death and the void, and the lower case voice contemplating a Stoical acceptance of these facts. The lower case voice asks

> Is it not right to attempt to be like God?
> To gain an equal acceptance of larks and cancer
> and to go gentle into that goodnight?

This is the crux of the intersection between an unremittingly pessimistic universe and the human capacity for appreciated beauty and love. God, in his omniscience, understands both cancer and larks (with a pun, one presumes, on high spirits). The very words, by the patterning of the open vowels and the repeated r and k sounds, begin to appear the same. The quote from Dylan Thomas is subtly altered; concatenating death (in the original, 'do not go gentle into that good night') with romance, and by implication, sexual satisfaction ('goodnight'). 'Accept, Reject' does not offer a final resolution between these voices. The next poems, 'Two' and 'Gods', like 'Mistaken' and 'The Experiment' beforehand, derive much of their meaning from the layout. The header titles are pushed together, creating in effect one poem called 'Two Gods'. 'Two' contrasts the unity of the self, indivisible into separate organs, with the disunity between the idea of a benevolent creator and the abyss of the universe. Thus, the only possible God is like Blake's Urizen, sustaining the clockwork of the universe with no regard to the happiness of its denizens: 'God is the iron grid of law upholding the totality'. Yet, in another *volte-face*, this line faces its opposite: the whole of the poem 'Gods' – 'God is the brightness without edge informing the totality'. The line, one third of the way down a blank page, seems set against the radiance in which it believes.

The final poem of the preliminary section attempts some reconciliation between these opposing positions. 'Reflecting Seashell' opens with a blank statement of the inevitability of death:

> That death will break this salt-fresh cockle-hand
> is simply wisdom.

The fear of death, more than death itself, is the cause of the horrors, which 'haunt the brain', and these horrors are no less real for being ill-founded. The simple, lyrical quality of the poem keeps one secret: whose hand is this? Is this the narrator finally accomplishing some act of self-healing, or is this the narrator at last holding someone else's hand and finding his resolution there?

Between Whiles 1957-61

Much of the mythology that would later develop into *Lanark* appears first in the second sequence of poems, *Between Whiles*, though of course it appears in print after the publication of that book. In this sequence we have references to Thaw, the hero of *Lanark*, as well as a Dragonman and dragon armour. These, however, are superficial connections, and occasionally even jar as seeming 'unintegrated' when compared to the over-riding imagery of *Between Whiles*, namely, the city. Whereas *In a Cold Room* took place predominantly within the head of the narrator, *Between Whiles* is set in an unidentified city. Nearly every poem makes reference to stones, mortar, buildings and streets.

The opening poem, 'Unfit', makes clear that we are in a different territory, dominated by 'terrible structures' and 'tainted light'. The residents of the city languish under some unspecified curse, an original sin – 'a crime has made us unfit to look upon'. But, as the poet reminds us, 'We were born here'. This is an embryonic version of Unthank, the conflation of Glasgow and Pandemonium. The problematisation of the body lingers on from the previous sequence. The body is still 'a box of bone'; but instead of the frailty conveyed by 'envelope' beforehand, we now have the encrustation of dragon armour, the callousing of the psyche under the continual struggle against the reality of pain and suffering. The female figure takes centre stage: rather than a yearned-after yet unobtainable 'other', she is an equal presence suffering from the same psychological torments of life within the city. The city itself is a form of the body: in 'I Assume', the narrator speaks of 'a wrong wish' that 'deranges this stone flesh'.

'I Assume' is in part a reworking of an Oedipal myth. The son falsely assumes the power of the father, receiving it as 'contraband'; an action that causes the city to 'fester'. The narrator forgoes the Oedipal conjunction, declaring he will 'love strangely no longer'. This leads him to father his child on a 'whore' – again there are overtones of *Lanark*. However, 'whore' is used metonymically to suggest any woman who is not a virgin. In the mythology of the poem, all mothers are virgins in that they should remain sexually unavailable to the usurping son. If, in 'Mistaken', the body was a generator for heat, it is here an engine of generation. Procreation will transfigure the 'whore' into a new mother-virgin and the son into a legitimate ruler of 'myself's own city'. However, this archetype that the narrator imposes upon the situation is not accepted without question, as the following poem elaborates. Reading 'I Assume' outside the context of the sequence could easily lead to the presumption that the only dichotomies Gray does not dissolve are those of gender – Man and Woman are absolute categories; Woman exists either as Whore or Virgin. The sequence, however, asserts that such an imposition of absolute categories is in itself a sign of awareness of the false nature of the dichotomies.

'I Assume' is the poem that undergoes most editing in Gray's errata slip for *Old Negatives*. Although most of this slip is a typical Gravian joke, and includes some points of textual fine-tuning as well as the correction of actual errors, 'I Assume' is fundamentally altered by the substitution of the word 'woman' for 'whore' throughout the poem. In an apologetic note, which seems to recant any implication of misogyny, Gray writes 'The writer took over a quarter century to see what was wrong with his first version'. In which case, one wonders why the changes were not made to the 1989 text; unless the importance is to chart the changing of the poet; acknowledging his development rather than over-writing it? One final note about the slip: it is dated 13th February, 1989 (a Monday, not a Friday, by the way). More importantly, the day before Valentine's Day.

'Vacancy' presents the same situation of pregnancy and its implications through the eyes of the female character. The female subject's thoughts are more concerned with the 'life enclosing a life' than with the repercussions for the parents; and in her 'vague thoughts', a more complex sexual politics is enunciated: 'Women, though not weak, are in weak positions'. Mandragon – as the male has become – has not found that prospective fatherhood has transformed him into the fit ruler of himself; instead, he remains sadistic and impotent, throwing off 'casual' words that hurt. The final sections of the poem employ the opposite of euphemism. The child's birth is the 'vomit[ing] debris of something human'. Indeed, each child is created from parts of its parents; its paternal chromosomes are the 'debris' of a complete being. Gray, through using language of emetics and damage, insinuates that all humans, even the most seeming perfect, are wounded from conception. Moreover, the female gives birth to 'a death'. Again, the child will surely at some point in the future, die. The deft perspective switches serve to undermine any easy mythologisation of the cycles of birth, copulation and death. The unremitting and almost gratuitous imagery forces the reader into making a judgement on the validity of those images. 'Under the Water' feels like a lyrical respite from the insane viciousness of the previous poem, set in a Glasgow transformed, briefly, into Venice. The second stanza introduces the name 'Carole', making an individual of the archetype. Only gradually does it become apparent that the (male) narrator is contemplating suicide by drowning; again, a prefigurement of *Lanark*. His heart 'aches that its ache for you must end'. But is it suicide, or is this to backwrite Thaw onto the narrator? Might it not be that the narrator, no longer loving the pregnant Carole, is contemplating *her* death by drowning? The 'sweet belly' becomes 'this memory': the memory as intact in the narrator's brain or the memory committed to paper? By either interpretation, a crisis is forced through the failure of reality to conform to a series of gender stereotypes and psychological archetypes.

The final four poems in *Between Whiles* seem slightly disjointed, given the tight inter-relation of the previous section. 'Lamenting Alan Fletcher' is a fine elegy, presumably included here because of Fletcher's 'appearance', as the character Aitken Drummond, in *Lanark*. Whilst 'Mistaken' was one line over the sonnet form, 'Lamenting Alan Fletcher' is one line under, suggesting the lack of resolution caused by his death. There is a stark and poignant contrast between the virtues of the man when alive and the sparse factuality of 'They have been put in a box to rot'. Fletcher, the poem maintains, was a positive *alter ego* to the narrator figure: successful both in love and art. Neither of these triumphs staves off mortality. 'Cowardly' continues the melancholy theme, opposing the organic tree, which blooms and fades, with an attempt at transcending the ravages of time in and inside the inorganic stone tower. The final stanza is clear in its equation of life and love; the vitalism of the loving man who makes his 'facts catch fire' in contrast to the coward who uses facts to fend off life. 'Lost Absence' articulates what Gray expressed on the cover of *Old Negatives*: 'They [the poems] are negative because they describe love mainly by its absences and reverses'.[4] Loss, in the poem, is a measure of the extent of love; and the sombre tone is developed in that even the absence eventually disappears. Like the coward in the previous poem, the narrator is immured through lack of love, he

> has nothing to do
> but sit in a room where dusk and the dust thicken.

The final lines have a Beckettian quality, repeating 'And there is nothing to do' thrice. This sense of immurement makes explicit a connection between death (the 'box' in 'Lamenting Alan Fletcher') and the loveless life. The wry cynicism of the 'union of two voids' is replaced by the necessity of love as a bulwark against the void.

The final poem is in the voice of Thaw. The city, he claims, is 'built over the desolate garden' – Eden – and they are suffering the consequences of the expulsion. Whereas the voice in 'Cries/Statements of Unceilinged Blood' had regretted his exit from the 'quilted womb', Thaw's experience is of an 'uncushioned womb'. Regression to a perfect state – whether Eden or the womb – is revealed as another palatable fiction. Thaw, unlike the previous narrators, has accustomed himself to the world's brutality, to 'the necessity of dragons'. The third stanza is in some ways a miniature synopsis of *Lanark*, showing how the child's dreams were gradually extinguished by events; leading to his decision in stanza four to sustain himself on this disappointment, to accept the role of outsider, prophet, 'leper in armour'. The poem concludes with Thaw forgoing the 'rostrum' for the 'pinnacle/no one uses for pedestal'. The image comes full circle: 'Time and Place' ended with the narrator awaiting revelation like a prophet; 'Announcement' transforms Thaw into a prophet ascending into the unknown. In the opening stanza, Thaw mentions that the Fall involved grandparents. The first grandchild of Adam and Eve was Enoch, the son of Cain, after whom Cain named the first city. City and Curse entwine around the figure of Thaw.

Inge Sørensen 1961-71

The opening poem of the third sequence, 'Woundscape', might seem as if the Thaw persona has disappeared into the ether at the end of 'Announcement'. Emotions may still be represented as diseases and wounds, but there is the possibility of cure.

> A wife, a baby, a cat and domestic repose
> might flatten the torn ground.

Moreover, the imagery of the previous work is challenged directly – 'Must everything the heart feels be a sort of illness?' Above all, the poem is a plea for 'companionable silence': a feeling pervades the poem that words are only of use in crises, that if 'love' has finally been accomplished, there should be no further need for the catharsis of poetry. T. S. Eliot's 'Poem to my Wife' expressed a similar sort of urge; a belief in the near-telepathy of those truly in love. Gray's poem is more complicated: when the poet starts mistrusting expression, there is more going on than contented quietness. Gray said in an interview with Elizabeth Donaldson for *Verse* 'I only do it [write poetry] when suffering a strong feeling of personal loss'.⁵ Despite his notorious evasiveness in interviews, this comment provides a critical key for the poem. The loss is not erotic but literary. The poem begins:

> He had wounded himself in the traditional places
> but no new crop came from the harrrowed [sic] flesh

i.e., the traditional methods of composition no longer yielded results. The nihilism that typified the first sequence has infected the whole basis of communication: 'Love talk, like all talk, is a way of saying no'. 'Woundscape' ends with a plea to be 'wounded regally'. It is a masochistic, high Romantic exposition of the connection between pain and poetics in the manner of Lautréamont. The Thaw persona still exists, as a Trappist desperate for martyrdom.

The two subsequent poems engage the reader again with the ricochet perspective changes that characterise Gray's sequences. 'Married' is one of the least acerbic poems in *Old Negatives*. The hermit and his wife become a king and queen, walking with a dignified gait, mutually supportive. Nonetheless, elements of ambiguity creep in: the people are revealed as sculptures, in which the sculptor has captured 'the solitude of being me and you'. Is this 'me and you' or 'me' and 'you'? Is this the privacy of lovers or their ultimate exclusion from each other? The poem ends with a seemingly triumphant celebration:

> Not sad to live they advance without fear
> to an end they cannot see.

If these are real people, the ending is positive. If they are statues, they will only appear to advance, and the ending will not be seen because it will never be reached.

'Mishap', contrariwise, is shockingly intimate and embarrassing. Ostensibly, the poem deals with premature ejaculation – 'the sun began setting an hour before noon'. This leads to recrimination not only for the action in itself, but for the inefficacy of language to solve the problem. Gray is at his most numbingly blunt with the line 'Soft pricks won't be stiffened by verbal alloy'. Sex, like, one presumes, death, is an inarticulate experience. Jock McLeish in *1982, Janine* could use language to reach the point of orgasm, but the event itself was below or beyond language. Thus, a new dichotomy has entered into the maelstrom of emotions in *Old Negatives* – sex versus poetry. The humiliation felt by the narrator in 'Mishap' festers into full-blown self-disgust in 'Declaration'. Whilst his wife sleeps, the narrator sits,

> drink[s] cheap wine
> and stir[s] the source of what is foul in me.

The image conveys not only the self-lacerating nature of his depression but hints at a masturbatory undertone. Again, we are in the territory of *1982, Janine*. The self-loathing is concentrated on the phallus as the visible symptom of psychological impairment. Sex is linked with pain and dirt; 'the strong dung that feeds my root the most'. As the second stanza puts it – 'I know that increase cannot come of good'. It would be a mistake to read the poem solely as a *Confessio Amatis* of the sexual sociopath. Although the 'surface' meaning exposes the narrator's shameful urges needed for arousal, on a deeper level we have the penis as stylic symbol, rather than the pen as phallic symbol. Writing is another unspeaking activity. The poem is, in a way, about inspiration, about the exploration of the deviant impulse and dark recess necessary for honest writing. The poem concludes with an imprecation to be inanimate, 'a grain, a stone, a shell' that could be pulverised by natural forces. Gray has, partly playfully, intimated in articles that he struck a Faustian pact with God, exchanging sexual fulfilment for authorial genius. 'Declaration' is a declaration of regret for the decision. It was not losing fulfilment that 'allowed' writing, but accepting frustration.

'To Andrew, before One' develops the fixation with the non-verbal and the costs of authorship. The child, unlike the narrator, in his pre-verbal stage, sees no separation between nouns and verbs. The first stanza is worth quoting in its entirety for the punchy rhythm, subtle repetition and clever lack of enjambment:

> He holds a spoon, certain of what he holds:
> nothing more solid-certain than his spoon:
> fat clenching fist and hard thing clenched, the same:
> no separation between noun and noun.

The world of words comes into existence with the Biblical imperative 'Thou shalt not', harking back to the awareness in 'Woundscape' that all words are a way of saying no. 'Home' becomes 'a place minced into tiny words'. With words come the possibility of possession and separation, they deprive rather than enrich. Words, fundamentally, signify difference, whereas the author wishes for a universe where differences are merged. The medium of poetry has succumbed to the pressure for dichotomies and exclusions against which it has been preaching.

'Both Perspectives' places the urge to assimilate and the urge to differentiate in sharp contrast, although this time it is the subsuming into multitude that is viewed as potentially more dangerous. History, from one perspective, is 'crowds oppose crowds and beget crowds' occasionally punctuated by a 'tiny criminal or legislator'. This is set against an individual man, woman and child in a room, the man 'pondering a debt he cannot pay'. Gray recalls Charles Olson, in the second part of the sixth letter of Maximus:

> There are no hierarchies, no infinite, no such many as mass, there
> are only
> eyes in all heads
> to be looked out of.[6]

Where this further links to the problems enunciated in 'To Andrew, before One' is the perspective from which the mass exists: 'from mountain tops and history books'. Literature, even when praising the triumph of the French Revolution or October Uprising, will lump together the individuals into the 'mass' or 'morass', the very identification against which they were fighting. In these poems, Gray's style becomes beautifully unadorned, simple and unconvoluted; as if he were trying, and failing, to write an 'anti-poetry'.

The final three poems of the *Inge Sørensen* section continue along the theme of the falsity of literature and the deleterious consequences of writing to the writer. In 'Awakening', the narrator has achieved the 'regal wound' he hankered after in 'Woundscape'. He is again alone, and pain, 'so near, his head [...] was my head' is a constant companion. The poem has a lightness of touch reminiscent of Berryman's *Dream Songs*; a lilting quality:

> He feeds at every meal, beckons down every street
> and yet could not withstand
> one pressure of your hand.

In pleading for the return of his lover, the narrator has inadvertently allowed poetry to return. The sweetness of the plea is soured by the veiled threat that he is becoming 'calm and brutal on beer and thick meat'. She does not return. In 'Unlovely', the eponymous characters begin stating, 'Love is an evil God'. In disdain, they turn to 'murderous games', including wealth, war and, most importantly, words. All senses, including language, have becomes 'ways/of not having you'; a return to the nihilistic imprisonment feared at the end of *Between Whiles*. In the loveless state, sight becomes blindness; the means of experience become its preventative. In the final poem, 'Not Striving', the narrator's solution to the predicament that plagued the *Inge Sørensen* section is the unification of love and pain; the very concept against which it was supposed to be a defence: 'love cannot last without doing and suffering harm'. The poem is not, however, unremittingly bleak. The narrator, observing his rented room, notes:

> Who built this room were badly paid.
> Even gifted carpets had a weaver.

Although the cover of *Old Negatives* maintains that it 'omits politics'; the third section has witnessed the growth of a social conscience as well as an infant; an awareness that there are other loves than just that of God and Women.

To Lyric Light 1977-83

The fourth and final section of *Old Negatives* signals a change in direction even from the opening illustration. The contents page had featured a gaunt figure, with Urizen style dividers, engaged in a vivisection of a model of his own head. A pen was placed in the lips of the model, from which a spume of smoke, representing, perhaps, the Logos as Word and Spirit, emerged. *In a Cold Room* featured a snake with an egg in its mouth – the image from the poem 'Loneliness' – curling from the head of a man. Images of women begin to appear with *Between Whiles*:

a female form, apparently ablaze, in the furnace-style stomach of a Greek-inspired male figure, fending off missiles from the city, above which banners read 'No' and 'Yes'. The female form becomes a manticore in *Inge Sørensen*, piercing the heart of a man with a spear, the end of which is elided with a burning tree in which a bird nests. The bird may be a phoenix; but may be merely in pain. *To Lyric Light* has a monumental, Rubenseque female figure presiding over tiers of humans, in the pose of God as Supreme Judge. Looking at the tiny figures beneath her, one notices that many of the people are couples, holding hands or resting against their partner's shoulders. From the illustration, one might assume that the final section will move towards *Amor Vincit Omnia*.

The opening poem, 'The Thinker', depicts a similarly Titanic female figure, Sum, sought by 'Smug Cogito, with flashing spectacles'. Cogito, like Monkey in Wu Ch'eng-en's novel, traipses over a landscape in search of his object, unaware that the landscape is the object – 'what he thought were foothills, but were feet'. Cogito eventually becomes aware of his smallness, and in that moment becomes the equal of the female. This does not, however, end with the epithalium of Cogito and Sum: 'Cogito walked away because he did not know'. Thus, a tripartite struggle emerges between being, knowing and thinking. The knowing and thinking dichotomy had previously been asserted in 'Cowardly' – thinking is depicted as a process, whereas knowledge is an object. Similarly, being and thinking had been challenged in *Inge Sørensen*'s radical destabilisation of expression and existence. 'The Thinker' plays around Descartes' maxim, 'I think therefore I am', which Gray renders problematic. 'Thinking' begs the question 'what?' Does one exist if one's thoughts are false, or incorrect? Does thinking of an object or situation imply that it should necessarily be? The male narrator is as yet unwilling or unable to forgo the cerebral in favour of the physical.

'Wanting' and 'Awaiting' are two of the most charming poems in the collection. Again, Gray plays with the space in which the poems exist; each line mirroring a line on the opposite page. The poems, for all their elegant simplicity, are not unambiguous. The poems read:

'Waiting'
I am new born
I want to suck sweet and sing
and eat and laugh and run and
fuck and feel secure and own my own home
and receive the recognition due to a man in my position
and not have nobody to care for me
and not be lonely
and die.

'Awaiting'
He was, and educated, and became,
residing and remaining and intending,
then on became in, and again,
and later and later again.
He still is, and hopes, and intends,
and may
but is certain to –
one day.

The fulcrum of the first (left hand) poem is whether or not the negative modifiers from the penultimate two lines carry on to the last line. Does the narrator, who asks for so little, accept death or insist that it should not happen to him? In contrast, the second poem, where objectless verbs accumulate, forever deferring the revelation of the 'point' of the existence, becomes more sombre in that 'one day' mirrors 'and die'; as if the verbs were straining to conceal the inevitability of death.

'Renewal' introduces an important leitmotif in the fourth section; namely, a desire for love that avoids possessiveness. The eroticised chastity of the 'Virgins who touch no body, even their own' becomes a destructive and solipsistic force; so full of ardour that it becomes unable to 'lose' itself in the partner and instead seeks to possess. The gaze 'turns anyone into meat', into the merely physical. The finale of the poem longs for a love not founded on the other as object or possession: 'I don't want to keep anyone', although Gray still figures this in terms of masochism, 'the pain/that makes me virgin again'. 'Cares', closing on the word 'shared', intensifies this new direction. The God of the poem is no longer the vengeful Urizenic despot or the ineffable and ultimately unknowable brightness; rather, it is a God found in the simple things like 'plain new bread'. It is a God that nourishes, but despite this the narrator is still too self-involved to accept the nourishment unconditionally. 'Care', etymologically from the Latin, *caritas*, is the highest form of love in St Paul's dictum on faith, hope and love. As such, it is to carefulness that the poet turns:

> Oh carefulness, inform all I do,
> then the good bread can be shared.

This image, through reference to the Eucharist, transforms the 'cannibalistic' virgins of the previous poem. Although in *Lanark* the Eucharist was seen as a substitute for cannibalism, the religious cadence of these lines implies that this is no 'transference' at work here. In many ways, the liturgical feel to the line derives from a lack of transubstantiation: the bread is just wholesome bread, rather than veiled flesh.

In 'For Grass', we can appreciate the extent of the progression in the central figure of *Old Negatives'* character. The bitterness that characterised earlier pieces is here the wistful, and wise, 'Avoid the enemy made in the valley of cunt'. The proximity of death is still tangible, the narrator still knows that 'All flesh is grass'; however, the tender emergent sexuality is one that provides a genuine alternative to the equation of Eros and Thanatos. The poem, on a literal level, describes cunnilingus; and the nature of the sexual act is important. The pleasure is transferred onto the pleasure of the partner – in contrast to, say, 'Declaration' in which the narrator obsessed on his own pleasure at the cost of the partner's pain, or 'Mishap' where the desire for self-pleasure ends in mutual dissatisfaction. With 'Ripeness', the reader reaches the apex of the redemption of the narrator-figure

> [...] old, ill-smelling,
> a body with whom nothing good can be done.

> Untrue of course. We can join again if
> love is more than a noise made in bed.

The assertion that 'love can be fun' represents a maturity at odds with the hysteria, mythologisation and resentment that had gone before. The poem is not wholeheartedly contented: the narrator still needs to elicit trust in his partner –

> [...] I will show
> that when you chose me, you chose right.

Nonetheless, the air of desperation has disappeared.

'Unlocks' revisits the same situation as 'Awakenings', but again there are signs of progression and indications of a more stable psyche. The narrator, again, confesses to the difficulty of separation from the partner, although this time there are no malign threats. Indeed, the surprise of the poem is to realise the extent to which they are parallel pieces: the lover will not return this time either. Instead of recrimination, the narrator admits to 'loving the delight you unlocked in me', and regrets his incapacity to reciprocate. There is still the hankering self-pity, that the narrator wishes to take sole responsibility for the failure of the relationship; but this is tempered with a sense of understanding. Most important is the connection between love and freedom. Although we had experienced the inverse – that lovelessness was a form of imprisonment – the poetry had not yet asserted the converse of the equation. Ideal love, as ideal freedom, precludes the possibility of possessing the partner.

The final three poems in *Old Negatives* seem slightly like a coda. The humane wisdom eventually achieved in 'Unlocks' represents the emotional closure of the collection. 'A Burning' reiterates some of the notions of liberty and self-imprisonment: the child 'locked himself in [...] himself the governor'. The ending can be compared to many Gaelic poems of a similar period, in the ambivalent relationship to notions of the home:

> Home is a place we had to leave.
> Love it, but don't return.

Even here, with the effective focus of the poem being something other than a relationship, there is an acceptance of the inevitability of change, and the positive nature of that. The narrator does not advance by taking revenge or slighting. 'Lyrical', the penultimate piece, is to all extents and purposes a riddle. The opening line poses the question: 'Who is all fire and wings and hearts and seed?' going on to elaborate on this unknown entity that 'changes everything we need?', that demands constant progress, and 'makes all we joyfully, painfully love march away?' Whatever the presence is, it is unspeakable, beyond language. As such, we are left to wonder again, if this is Love, or Death, or God, or, as exam papers used to say, 'All of the above'.

The final poem is unlike any other. The greatest dichotomy in the book is black and white, ink and paper. 'End' is a chromatic poem, with the lines coloured black, maroon, purple, blue, green, yellow, pink and palest grey. The poem fades from the page, describing how:

> The grave colours of earth
> Brighten towards
> An
> Open book
> Of
> Light unstained
> By
> Word

The poetry of the *Inge Sørensen* sequence had challenged the role and necessity of poetry. This uneasiness has not departed; indeed, almost all good love poetry foregrounds the paradox of writing for a specific, known other and an unknown reader, as in Donne's *Triple Fool*. The blank book is the book we write ourselves. *Old Negatives* ends by returning the reader to the world of their own emotions, unlocked from the psychodrama of another's.

Sixteen Occasional Poems 1990–2000

With the very title of *Sixteen Occasional Poems*, Gray warns the reader not to expect the taut, interconnected and inter-textual universe of *Old Negatives*. It is a sequence of chance encounters rather than an extended narrative. The cover image, does, however, link us back to *Old Negatives*. *Old Negatives'* paperback cover illustration depicted a foetal angel entombed, or enwombed, inside a skull. *Sixteen Occasional Poems* shows the angel stepping out from a skull, looking at a red sun on the horizon. The image 'detournes' a Blakean etching from 'The Gates of Paradise' in which the angel steps from an egg into a world of uncertain clouds. Without the sun, Gray's image would be a clear metaphor of rebirth, renewal; with the sun, a deep red colour, we must ask: is this sunrise or sunset? That question simmers beneath the opening poem, 'First of March 1990'.

Gray informs the reader in the notes to *Sixteen Occasional Poems* that this piece is all that was completed of a projected verse diary of a trip to Berlin. In form, the poem resembles arrows pointing North East, or track headed in the same direction, and the style is unlike anything we encountered in *Old Negatives*; breezy, disjointed, like sparks flying from an anvil. The narrator is still as self-critical, if less self-torturing:

> HATE change always hoped each home
> where i came to live would be where i would die

The acceptance of change gleaned at the end of *Old Negatives* was, it appears, impermanent. Words, however, are not the sleekit double-dealers they were but a means of holding on to the past, even though they too are subject to the ravages of time. Words, moreover, are a means of freedom; yet they are turned into a form of obligation by pusillanimous teachers forcing a 'canon' on students.

> now teachers tell children it ought to be read
> does all free work leave a chain?

Gray – it is pointless to refer to a narrator in this poem, which so explicitly identifies the speaker with the Author of *The Book of Prefaces* – is running away. He is '55 my best work done'; hence the previous reference to the ambiguously rising/setting sun. The only thing he claims not to be running from is *The Book of Prefaces*, whose 400 pages are 'in this bag/& also in this brain'; a book so intrinsic it has become part of the author. How seriously should we take the claim that Gray's 'best work' is done, given the central position of the Anthology? Very seriously. *The Book of Prefaces* is nothing if not pedagogical; a final attack on the educational establishment that reduces books to texts. 'First of March 1990' may be almost a self-elegy, but it is also a Preface to *The Book of Prefaces*.

Politics, as mentioned above, was supposedly banished from *Old Negatives*, though it made some surreptitious appearances. *Sixteen Occasional Poems* is explicitly a political text. The 'occasional poem' as genre, in the hands of a writer like Dryden, was a tool for bolstering state power and endorsing state culture; a format used to eulogise the birth of an heir or mourn the passing of a ruler. In the late twentieth century, political poetry is a more ambivalent prospect. Poetry, despite Roman Jakobson's analysis of Eisenhower's election slogan, sets itself outside the rhetorical constructs of propaganda. To be subtle without becoming opaque, and to be ideological without descending to tub-thumping is a precarious path to tread. The next three poems in *Sixteen Occasional Poems*, 'Winter Housekeeping', 'Waiting in Galway' and 'South Africa April 1994', can be classified as contemporary political poems. All three poems hint at the ubiquity of pain, whether through poverty or political conflict, without blatantly stating this. There is a sense of irreducible complexity about them:

> I give to beggars of course, though charity
> prolongs their pain. So do market forces.

In 'Waiting for Galway', the first two stanzas are clear about the undercurrents of potential violence, which even the snug of the pub cannot wholly evaporate. The reference to dominoes is more than description; suggesting unseen powers that can initiate a chain of events that ends in falling. 'South Africa April 1994' celebrates the sense that despotic structures succumb to their own destruction through a form of political entropy; that the resistance itself can implode them:

> we [...] tell lies
> until we make you make them come true.

Whether one agrees or not with the analysis of totalitarian regimes – deflated in the final line, since 'they could not be, everywhere, the same' – the poem's quiet insistence manages to say more about political struggle than the more obvious 'poetics of protest'.

The poem 'Postmodernism', though witty, seems to me insubstantial. No doubt there have been postmodernist theorists that are a mixture of snake-oil salesman and blindly-led sheep; however, there are a great number of contemporary theorists and practitioners with daring thoughts and integrity. Perhaps one of the problems is that *all* experimental writers tend to be categorised as 'postmodernist', even when they themselves argue from a dialectically opposite position to other so-called post-modernists. Many would argue that Gray himself is in a postmodernist tradition that includes Borges, Calvino and John

Barth (and Melville, and Sterne …). If the target had been more specific, the satire might have been more biting. In terms of Gray's cohesion as a writer, the interest in the Logos-created universe extends back as far as *In a Cold Room*, where the 'Word' was a misconstrued scream. 'Genesis' argues against the 'commanded' Universe in favour of an evolving and collaborative one. The line 'God [...] is to be achieved' shows a debt to utopian Socialist thinkers, such as Marcuse, for whom the evolution of man was towards perfection, rather than decaying away from it. As a poem, though slight, it has undeniable charm. The complex origins of language are neatly encapsulated in the line 'Crying, crooning make language', linking pain and comfort, and other inarticulate expressions, as the root-note of language. These ideas previously had been approached with trepidation, rather than compassion.

'Dear Colleague' is a more perceptive satire, on the language of 'management' as a particularly vague form of euphemism, concealing unpalatable truths in polysyllabic terms. As any worker who has suffered from 'downscaling', 'rationalisation' or 're-organisation' understands, it is also pernicious. 'Epitaph 1998', by tactfully avoiding naming Diana, Princess of Wales, is able to universalise her death and at the same time make valid criticisms. It is a clear-sighted and measured poem, miles from the public lamentations and legend-building. Gray, as always, is on the side of the disadvantaged whilst being able to appreciate that the privileged suffer in different ways.

Poems 9 through 15 were written to accompany prints by Ian McCulloch, published as *The Artist in his World*.[7] The reception of these poems in *Sixteen Occasional Poems* is therefore somewhat altered. The poems do stand on their own, not exactly as a conceptual sequence, but in a similarity of diction and tone, and their approach to ancient and modern mythology. Many of Gray's continual concerns are revisited. In 'Eden', a petty and vengeful God understands that 'naming' is a form of 'taming', of compartmentalising reality. 'Agamemnon's Return' counterposes Agamemnon's sacrifice of his daughter for political ends with Clytaemnestra's murder of Agamemnon for personal reasons. The two characters' thought rhythms convey their mind-sets with tact, ranging from the matter-of-fact 'Girl bleeds. Gale blows. Fleet sails. King conquers Troy', to the mock-innocence of his wife's 'The king is soon very wet', with a rhythm that artificially stresses the beginning of 'very'. Thought versus action is again a concern. Gray does not depict Agamemnon as utterly callous:

> Agamemnon thinks twice
> about ordering the sacrifice
> but orders it all the same.

'Tales from the Polish Woods' seems like the title of a lost volume of children's stories, and the poem mimics the lilt of children's rhymes whilst describing the atrocities of the Holocaust.

> So sights too vile to be seen were seen
> tales too vile to tell get told

The 'so' is a particularly neat artifice; logically connected to the previous line – that the Nazis lost the war and therefore the truth about the camps was revealed, yet echoing the sing-song of a different kind of poetry. 'Bosnian Heads' on the other hand, can be about little else. It is exceptionally sparse as a poem – indeed, such events are diminished by decoration. Sheer statement is more eloquent than embellishment. Instead of the word 'one', Gray uses the numeral '1'; giving an odd feel to the line:

> 1 grief distorted, 1 grief bemused
> 1 enraged with his broken sword.

The numeral serves a double function. Visually, it echoes 'I', insinuating the self as an act of impossible empathy. More sinisterly, it reads like a tally.

'No Way' and 'Alba' are companion pieces, written in a 5 line stanza followed by a 4 line stanza diminishing the syllable count of each line down to one. These seem to stand less steadily on their own. Both poems depict imprisoned people in impossible prisons; and each poem offers death as an escape from the chaos and turmoil within the prison. 'Alba' sustains itself more effectively, with a whole tradition dwindling into the person of one woman – Mary, Queen of Scots – who, in accepting her role as myth ('opens herself to the past'), can accept execution.

The best poem in the sequence is 'Biblical Themes (shuffled like dreams)'. There is an almost Dadaist quality to these off-kilter tableaux, and the language similarly has a prose quality that disconcerts. What these images and fantasia *mean* is a different matter. They mean what the reader chooses to take from them. I quote in full my favourite lines and leave it to readers to decipher them at their leisure:

> Saint Francis, elephant-masked, addresses two
> dangerously huge white pigeons without seeing them,
> beside lines suggesting King Herod and a bamboo shoot
> without necessarily being them.

The collection closes with 'To Tom Leonard', an optimistic envoi. At the beginning of this section, the question was raised about *Sixteen Occasional Poems* as a swan-song, a signing-off to accompany and commemorate *The Book of Prefaces*. In 'To Tom Leonard', there is a sense of indubitable continuation. Even 'the blighted prove' Scotland is 'no dead stick'. The poem is like the hidden 'icons' of the stump and shoot: despite the manifold and not-to-be-underestimated difficulties, the vibrant culture survives.

Remarks by Way of Conclusion

I hope the anthologists of the future will take time to read Alasdair Gray's poetry. What he contributes to the range of possible poetry is unique: a dispassionate, confessional voice; technical accomplishment utilised to convey meaning rather than for its own sake and a hard-won sense of the complexity of the universe, imparted often through the subtlest of means. His poetic work, especially when dealing with the relationship, or lack thereof, between the sexes, is memorable and disconcerting in the way only good poetry is. That his work as a poet is not as well known is regrettable: however, those who do know it do not forget it.

Notes

1. Anthony Burgess, *Ninety Nine Novels: the Best in English Since 1939* (London: Allison & Busby, 1984).

2. Thom Nairn, 'The Necessity of Dragons', in *The Arts of Alasdair Gray*, ed. by Robert Crawford and Thom Nairn (Edinburgh: Edinburgh University Press, 1991), p. 136.

3. Compare especially, Philip Larkin, 'Reasons for Attendance', in *Collected Poems* (London: Marvell, 1988), p. 80.

4. Alasdair Gray, *Old Negatives*, pbk edn (London: Cape, 1989), cover.

5. Interview with Elizabeth Donaldson, *Verse*, I:I (1984), p. 31.

6. Charles Olson, *The Maximus Poems*, ed. by George Butterick (Berkeley: University of California Press, 1983), p. 33.

7. Ian McCulloch, *The Artist in his World: Prints 1986-1997* (Glendaruel: Argyll, 1998).

ART FOR THE EARLY DAYS OF A BETTER NATION

ELSPETH KING

THE ART OF ALASDAIR GRAY IS AS ORIGINAL AND AS CREATIVE IN its conception and execution as his novels, short stories, plays and poems. Sadly, this is a view that is not widely shared, otherwise this piece would be being written by a professional art historian, our galleries and public buildings would be rich with Gray's works, and his international reputation as a muralist in his native land would be as secure as that of Diego Rivera in Mexico and John Singer Sargeant in the USA. This view is not even entertained by Gray himself. In a television programme that presented him as 'one of the greatest novelists of the second half of the twentieth century', he was asked to comment on his work as a painter. 'I'm one of these interesting second raters' was his instant and self-deprecating response.[1]

A second argument of this essay is that his work as an artist is complementary to, and inseparable from, his work as a writer and novelist. In a world of increasing specialism and low expectation, it is sometimes difficult for people to appreciate and acknowledge that others may be greatly talented in more than one area. The desire to classify and categorise in order to comprehend invariably results in 'Alasdair Gray, the writer' being the only aspect of the man that is understood. In the year 2000, the Scottish National Portrait Gallery commissioned Calum Colvin to produce 'a group portrait of eight Glasgow-based writers centred around Alasdair Gray' as a companion piece to Sandy Moffat's 'Poet's Pub' portrait of an earlier generation of writers with Edinburgh associations. 'The Kelvingrove Eight' is a true museum piece, embracing both taxonomy and taxidermy, for it bags all eight writers within the one frame for the gallery, with Gray as its centre, safely pigeon-holed as a writer, and looking as if shot and stuffed. The other subjects of this photomontage look equally uncomfortable and out of place. It is ironic that Gray has sketched and painted portraits of most of them in the past, in congenial surroundings of their choosing, and to better effect. In the Colvin work, he tellingly has a small portrait of Morag McAlpine on his lap, and books that he has both written and designed are strewn around in an uncharacteristic mess. It is sad that Gray, himself a portrait artist of enduring and consummate skill, should be represented thus in the Scottish National Portrait Gallery.

Showing concurrently at the Scottish National Portrait Gallery with the 'Writers of Our Time' exhibition, was another on Scottish artists and self-portraiture. The work of Alasdair Gray, who throughout his life has drawn and painted dozens of self-portraits, often in a very challenging way – reflected in a hand-held mirror, giving the viewer the same viewpoint as the artist, as an artist painting his own portrait, as a scientist dissecting himself, as 'a bankrupt tobacconist' and even as Sloth, curled round the Tree of Life in his Genesis mural of 1958 – was notable by its absence. Not all artists can rise to the challenge of a successful self-portrait, which demands a rigorous analysis going beyond mere likeness. Gray has a lifetime of achievement as a painter, and often thinks nothing of supplying a self-portrait as an illustration to a piece of writing. So where was he?

It is evident that Scottish National Portrait Gallery curators have decided that Gray is a writer. The Gallery has a very fine photographic portrait of Alasdair Gray, purchased in 1985 but taken by Oscar Marzaroli (1930-1988) in 1961. Tellingly, in defiance of the subject matter, it is captioned to the effect that Gray's *Lanark* 'achieved great critical acclaim and its experimental and innovatory treatment of language prompted comparisons with James Joyce'. Yet the photograph was taken twenty years before the publication of *Lanark*. It shows Gray, a tousle-headed young artist, leaning over the stairway of 10 Kelvin Drive, Glasgow, where he is producing a great phantasmagorical mural on the theme:

> The world is so full of a number of things
> I'm sure we should all be happy as kings.

The mural has a fantastic land and seascape, full of mythical beasts, floating islands, paddle steamers and flying snakes. It is in Gray's linear, monochromatic style, and is one of his few private murals that survives to the present day. The gallery label made no comment on any of this.

The conspiracy of silence on Gray's contribution as an artist is strong. He was commissioned by Canongate to write a narrative history of classic Scottish writing, published along with a boxed set of six Pocket Classics in 2001, artwork for the covers of which was 'commissioned from six leading Scottish artists'. The artwork was exhibited in the Scottish National Gallery of Modern Art, and it is noteworthy that of the seven books, the cover with the simplest design but the greatest visual impact is that devised by Gray for his volume. The 'Scottish Literary Lion', with his quill pen and computer, in black and red on a silver background, has the economy of line employed by the heraldic artist combined with the knowledge of the skilled book illustrator. Gray, who has been producing book illustrations since childhood, and designing and producing fine books for the last quarter of a century, may not be considered as a 'leading Scottish artist' but he knows how to produce a cover that will sell a book. Moreover, his covers accurately reflect the intellectual and emotional content of the book, something seldom achieved by the finest commercial designers.

There are historical reasons for this lack of appreciation of Alasdair Gray's art. These include: the poverty (financial and cultural) of Scotland itself, which is unable to sustain artists in full time employment; the manipulation of art as a commodity, and the creation and control of a particular art market; the failure of curators in public galleries to pursue an acquisitions policy independently from this market; the absence of art criticism, beyond promotion of personalities and advertorial puffs for exhibitions; the connivance of these so-called critics in sustaining the market; the prejudice against public art commissions; political prejudice and the prevalence of a kind of McCarthyism in post-War Glasgow. In the present day, there is the cynical nihilism of the art schools in the promotion of installation and contemporary art, the constituent parts of which appear to be literally 'con' and 'temporary'. Within this quagmire that is Scottish Art, Alasdair Gray has acted with integrity and always according to his own conscience, which means that his art has brought him no profit and little acknowledgement, and has sometimes cost him dearly.

I will address each of these factors in trying to offer an analysis of the nature and strength of Gray's work, and indicate where his art could have been, had he been lucky enough to work in the early days of a better nation. In advance, I must declare my own myopia and lack of impartiality towards Alasdair Gray's work. I have had the privilege of working with him formally on three occasions in the last 25 years: in 1977-8, when he was artist-recorder and I was curator of the People's Palace, Glasgow; in 1994-5, when he contributed a major work for the Abbot House heritage centre in Dunfermline, and in 1996, when his design work and painting lent some credibility to the Brave Art exhibition at the Stirling Smith Art Gallery and Museum.

During this time, I have come to know Alasdair Gray and to have the honour of his private friendship and public support during the most adverse of personal circumstances. From 1989, when I heard by rumour that my services would no longer be required as curator of the People's Palace, through 1990 (Glasgow's City of Culture year), when my position was made untenable and my partner Michael Donnelly sacked, until 1991, when I parted company with Glasgow District Council, were three personally painful years, lived in the full glare of media attention, sometimes on a daily basis. This long-running saga, dubbed by the newspapers 'the Elspeth King affair', was made bearable only by the overwhelming support of the people of Glasgow and the friendship of Alasdair Gray.

As well as writing in my support,[2] Alasdair took part in the very public demonstrations that divided Glasgow down the middle in 1990. There were protests against the 'Glasgow's Glasgow' exhibition, a sanitised alternative to the People's Palace, that ran up losses of four million pounds, against the proposed privatisation of Glasgow Green, against the sacking of Jude Burkhauser, the curator of the 'Glasgow Girls' exhibition, and against the removal of Ian McCulloch's murals from the Glasgow Concert Hall. In essence, the struggle was for the soul of Glasgow. The disquiet started in October 1986, when the Tory Arts Minister Edward Luce announced the award of the European Capital of Culture status to Glasgow for 1990. It became apparent that the culture of capital was the main driving force for the capital of culture.[3] The economic miracle of turning welders into wine waiters, of gentrifying central Glasgow to make it the preserve of the middle classes and the international tourist, was least appreciated by the welders themselves, smarting from the pain of a de-industrialisation process that seemed to be without end.

With the clearance of the traditional industries and those that worked in them came the assault on the philosophy and culture that had sustained them. A heavily funded attempt was being made to defuse their radical and revolutionary history by re-writing and re-presentation. At the same time, Scotland was being used as the testing ground for the new Poll Tax, the poor were being disenfranchised or pursued for money through warrant sales and evictions. Glasgow was divided into payers and non-payers of the Poll Tax, and Alasdair gave away his paintings to avoid having them poinded and sold.

Friendships forged on the anvils of such struggles are not easily broken. They colour both past and present. Several of us came to share the services and friendship of Alasdair's solicitor, Angela Mullane, a champion of artists, writers and peace campers as well as the dispossessed of the Drumchapel housing scheme, where her practice is based. My understanding of Alasdair's work is unavoidably informed and influenced by these relationships.

Like many people, I started out knowing only a part of Alasdair Gray – Gray the artist. In 1974, a retrospective of his work was organised in the newly established Collins Gallery of the University of Strathclyde.[4] The exhibition showed over 100 works from Gray's schooldays onwards, covering a twenty-five year period and demonstrating his development as an artist. It was accompanied by a carousel of slides featuring his public and private mural work. One of the most remarkable things about the exhibition was how the recent portrait work reflected contemporary Glasgow. There were portraits of children and families in ordinary domestic settings, sitting at kitchen tables, playing games, reading books and newspapers, relaxing in the sitting room with the cat on the rug, reading in bed. Some paintings had views from the window, to a Glasgow landscape beyond. Meticulously executed in rapidograph pen, watercolour, gouache, and in a variety of media, the paintings were a revelation. Traditionally, Glasgow artists went outwith Glasgow to find their subjects. The Glasgow Boys were more at home in Kirkcudbright and in the south of France. Few considered the Glasgow cityscape as an appropriate subject, almost as if the source of the wealth that made painting possible was too dirty a subject for the fine arts. Those that painted portraits omitted any recognisable backgrounds, editing out the associations of place, focussing on the figure alone. The ability to combine portraiture with landscape is rare.

Portraits by Alasdair Gray were commissioned by people that liked and could afford his work, and shown in the 1974 Collins exhibition were works owned by Glasgow solicitor Keith Bovey, George and Rose Singleton of the cinema chain, Neil Carmichael MP and his wife, social worker Kay Carmichael, author Archie Hind, playwright Joan Ure, music historian John Purser, poet Liz Lochhead, and professor of sociology Andrew Sykes. There were also portraits of those that could not have afforded the purchase, such as inventor Bill Skinner, and Alex Hamilton, one of the unemployed. These were executed with the same meticulous skill and respect accorded to paying customers. Alasdair Gray, unlike younger generations of Glasgow artists, has never exploited or monstered disadvantaged people, either in pursuit of his art or for profit.

The overall effect of seeing Alasdair Gray's exhibition in the Collins Gallery was one of pleasure and recognition of a type that must have been experienced by Florentines viewing an ecclesiastical mural cycle by Domenico Ghirlandio on the day of its completion and in the centuries since. Ghirlandio's Bible stories and saints' lives are peopled by contemporary Florentines and set in Italian landscapes. Similarly, in Gray's exhibition, all Glasgow life was there, observed with love and attention to detail, and drawn with the mastery of line possessed by Blake and Beardsley.

Although Alasdair Gray paints portraits well, he did not set out to become a portrait painter. As a child, he was exceptionally gifted, both as a creative writer and as an artist, and his unusual record at Whitehills Secondary School has been recounted well in a study by Robert Crawford.[5] His scraper board drawing, *Theseus and the Minotaur*, published in the school magazine in 1952, is still remembered by those who saw it and found it hard to believe that a teenager could have such control of line and spatial sense. As recounted in *Lanark*, it was the Registrar of Glasgow School of Art, who on seeing Alasdair's portfolio, intervened with his father to have him admitted as a full time student. The then-Registrar was Harry Jefferson Barnes (d. 1982) who became Director of the School of Art from 1964 to 1980. The then-Director was Douglas Percy Bliss, and both of them appreciated the special gifts of Alasdair Gray.

Gray had great ambitions, beyond what was being taught in the painting department. His frustration at mundane exercises such as being 'taught' how to draw a light bulb, and producing a drawing on the subject of 'Washing Day' are well recorded in *Lanark*:

> What grandeur can be shown in that? I want to make a series of paintings called Acts of God showing the deluge, the confusion of Babel, the walls of Jericho falling flat, the destruction of Sodom. Yes, yes, yes, a hymn to the Old Testament Catastropher who makes things well but hurts and smashes them just as well. Or I would make a set of cityscapes with the canal through them. Or ....'[6]

What is not recorded in *Lanark* is the triumph of the resulting 'Washing Day' painting, an 'essentially linear image in which the back court of an ordinary Glasgow tenement was transformed into a Piranesi labyrinth where certain elements – tall, narrow, close-mouths, female figures, basins of washing, etc – came in threes, to be played with in a visual game, without repetition'. The drawing was of such extraordinary quality that former art student Cordelia Oliver could recall the image clearly in those terms almost forty years later.[7]

Lanark is in essence a personal Odyssey about the difficulties of trying to survive as an artist in Scotland. Regardless of the complexity of the plot, the fantastical story line that envelopes and masks the pure autobiography, the brilliance of the language in which it is told and the erudition that underpins the whole, we should never lose sight of this. To reinforce the point, the author has jacketed each of the four separately bound books of the Canongate 2001 edition of *Lanark* with a different and appropriate painting. The Volume 1, Book 3, image is his masterpiece *Cowcaddens Landscape 1950* (1963, oil on hardboard, 47.5 x 95 inches, Collins Gallery/University of Strathclyde collection), which sets the scene. The painting shows a brooding, dark, industrial, smog-plagued Glasgow, which nevertheless has its industry intact and is full of a warmth and vitality emanating from the tenement windows, the street lamps, the public house, and the people. It is an enduring portrait of this part of Glasgow in the 1950s, before the M8 motorway smashed through, fragmenting and destroying it. The artist has used the skills of the panorama painter, creating several vistas within the work, as well as using the medieval device of showing the same people twice, on a different part of their journey, within the picture.

The jacket of Volume 2, Book 1, the first autobiographical book of *Lanark*, is illustrated with a gouache entitled *Two Hills* from 1951. This very neatly ordered stylistic Glasgow scene, with its school, churches and tenements on one hill, linked to the other hill with its phalanx of factory chimneys by a railway tunnel, is obviously influenced by Lowry, but drawn with a style and precision instantly recognisable as that of Alasdair Gray. Gray was only seventeen when he began the work. Volume 3, Book 2, has the painting *The Garden of Eden* (1967, oil on board, 24.5 x 21.5 inches; private collection). This small piece features a section of the Genesis mural, begun in Greenhead Parish Church, Bridgeton in 1958, with Adam and Eve embracing, reflected in the still waters of Paradise. Other episodes, the Tree of Knowledge, the expulsion from the Garden, the Destruction of Sodom and Gomorrah and Noah's Ark, are depicted, with Calvary in the far distance. As Volume 3 deals with Gray's art school years and the painting of the Genesis mural, the choice is particularly apt.

The jacket of Volume 4, Book 4 features a large work, *The Triumph of Death* (also known as *The Fall of the Star Wormwood*, 1959, oil on canvas, 71 x 134 inches, collection of Angela Mullane). This is a powerful piece, and a more mature working of Gray's first mural, for the Scotland-USSR Society in 1957. The subject is a nuclear attack on Glasgow. In Revelations ch.8 v.10-11, the star Wormwood falls to the earth, poisoning a third of the waters, and causing death and destruction. Gray sites the fall of Wormwood right in the heart of Glasgow, on a site close to the former Tenant's chemical works, where the malodorous slag heap-ringed loch of effluence was known as 'the Stinky Ocean'. Although multi-storey tower blocks were built over the site in the 1970s, the choking sulphurous smell still pollutes the atmosphere there in cold weather. The Stinky Ocean is at the centre of the work. The Horsemen of the Apocalypse ride past in the foreground and multiple fires burn all over Glasgow. Genetic mutations create faceless monsters, whilst the people of Glasgow stand by, helpless.

For the first time, Gray is presenting his paintings with the text of *Lanark*, the story of the artist as a young painter in a country that has not much use for art.

The sequel to *Lanark* is *1982, Janine* where the author analyses the state of Scotland to explain why this should be. Along the way, Gray has written factual essays that elaborate on the subject. In 'The Mean City' (1962), he recounts the lack of gallery and exhibition space in Glasgow for contemporary artists at that time, and writes of his need to paint:

> I get a satisfaction from painting which nothing else gives, and cannot stop painting for two or three months without feeling guilty and cheap. This mental condition has made me give up teaching several times since I graduated from art school five years ago.

He asks the question, 'What use is Art?' and answers it for himself:

> No use at all. It won't help you earn money or get a job, or make friends and influence people, but if you enjoy it, you have an extra pleasure in life, a pleasure as strong as religion and almost as strong as money making or drink. And unlike drink there's no hangover after.[8]

In a lengthy interview in 1982, Gray summarised the problem his family had with a son becoming an artist:

> My parents did not mind me painting, but they feared correctly that living to do it would bring me to dole queues, and wearing

second hand clothes, and borrowing money and having my
electricity cut off – bring me to the state that many respectable
working folk are forced into, during depressions, for reasons they
cannot help. That I should become a seedy parasite in order to
make obscure luxury items hardly anybody wanted, depressed
them.[9]

Making a living as a painter in Scotland has always been extremely
difficult, because of the lack of patronage and the restrictive nature of
what little patronage there is. Most artists have found it impossible to
live by their paintings alone. Some have been lucky enough to have a
private income. The rest have had to seek the regularity and the thraldom
of a public income, in the form of a teaching post. During Gray's time at
the Glasgow School of Art, 1952-1957, the understanding was that the
better students would graduate and make a living by teaching, and find
the spare time to pursue their art wherever possible. Painting pictures
has never been considered a 'real' or full time job by the majority of the
Scottish public. It is regarded as a hobby or a therapy, and those that are
artists by profession were, and are, characterised as eccentrics and
lonely tortured souls in the popular press.

In a treatment for a television documentary on art in the New Towns
in 1974, Gray dealt with the history of art in Scotland in the twentieth
century, the relationship of art to industrial wealth, and the difficulties of
surviving as an artist with and without a teaching post:

> When prosperity sailed south in the 1930s it left Scottish painters
> clinging to their art schools like drowning seamen to so many
> rafts. [...] The art schools were unimportant to an earlier
> generation of painters. The staff was smaller, foreign, and most
> RSAs and RGIs would have nothing to do with them. Now the
> committees of the Royal Scottish Academy and the Royal Glasgow
> Institute are almost all painting teachers. [...] Eighty per cent of
> our artists paint in the time left from educating people, and the
> domine is our most obvious type of artistic life. [...] The force
> which turns artists into dominies or hermits is the force which shut
> the shipyard that developed the hovercraft.[10]

A watershed exhibition on post-war Scottish painting, 'Painters in
Parallel', mounted by the Scottish Arts Council in Edinburgh College of
Art, 1978, emphasised this relationship between painting and teaching.
Of the seventy-six selected artists, only thirteen did not mention a

teaching post in their curriculum vitae. The majority held, or had retired from, posts in the four major Scottish art schools.[11] Art must be the only profession where the practitioner has to work in another profession in order to obtain the money necessary to purchase the privilege of pursuing it. For Gray, the time and creative energy left from teaching was not enough to pursue his art adequately, although he admires others, the singular few, like Klee, Kandinsky and Cowie, who managed to teach and paint well.

Patronage has always been a major issue in art. It is, for example, very difficult for a portrait painter if he does not share the same opinions and outlook as his patrons. Alexander Nasmyth (1758-1840), a radical in his politics, turned to landscape painting on that account. For his generation, portrait painting was a main source of income for artists. However, it was also the generation prior to the establishment of the public galleries in Scotland, and artists such as John Knox (1778-1845) could, and did, make their living by painting huge panoramas that travelled from town to town, with lighting, sound and special effects, as the precursors of cinematograph entertainment. Theatre backdrops were another source of employment, and often the scenic canvases in nineteenth century Scotland were considered as much of an attraction as the plays and performances that went with them.[12]

It is interesting that in 1962-1963, Gray found himself working in this tradition, as a scene painter in the Glasgow Pavilion and the Glasgow Citizens Theatres. By the 1960s, only a handful of theatres, the remnants of a once-major entertainment industry, survived in the city, and whilst a guest artist may still be invited to do backdrops from time to time, such work is now the preserve of the specialist theatre designer.

Gray's talent for handling very large spaces became apparent during his time at the Glasgow School of Art when he decorated the Assembly Hall for the annual Christmas Ball. His skill in transforming the area left both staff and students in awe of his ability as a draughtsman. So when the Scotland-USSR Friendship Society (now the Scotland-Russia Society) approached the Glasgow School of Art with a proposal for a mural on their premises at 8 Belmont Crescent in Glasgow's West End, Gray was the natural choice.

The mural in the meeting room at 8 Belmont Crescent is Gray's earliest public work, and is remarkably extant and well protected, in spite of the fall of the Soviet Union. It is on two sides of the room, 5.5m in length, 3.27m in height and joined by a partition rail of 4.26m. Both walls have doors in them, and one an art deco fireplace, which the artist has incorporated into the painting. The work took over two years, and was still not complete when it was unveiled on 12 June 1957.

It is an astonishing work for a twenty-two year old student. Many themes and elements within this work appear again and again in his later works, echoing Blake's cry to Joshua Reynolds, that 'Man brings All he has and can have Into the World with him'. The overall theme of the work is 'Man's inhumanity to Man' and the east wall shows the supreme example of that – the crucifixion of Christ. The perspective has remarkable depth. In the foreground are a peaceful Adam and Eve, contrasting sharply with the tortured crucifixion scene where Glaswegians weep at the foot of the Cross and the landscape beyond is akin to the Firth of Clyde. In an interview some twenty-five years later, Gray said that a main theme of his painting was:

> The Garden of Eden and the triumph of death. All my pictures use one or both. Any good portrait shows someone at a point in the journey from the happy garden to the triumph of death. Any calm place where folk are enjoying each other's company is heavenly. Any places where crowds struggle with each other in a state of dread is a hell, or the doorstep of hell.[13]

The east wall in Belmont Crescent is painted with the Fall of the Star Wormwood. Although Gray painted a large canvas on the same theme two years later, there are important differences in this early work. The tiling of the fireplace gave him the idea of continuing the material at either side and above it as a broken brick wall, against which the figures in the foreground were either struggling or leaning. Unfortunately, the brick has since been painted out, and the trompe l'oeil effect of the original image is now lost. However, the device still gives greater depth to the perspective, which is heightened by the system of railway lines and tunnels that snake through the painting. The Star Wormwood and the Stinky Ocean are at the centre of the work, with stunted, dead trees framing a Glaswegian Adam and Eve in the foreground. The mutant monsters on the right hand side of the 1959 canvas appear separately on the partition rail in Belmont Crescent.

The subject of the painting is in itself both prophetic and apocalyptic. The Star Wormwood emanates from the Firth of Clyde on one wall, and falls in central Glasgow on the other. Three years later, in 1960, the United States Navy came with its Polaris submarines to the Holy Loch, only thirty miles away from Glasgow city centre,[14] and cast a shadow over central Scotland that has not yet lifted. The nuclear deterrent was aimed at the USSR, and here, on the walls of the Scotland-USSR Friendship Society, Gray was highlighting the horror of nuclear war.

The unveiling of the mural was a small event, and a letter of Douglas Percy Bliss, Director of the Glasgow School of Art, to George McAllister of the Scotland-USSR Friendship Society, explained the reasons:

> I am sorry that the prejudice that exists against all things Russian did a lot to keep away the people whom I invited. It will not surprise you to hear that some of my Governors told me later that of course they could not attend a function organised by your Society. This illiberal attitude is so much more the pity because it meant that I failed completely to draw the attention of the people I know in Glasgow who are in the best position for encouraging the talent of the young artist.
>
> I would be very glad if you would return to me any photographs which you still have. The 'Herald' reproduced one of these photographs in its first edition on Thursday, but owing to pressure of news the block was withdrawn and did not appear in the later, and, I presume, the Glasgow editions of the paper.

Bliss, who put his appreciation of Gray's skill before politics, supported the event by enclosing a personal cheque for the sherry, but the Governors of the School of Art, whose function and duty it is to promote the work of the School, could not, for whatever reason, attend the mural's unveilling. *The Glasgow Herald* withdrew the illustration from its Glasgow edition, preventing Glaswegians from seeing it for themselves. George McAllister's reply was to the point:

> We are sorry that your effort to draw the mural to the attention of important people in Glasgow was, in your opinion, a failure. This is unfortunate since we are sure it could have given great encouragement to Alasdair. Of course, we are not unaware of the

prejudice against our Society still shown by some people and regret very much the fact that this affected the attendance. It is just one of those things that we have to contend with.

We feel that people who take up this short-sighted attitude are wrong and that the time must come when people will realise to a greater extent than they do at present that there is very little hope for the future of any of us unless we recognise that despite political and other differences we have to try to get along together in this world. We feel that the Society's work is a necessary contribution towards this end and hope that as time passes and relations between our country and the Soviet Union improve, more and more people will be drawn to visit the mural and appreciate Alasdair's fine work.[15]

Alasdair Gray undoubtedly obtained his first 'Christmas tree file' as a political dissident with this mural. Paintings with a political or social message have never been welcome in Scotland, and murals by their very nature are not 'bankable'. For art to be part of the art market, it has to be portable, preferably within a frame, and suitable for the walls of the nation's banks, company offices and corporate headquarters, and thereafter the nation's galleries.

It is the purchaser who decides what is suitable. The industrialists and businessmen of Scotland have been the purchasers or consumers of art, and in Glasgow it was the bequests and gifts of Archibald McLellan, William Euing, James Orrock, James Reid of Auchterarder, James Donald and William McInnes that formed the municipal art collection. The main purpose of art curators in Glasgow Art Galleries was to manage these collections and purchase 'items mainly to fill gaps' in them.[16] This stamp collector approach to art curatorship was, and still is, dictated by lack of funds and marked by an acceptance of the canon created by the business community, coupled to a fear of dealing with living artists and general favour towards artists that are dead.

For most of the twentieth century, boardroom pictures were the main stock in trade of the few art dealers operating in Glasgow. Artists such as E. A. Hornel (1864–1933), who turned out endless compositions of three little girls in sylvan scenes, and David Gauld (1865–1936), who painted cattle, understood what was required in the boardrooms. By the time Alasdair Gray graduated from the Glasgow School of Art in 1957, the art trade was mainly in these boardroom paintings by a previous generation of artists and shown to the public through exhibition on the walls of the tearooms and coffee shops patronised by the local businessmen – Craig's, Brown's, Cranston's, the Rhul, Treron's. The Director of the Glasgow School of Art knew that the way for the next generation of artists to succeed was through the patronage of the business community, and his school's Governors were the main conduit to it.

Gray with his natural abilities, art school training and burning desire to paint great works of art had no outlet and no market for his creativity. He saw the future in the restoration of the medieval practise of commissioning works of art, a system in which artists were engaged and rewarded as other journeymen.

> Abbots and bishops hired artists to do jobs of work like weavers and builders. Painting became an unstable industry when the rich stopped helping to make art themselves and began searching for completed works by guaranteed, rock-bottom, gilt edged geniuses, preferably dead ones who couldn't spoil the market by flooding it in new pictures.[17]

The creation of public art works in public buildings means that the art is in public ownership and usually, if it is a mural painting, has no commodity value in the art market and is there to be enjoyed by all. There were several attempts in the nineteenth and twentieth centuries to create a movement for public art in this way in Scotland and all of them were short lived or abortive.

In his murals in Greenhead Church of Scotland, Bridgeton and in Belleisle Street Synagogue, Gorbals (1958-1962), Gray showed what was possible. Although his inability to finish the Greenhead Genesis mural within the church officer's timescale has been much commented upon, these were enormously productive years. In 1961, he illustrated the Book of Jonah on a bedroom wall as a wedding present for George and Rosemary Singleton, a work he had forgotten until it was re-discovered under wall paper by a new house purchaser in December 2000.[18] Since then, he has spent many weeks repainting and repairing the Jonah mural to perfection. It is fortunate that the work survives. Both the Greenhead and Belleisle buildings were victims of Glasgow's comprehensive demolition and redevelopment programmes.

These Biblical murals were unique, as such paintings were unheard of in Church of Scotland circles. Gray had no traditions or even examples on which to draw. The murals in Edinburgh churches by Phoebe Traquhair (1852-1936) were known only to the episcopal community until recent times.

In 1964, Alasdair Gray's work was featured in a fifty minute television programme in Huw Weldon's *Monitor* series for the BBC. As he wanted the full focus of the programme to be on his work, he did not wish the audience to be side-tracked by his person.

> This interest in artists as people degrades painting into an excuse for gossip. I wanted Bob Kitts to film my paintings and record my poems but to leave my personality where it belongs: in my private life. An artist's person adds nothing to the true enjoyment of his art, though nowadays it is widely enjoyed for itself.[19]

The only way the producer, Bob Kitts, felt he could achieve this was to imply that Gray was dead – until the last frames of the film. It was a carefully made and sensitive piece, which showed the genius of Alasdair Gray's work. To qualify as such, a genius should preferably be dead. It was said that as the credits rolled, the sound of cheque books being put away could be heard all over Scotland, as Gray, disappointingly, was revealed as young, vigorous and still alive.

Alasdair Gray is one of a handful of artists that have managed successfully to capture the spirit of Glasgow through painting its buildings and people. There have been fine topographical artists, such as John Q. Pringle (1864-1925), Muirhead Bone (1876-1953), Ernest Hood (1932-1988) and James Morrison (b. 1932) who have done some justice to its buildings and cityscape. Only a few have managed to also include a sense of the community. These include Joan Eardley (1921-1963), Harry Keir (1902–1977), Ian Fleming (1906–1998) and Alasdair Gray. A younger generation, which includes Lesley Banks and Avril Paton, have learned from them.

In 1977, when I was in charge of the People's Palace, the social history branch of Glasgow's Museums and Art Galleries, the opportunity arose to employ Alasdair on one of the new government job creation schemes. At that time, the People's Palace – 'an unsuitable building in an undesirable area' – had no long-term future, as other disused buildings in demolition-torn Glasgow were constantly being proposed as better alternatives. The museum had no purchase fund and the last major acquisitions of contemporary art were the watercolours of William Simpson RI (1823-1899).

It was a difficult and delicate matter, not only to interest an important artist like Gray in working for a pittance and to go through the humiliation of 'signing on' the dole as unemployed for the privilege of doing so, but also to convince the management, based at Kelvingrove Art Gallery, where only dead artists seemed to be appreciated and where painting was the sole preserve of the Art Department, that the scheme was appropriate.

An attempt to enlist the help of a former curator of the Collins Gallery to endorse the project resulted in such a negative conversation that I ended up begging the person not to mention our plans. For a time, I was too afraid to admit to the Kelvingrove hierarchy that Alasdair Gray was with us to paint pictures. Had my partner, Michael Donnelly, not already persuaded Alasdair Gray to take on the project, we might never have gone ahead. However, Alasdair was full of ideas and enthusiasm from the start, pleased that he would be working for the local authority, and in every respect was the exact opposite of the obstructive and difficult individual I had been led to expect.

The members of the job creation team were housed in a disused annexe to Templeton's Carpet Factory, at the east end of Glasgow Green, a short distance away from the People's Palace. Alasdair immediately got to work to make the premises habitable by painting the walls in Mondrianesque blocks of colour. Curtain material was found in a derelict textile depot, and shelving came from a disused factory in Gorbals.

The allowance for materials was minimal and Alasdair was restricted to acrylics, watercolour, pencil and rapidograph. We had fun working out who should be in the paintings, attempting to represent all of the political parties and as many of the different occupations as Alasdair could manage. The aim was to create a collection of paintings of Glasgow for Glasgow, a series that would reflect the Glasgow of the 1970s as well as the William Simpson series did the Glasgow of the 1840s.

At that time, the People's Palace collections did not reflect the story of Glasgow at all. The museum only became a local history museum when the 'Old Glasgow Room' at Kelvingrove had to be cleared to make way for the bequest of arms and armour of ship builder Robert Lyons Scott, who died in 1939. Before and since, it had been a dumping ground for items unwanted at Kelvingrove. For a generation, the People's Palace had been the Cinderella of the museums service and it was my private hope that the work undertaken by Alasdair Gray would help build a rapport between the museum and the people whose history and culture it was there to represent.

The political subjects were tackled first. To represent the Glasgow Labour Party, Alasdair drew the first Lord Provost of the recently created Glasgow District Council, Peter McCann, who was depicted with a map of Anderston, a district he been involved in re-shaping in the 1960s. His wife and son were also in the portrait. The Tories were represented by Teddy Taylor, MP for Cathcart with one of his councillors. There was a widespread belief at that time that Taylor would be the next Secretary of State for Scotland. Margo MacDonald represented the SNP and was sketched in an outfit she wore during the Govan by-election of 1974.

Jimmy Reid, the hero of the Upper Clyde Shipbuilders sit-in, was still in the Communist Party and Alasdair took for the typological inspiration of his portrait, the portrait of the Glasgow tobacco lord John Glassford and his wife and family in their mansion house in Trongate, Glasgow in 1760. Thus Jimmy Reid was similarly positioned, with his wife and family in their council house in Clydebank and the view from the window, which in the Glassford painting is a deer park, was a council estate.

Most of the writers in Glasgow were good friends of Alasdair, and most of those whom he drew for the People's Palace – Jim Kelman, Tom Leonard, Edwin Morgan and Liz Lochhead – chose to be painted in their own homes. The portrait of Liz Lochhead, although not a likeness with which the sitter identifies, had great subtleties in the portraiture. Each of the writers supplied, in their own hand, a text of a favourite poem, which was mounted and framed with their portrait.

The poet Alex Scott chose to be painted with his wife Cathy and family dog in their favourite pub, the popular Pewter Pot in North Woodside Road. The novelist Archie Hynd was depicted beside the Clyde at the Dalmarnock Power Station, a majestic structure that has now been demolished.

Among the new features of Glasgow tackled by Alasdair was the Third Eye, an arts council-funded arts centre in Sauchiehall Street, which from 1977–1990 offered some of the best exhibitions in town. Alasdair drew its first director, the playwright Tom McGrath, in an office well-stocked with cutting edge office technology of the times and shared with Linda Haase of the Scottish Society of Playwrights, who later became the first administrator of the Tron Theatre. The scene, created in rapidograph, was full of contemporary detail. To pack in even more, Alasdair made the walls transparent, with a view into Sauchiehall Street and the shops beyond.

Religion has always been of significance in Glasgow and one of Alasdair's most successful portraits was that of Pastor Jack Glass of the Sovereign Grace Baptist Church, who, because he sees himself as continuing the work of the Scottish Reformation, chose to be painted with the statue of John Knox in the Necropolis and the spire of Glasgow Cathedral. The foreshortening of the figure, with the emphasis on the Bible in the subject's hand, highlights the importance of the word of God.

Another particularly good work was the portrait of Frances Gordon, one of the teenagers on the People's Palace job creation scheme. She was painted in a t-shirt and the fashionable flared trousers of the time and on completion of the work, Alasdair asked her to empty her purse of the tickets and receipts kept from various teenage rites of passage. These included receipts for platform shoes and denim flares, tickets for Elton John at the Glasgow Apollo and a midnight disco in the Highlanders' Institute (both places of entertainment have been demolished since), her ticket from her first journey on a Glasgow late night bus, photographs with Spanish waiters in Ibiza on her sixteenth birthday, a £6 Glasgow to London bus ticket, a cinema ticket for *One Flew over the Cuckoo's Nest*. He glued these around the portrait, which was framed as a time capsule of the life of a Glasgow teenager of 1977.

Alasdair Gray worked with speed to get the subject and composition of his paintings and drawings, spending time later in filling out and completing details. The intention was to complete a body of work, to be presented as an exhibition reflecting contemporary Glasgow, for the eightieth birthday of the People's Palace, from 22 January 1978. After only a few months in the job and with only some of the works completed, he announced that he was leaving for a post as Writer-in-Residence at the University of Glasgow.

This came as a shock and disappointment. It seemed to be a waste of his time and talent as an artist, for writing was an even more difficult way of earning a living, always supposing he would find a publisher. I begged him not to leave the People's Palace, trying to convince him that Glasgow needed his singular talent as an artist. He promised that the works would be finished in time, even though he was working elsewhere.

They were. The People's Palace has a collection of thirty-two works by Alasdair Gray, which reflects the social, political and cultural colours of Glasgow in the mid-1970s.

The project was not without its problems, especially when it became known at Kelvingrove that Gray was actually painting for the People's Palace instead of recording the historic paintings in the collection. In a hundred ways, subtle and otherwise, disapproval was made known. On one occasion, an empty bottle of Black Label Whisky was discovered in the picture framing store at Kelvingrove and claims were made that Gray must have been drinking on the premises. The fastest way to discredit anyone in Glasgow Museums at that time was to allege secret drinking or alcoholism, for there was a prevailing culture of censorius temperance, a lingering relic of the directorship of temperance advocate Dr T. J. Honeyman. In retrospect, it is laughable to think of Gray, a social drinker of wine, being accused of drinking cheap whisky in such uncongenial surroundings. Nevertheless, the accusation was serious and unpleasant at the time.

Alasdair Gray's exhibition was entitled 'The Continuous Glasgow Show' and opened on the eightieth birthday of the People's Palace. We persuaded the Parks Department to open the winter gardens of the

People's Palace, which had been closed and awaiting demolition since 1966, for the occasion.

Alasdair designed the poster and invitation in rapidograph, taking portraits from several of his new paintings, providing a line-up of Glasgow faces that included a tobacco lord and set them against a Glasgow skyline terminating in a fine drawing of the People's Palace Winter Gardens. The image was printed in the *Glasgow Herald* in advance and had an immediate, spectacular effect. The day of the opening was freezing, blustery and icy, and we witnessed the strange phenomenon of several hundred people, battling against the wind and trying to keep their footing on the slippery, ungritted pathways of Glasgow Green, converging on the People's Palace for the private view.

'The Continuous Glasgow Show' was a turning point for the People's Palace, and helped secure the survival of the building to the present day. Alasdair's paintings brought in a new audience that identified with the ethos of the museum, and a new constituency that did not want to see it closed.

In retrospect, the work was wrong for him. He needed a number of major commissions for mural schemes in public buildings with a long-term future, and not a series of small paintings planned as a survival mechanism for an ailing, under-funded, struggling local history museum. Regrettably, we were not in a position to do otherwise. Even after the People's Palace had undergone extensive repairs, and was back in full operation as a museum and winter gardens, there was talk of the museums department vacating the premises to release the space as headquarters for the parks department, when Glasgow Green was planned as the site of the 1988 Garden Festival.

Regardless of the troubles of the People's Palace, the public art movements of the 1970s and 1980s, which had been the hope of those who wished to see art in public ownership and free from the prison of the art gallery, came to nothing. Gray, looking at public art schemes in new towns, and in particular, in Glenrothes, where David Harding was employed as a 'technician' (the acceptable terminology for 'artist-in-residence') in 1974, saw this as the way forward. There was an arts council-supported, halfhearted scheme for murals on gable ends of tenements in Glasgow in the early 1970s. The sites selected were not meant to survive, and almost all of them have disappeared through demolition, redevelopment and neglect. Alasdair Gray submitted in 1973 a scheme for gable end murals in Garnethill overlooking the M8, but the proposal was not accepted. The winning scheme was for some anodyne, inoffensive geometrical patterns in beige and blue, which are long since gone and forgotten. The lack of investment in, commitment to, and above all, vision for, public art, has reduced the form to amateur daubs on the walls of badly-built community centres, and the very term is now redolent of amateurism and the second rate.

In the 1970s, there was still a belief that art could affect people's lives, enhancing them if not changing them for the better. In the past, murals in public buildings had been used as vehicles to express national and local identity, shared values and beliefs and human aspiration. Developments in conceptual art in the past twenty years have destroyed such philanthropic intention. Vision is now introspective and limited to that of the individual artist, who, without knowledge of or concern for either art history or the wider community, focuses on his or her private dreams and nightmares. The end product is so esoteric and unintelligible that it requires a new breed of art critic to interpret it, as well as arts managers to present, promote and sell it to an unbelieving public.[20] Such art requires the life support machine of the gallery system and the regular charades of the British Art Show and the Turner Prize to sustain it.

In direct opposition to this trend, Gray has always maintained an unfashionable belief in the power of art to both change and reflect lives. His mural in the Ubiquitous Chip Restaurant in the west end of Glasgow, painted between 1976 and 1981, and restored and extended in 2000-2001, is a decorative Eden that enhances the pleasure of the diners and also depicts many of the restaurant's regular customers. His mural of 1974 in the exhibition centre of the Palacerigg Nature Reserve, Cumbernauld, is a teaching piece on natural history and ecology.

In the ceiling painting for Abbot House heritage centre in Dunfermline, the commission was for a contemporary work that would pay homage to the Scottish painted ceilings of the sixteenth and seventeenth centuries, many of which are extant in other historical buildings in Fife. Abbot House is a medieval building extended in the seventeenth century but which had all of its internal historical features erased in a refurbishment of 1964. In 1991-1994, the building was refurbished again for Dunfermline Heritage Trust. The fabric of the building was restored and re-worked as a palimpsest, with many of the surfaces decorated in historical styles and embellished with murals telling the story of Dunfermline from Pictish times to the present day. Thirty-two artists and craftspeople worked on different parts of the project, to give Dunfermline a visitor centre of quality that would reflect the historical importance of this ancient capital of Scotland and act as a focus for the local community as well as area tourism.

Alasdair was asked to fill a difficult space – the long gallery ceiling that stretches the length of the centre of the building on the top floor, and which is so low that it can only be viewed in sections at a time. The surface is cut by a number of windows and attic skylights. Together we looked at ceilings in Culross and at Earlshall Castle, where Dame Agnes Lindsay, a former resident of Abbot House, had commissioned the decoration of the long gallery ceiling there.

Although the commission was framed in terms of ceiling decoration, Alasdair took the project further by miles. He embraced the concept of the palimpsest in its entirety and in his work offered a schematical summation of Scottish history with Dunfermline's place at the heart of it, a navigational chart for the townspeople from prehistory to the future, combined with a portrait gallery. This was executed with mathematical precision, in the spirit of the labyrinth makers of Chartres Cathedral, but offering a very fulsome graphic and textual interpretation of past and present, whilst challenging common perceptions.

The central idea was to present a Tree of Scottish History with events and episodes springing from the branches. Working with sign writer Robert Salmond, he divided the trunk with branches extending down the cove of the ceiling, terminating in thistles, and dividing the space into centuries. In the roots of the tree is a meticulously drawn choice selection of the best archaeological finds from the National Museum and elsewhere – the Lewis Chessmen, Pictish stones, axes, brooches, combs, musical instruments and masks. The introductory text proclaims that

> All Nations are made of earlier nations and over 150,000
> generations of forgotten folk as wise and important as us

The scheme is punctuated with important pieces of information, such as:

> James Blake, Dunfermline weaver steals the design of damask
> making loom from French tradesmen: giving the Burgh an
> advantage on which its weavers & merchants worked & made
> Dunfermline Britain's main exporter of table linen throughout the
> nineteenth century.

The whole political, social and cultural make up of the town are explored through such texts, and the main tree trunk has additional time lines running from it. The black line of coalmining starts in 1291 and runs through the abolition of serfdom, 1799, the eight-hour day of 1870, the first pit head baths in 1920, and into the future with Longannet, Scotland's last surviving coal mine. Similar lines run for royal residence, royal burials and linen production. This is no establishment history, however. The client was surprised to find Alasdair including local aphorisms:

> Copper wire – invented by a Dunfermliner and Aberdonian
> fighting for a penny.
> Perpetual motion – a Dunfermliner collecting a debt from an
> Aberdonian.

Along the coving are portraits of Dunfermline people, past and present. The north wall has those who worked on Abbot House, 1991-1996, from the architect to the cleaner. The south wall has portraits of historical and contemporary figures which, where there are known portraits (James IV, James VI, Charles I, Communist MP Willie Gallacher, Singer Barbara Dickson, Dancer Moira Shearer etc) are instantly recognisable. Others may look familiar. The heresy-hunting Abbot Durie has the face of Alasdair's fellow writer, James Kelman. There are seventy-five head and shoulder portraits in total, painted on brown paper and incorporated in the scheme, comprising a portrait gallery for Dunfermline.

Like the People's Palace commission, this was a low budget work. It was begun in July 1994 and completed in January 1996. Gray lives by the maxim which decorates the boards of his books – work as if you live in the early days of a better nation. The Abbot House commission was

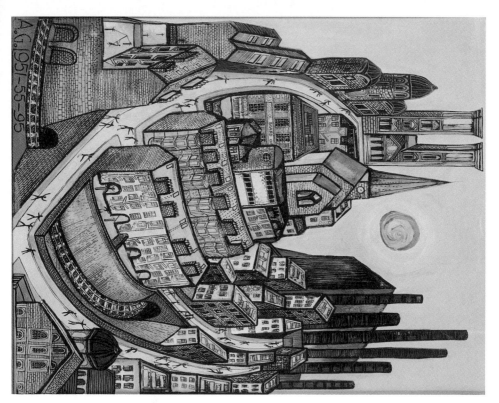

1951 – TWO HILLS – gouache & ink on paper.

1951 – SAINT CHRISTOPHER – ink & watercolour on paper.

1952 – AFTERNOON TEA – gouache on paper, 23 x 18 inches.

195? – THE BEAST IN THE PIT – ink & watercolour on paper.

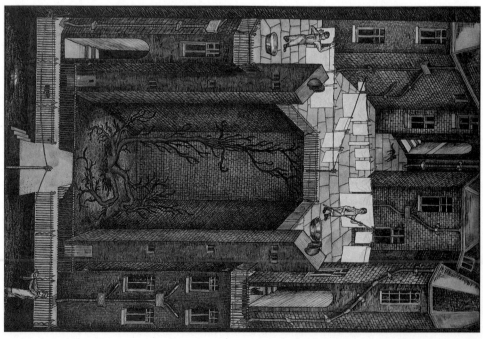

1960 – THE FALL OF THE STAR WORMWOOD – oil on canvas, 71 x 34 inches. Though never satisfactorily completed, this was painted for an exhibition called *Artists Against the Bomb* arranged by Church of Scotland clergy who supported the CND, and in 1961 was exhibited in Glasgow and Edinburgh. Present owner, Petra Boyce.

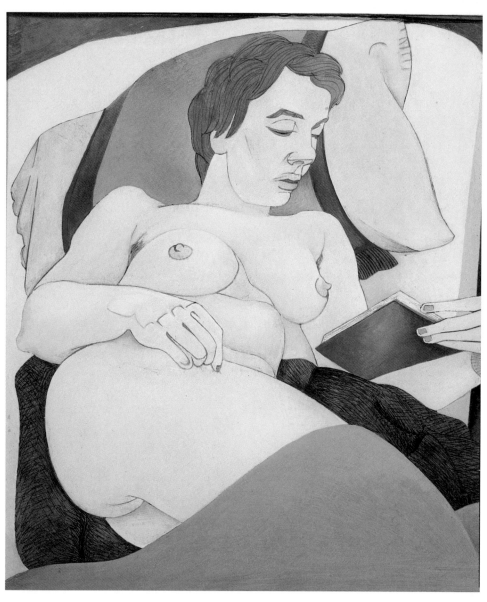

1963 – INGE READING – pen, watercolour, oil on paper mounted on wood, 17 x 14.6 inches.

1966 – UPLAND ROAD – oil on canvas, 15.75 x 22.75 inches.

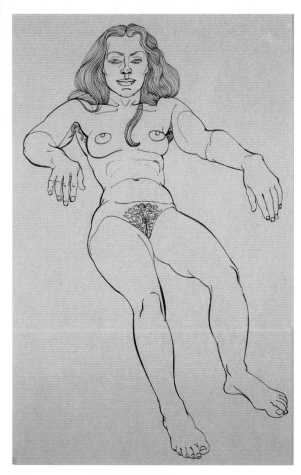

Circa 1987 – MAY HOOPER
ink on craft paper, 26 x 27 inches.

1969 – ANDREW AS REDSKIN
tinted drawing, 20.25 x 6.25 inches.

Circa 1970 – NELLIMEG & ARCHIE, ballpoint on newsprint, 16 x 31 inches.

1975 – DAVE, PAT, KIRSTY STANSFIELD – oil & pencil on wood & paper, 17.5 x 25 inches.

19? – SKYE LANDSCAPE – oil & acrylic on wood.

1966 – EDEN & AFTER – oil on wood, 24.5 x 21.5 inches.

1968 – FIRTH – acrylic & oil on board, 11.25 x 23.26 inches.

1974 – MOST OF A MURAL SHOWING WILD LIFE THRIVING AROUND AN OAK TREE – emulsion, acrylic & oil paint, in the exhibition centre of Palacerigg country park and nature reserve near Cumbernauld, in Lanarkshire, and restored by the artist in 2001.

conceived as a piece of mere ceiling decoration, but Gray delivered a modern *mappa mundi*, a focus for the identity of the people of Dunfermline. It is a detailed work of great complexity and rare insights, combined with good signwriting and precision geometry.

Alasdair Gray is an addict to perfection, and will spend hours, days, weeks, and months on a work, regardless of the cost to himself, to ensure the effect he desires is obtained. He has the ability to return to a work after many years and extend and complete it. A better nation would have employed his talents to the full, utilising his skills as a mural painter in public buildings, especially great libraries, like the Mitchell in Glasgow and the National Library of Scotland. The mural spaces created by classical architecture in Scotland have been kept calvinistically blank.

Deprived of a market and an audience for his talents as a muralist and public artist, Gray did as others in his position have done. He concentrated on book illustration and on writing. It was a path well worn before him by William Blake, who starved as a history painter before returning to engraving, book illustration and poetry.

In 1975, Gray first demonstrated to the Scottish publishing world what could be achieved with good book illustrations, when he illustrated Carl MacDougall's collection of folk tales, *A Scent of Water* for the Molendinar Press.[21] The end covers were printed in dark green on yellow. Fifty separate illustrations complement the text, both as marginal illustrations and illuminated drop capitals, where line drawings flowing around a single letter, summarise the narrative and greatly heighten the pleasure of reading it.

Gray has always worked co-operatively with other writers and artists to great effect, and it is known that an Alasdair Gray cover will always sell a book. His illustrations helped sell the literary magazine *Chapman* for much of the 1980s, and he designed all seven books of the short-lived Dog and Bone publishing house in 1988-1990. Conversely, he also writes to illustrate the art of others. His poems written to accompany a book on the art of Ian McCulloch, and his essay introducing the collected poems of Jack Withers, are pieces produced with the same care as any of his linear book illustrations.[22]

The reading of a book by Alasdair Gray provides an aesthetic, sensory pleasure, from the dust jacket to the valediction on the last page. Every part of his own books has been designed by him. No other Scottish writer has sought and obtained involvement in the design and production in this way. His commitment to perfection and to producing work that contributes to re-enforcing local and national identity has raised publishing standards. There is so much visual interest in each work, with board papers either profusely illustrated (as in *Unlikely Stories, Mostly* and *The Book of Prefaces*) or in primary colours (*Something Leather, Ten Tales Tall and True*), and followed by end papers, title and contents pages that pay homage to the best traditions of book production, that readers sometimes omit to remove the dust jackets and discover the boards themselves, beautifully stamped in gold and silver with bold designs and Gray's guiding principle: Work as if you live in the Early Days of a Better Nation.

Gray has always used typography to change mood, enhance the meaning of the text or convey a mindset. The changes in typeface are never gratuitous. The appearances of words have been selected with the same care as they have been written, and work together for a purpose. His encyclopaedic knowledge of the printer's art has enabled him to invent historical title pages (as in *Poor Things*) and his love of beauty in books has led to the re-introduction of the book ribbon (*Poor Things, Mavis Belfrage, The Book of Prefaces*) by the publishers Bloomsbury. Two errata slips were issued in red and black type for Prefaces within days of its publication. It was his love of printing conventions that led to the issue of the first slip in *Unlikely Stories*, proclaiming 'Erratum: This slip has been inserted by mistake'. The dropped capitals containing portraits (*Something Leather*) and animals (*Ten Tales Tall and True*) are stunning in their economy of line, and in their effect on the page.

In short, the books written and designed by Gray are beautiful works, which do homage to the arts of the type setter, printer and bookbinder, and his fellow artists – 'the compositors employed by Kingsport Press of Kingsport, Tennessee to typeset this bloody book' – are always given full acknowledgement.[23] Each publication by Gray is as much a work of art as it is a work of literature.

Acknowledgement to Alasdair Gray himself has come late in life. The publication of *Lanark* at the age of forty-seven secured his reputation as a writer. In the years since, his skill as a maker of fine books has become well known. His appointment as Professor of Creative Writing in the University of Glasgow at the age of sixty-six is gratifying. It is not yet too late for his creative genius as a muralist to be allowed to flourish. A full-colour catalogue showing the scope of his paintings to date would be a prerequisite and long overdue. Given the resources and a team of artists working under his direction, he could transform the public spaces of the newly refurbished National Library of Scotland, the Museum of Scotland and the new Scottish Parliament which is now under construction.

A better nation would have no difficulty in doing this.

Public Collections Where Alasdair Gray's Work Can Be Found

Abbot House, (Dunfermline Heritage Trust), a mural
Artemis (Leeds School Museum and Art Loan Service)
Collins Gallery, University of Strathclyde
Hunterian Art Gallery, University of Glasgow
National Library of Scotland, Edinburgh
North Ayrshire Council Museums Service
Palacerigg Country Park Visitor Centre (North Lanarkshire
 Council), a mural
People's Palace (Glasgow Museums and Art Galleries)
Stirling Smith Art Gallery and Museum
University of Stirling Fine Art Collections

There are also large elaborate but not quite complete murals in Greenbank Church of Scotland, Clarkston, and the Ubiquitous Chip restaurant, Glasgow.

Notes

1. *Gray Matter*, directed by Donny O'Rourke for Scottish Television, 1993.

2. See James Kelman, 'Storm in the Palace Summer 1990' and Alasdair Gray, 'A Friend Unfairly Treated', in *Beyond the Culture Rip Off: The Reckoning*, ed. by Farquhar McLay (Glasgow: Clydeside, 1990), pp. 50-56. Also Alasdair Gray, 'Elspeth King' *Independent Magazine*, 13 July 1991, p. 46.

3. Alasdair Gray has written eloquently of this in *Something Leather* (London: Cape, 1990), chapters 8 and 10, pp. 134-153, 171-186, and in his introduction to *A Real Glasgow Archipelago* by Jack Withers (Glendaruel: Argyll, 1993), pp. 11-21.

4. *Alasdair Gray: Retrospective Exhibition Descriptive Catalogue* (Glasgow: University of Strathclyde, 1974).

5. Robert Crawford and Thom Nairn, *The Arts of Alasdair Gray* (Edinburgh: Edinburgh University Press, 1991), pp. 1-12.

6. Alasdair Gray, *Lanark: A Life in Four Books*, rev. edn (Edinburgh: Canongate, 1985), p. 236.

7. Crawford and Nairn, *The Arts of Alasdair Gray*, pp. 22-23.

8. 'The Mean City', 1962. Article composed at the suggestion of Andrew Sykes. Typescript, National Library of Scotland, Acc 9247/37.

9. Replies to Christopher Swan and Frank Delaney, August 1982. Question 20. Typescript, National Library of Scotland, Acc 9247/51.

10. Treatment for a documentary on art in New Towns, 1974. Typescript, part 1, National Library of Scotland, Acc 9247/40.

11. *Painters in Parallel: a Scottish Arts Council Exhibition selected by Cordelia Oliver*. Catalogue (Edinburgh: Scottish Arts Council, 1978).

12. Elspeth King, 'Popular Culture in Glasgow', in *The Working Class in Glasgow 1750-1914*, ed. by R. A. Cage (London: Croom Helm, 1987), pp. 142-181.

13. Replies to Swan and Delaney, p. 7.

14. Kevin Dunion, *Faslane, Diary of a Peace Camp* (Edinburgh: Polygon, 1984), pp. 1-7.

15. Correspondence in the archives of the Scotland-Russia Society. I am indebted to Alan Burton, Secretary, and the Society members for allowing me to consult the archive and photograph the mural for this paper.

16. *Glasgow Art Gallery and Museum: the Buildings and Collections*, ed. by A. Auld (London: Collins, 1987), p. 101.

17. New Towns Documentary.

18. *Glasgow Evening Times*, 26 December 2000.

19. 'An Apology for My Recent Death', 1965. Typescript, National Library of Scotland, Acc 9247/38.

20. For a cogent description of this phenomenon, see Alasdair Gray's story 'The Bum Garden' in *Something Leather*, pp. 134-153.

21. This successful little press did not last long.

22. Ian McCulloch, *The Artist in his World: Prints 1986-1997* (Glendaruel: Argyll, 1998) and Withers, *A Real Glasgow Archipelago*.

23. Gray, *Lanark*, p. 499.

POLITICS, SCOTLAND AND PREFACES
Alasdair Gray's Non-Fiction

ANGUS CALDER

1

A FRIEND JUST NOW GAVE ME SOMETHING SHE'D PICKED UP IN a charity shop. In 1993, Argyll Publishing brought out a wee book by Jack Withers, with illustrations by Ian McCulloch, *A Real Glasgow Archipelago*.[1] In verse and prose, Withers projects 'the way individual people' – in Glasgow, that is – 'have become like a chain of separate islands – deeply touched by, but unable to connect with the forces of politics, economics and culture'. Alasdair Gray contributes an introduction, which describes with cold scorn certain goings-on around Glasgow's sleazy repackaging in 1990 as 'European City of Culture', and provides the most eloquent, succinct presentation I've seen from him of his own Scottish Socialist position and where it comes from.

He mentions that in 1988, together with Tom Leonard and Philip Hobsbaum, he was invited to meet a Japanese-Canadian lady deputed to organise an exhibition for Culture Year to be called *The Words and the Stones*. It would celebrate Glasgow's history, its fine writers and wondrous architecture. It would counteract Glasgow's 'bad reputation'. She would value their advice:

> Alas, we had none to give her. I said that Glasgow's best civic architecture this century had been good pre-war housing schemes built as a result of the Wheatley Acts – how could the District Council celebrate its achievements as a public landlord while selling its best housing stock to private buyers? Tom Leonard said that what outsiders thought of Glasgow was *their* problem, not his.[2]

The exhibition found other advisers. My friend, and Alasdair's, Carl MacDougall was enlisted to edit the Book of the Exhibition. I contributed three short bits. That wee darg, and attending one or two 'advisory' meetings constituted, I think, the only work I've ever done in my life for which I felt I had been overpaid. Seated, as it were, in the commodious, smartly-painted gravy train, I said I thought the exhibition proposals said too little about women and non-white people, and recommended that the anti-black Glasgow race riot of 1919 should be commemorated, to counteract sentimentality about the 'Red Clyde'. Needless to say, it did not feature in the sanitised presentation of the history of the Dear Green Place that opened in the vaults under Central Station in 1990. Nor did Glasgow's gains from black slavery and the rape of India. As Alasdair goes on:

> To stop *The Words and the Stones* being shortened to the acronym TWATS the show was renamed *Glasgow's Glasgow*. Though intended to pay for itself by the sale of entrance tickets, the District Council have since admitted that it lost £6,000,000. Nor is it strange that a transatlantic lady with an English assistant had been put in charge. The show, like the Culture Capital Year itself, was not meant to send Glasgow goods and examples outward, it was designed to pull foreigners and their money in. And surely foreigners must know what they want better than the natives can![3]

Such outrage against deference to international capitalism and to England is wholly typical of Alasdair. (Forgive me, please, as I refer to him throughout this article by his given name. Not only have I known him pretty well for a couple of decades, it is one of the cherishable peculiarities of Scotland that our favourite writers are universally known by first names. People whose closest contact with the late MacCaig occurred when they shyly handed their copies of his *Collected*

Poems to him for signature after a reading are not thought to be name-dropping unwarrantably when, like everyone else, they refer to 'Norman'.) Alasdair, as we will hereinafter denominate him, might seem quite bitterly anti-English. So what are we to make of the fact that his biggest work since *Lanark*, the much-anticipated product of sixteen years labour, amounts to a paean of celebration of the English literary tradition, and was acclaimed as such in an exceptional two-page spread in the London *Times?* [4]

2

Another peculiarity of Scottish literary culture is that leading creative writers quite commonly sound off *in extenso* on general as well as particular political issues. The modern tradition in this matter was established by C. M. Grieve as 'Hugh MacDiarmid' and under other bylines and pseudonyms. While English counterparts content themselves with the occasional well-paid grumble in the *Guardian*, the novelist William McIlvanney, as newspaper columnist, was a prophet for the new Scottish Parliament, and Allan Massie, one of very few intellectuals to give support (however idiosyncratically) to the not-so-romantically doomed Scottish Tory Party of recent years, has always been a regular, respected and well-informed political commentator as well as a prolific publisher of fiction. The poet Douglas Dunn produced a pamphlet against the Poll Tax.

Since *Lanark* and *1982, Janine* are as thoroughly 'political' as *Nineteen Eighty-Four* and *Catch-22*, it was, therefore, no surprise that Alasdair intervened in the 1992 General Election with a long pamphlet called *Independence: Why Scots Should Rule Scotland.* Passing from Malaga Airport on my way to a family holiday in Andalucia, about a week before that election, I bought that admirable newspaper *El Pais*, and was delighted to learn that its correspondent covering the election believed (as I did at that point) that the Tories would be wiped out in Scotland and that autonomy for our bonny country was near, but was somewhat amused that he adduced as proof of this that the great writer Gray had declared for independence. Such is the prestige of writers in other countries. Alas, as I learned from the local expat station, Radio Nerja, in the small hours of a subsequent dreadful night, Prime Minister Major bucked the opinion polls, the Tories actually boosted their number of seats in Scotland, out of 72, from 10 to 11, and we had to endure five more years of 'democratic deficit' before Blair's landslide in 1997 (when Alasdair again chose to pamphleteer at length) secured the referendum that gave us our Parliament back after nearly three centuries of Westminster rule.

Alasdair's 1992 pamphlet was somewhat hectically put together. Confessedly, it was more or less dictated to his publisher at Canongate, Stephanie Wolfe Murray, who is 'heard' urging, querying and ticking him off. She reminds him that to be of any use during the election campaign he must meet her printer's deadline. It is 7.45am on Monday 16 March and the printers must have copy by noon. The book has a most explicit topical thrust. It is a work of agitation (in more than one sense of the word).

But it is not partisan. 'Since I argue that Scotland should have a strong government elected by its people this pamphlet is propaganda for the Scottish National Party, *or for candidates of other parties who have declared for such a government without swithering from side to side on the matter'.*[5] Who might have been intended by the lines I have italicised it is hard to say. It depends on what Alasdair meant by the word 'strong'. In the disastrous Referendum of 1979 – when the Labour Party offered an Assembly to Scotland with very limited powers – Labour MPs campaigned on both sides, and the notorious '40%' rule had been introduced, whereby the votes of four-tenths of the total electorate was necessary, a straight majority was not enough. Thereafter Scottish opinion gradually firmed up. The Tory vote span into decline as Thatcher introduced policies offensive to Scottish opinion. The Labour Party gradually swung behind 'a devolved *Parliament*' – not Assembly – as a way of making up the 'democratic deficit' and ensuring that such notions as Thatcher's Poll Tax could never again be imposed on Scotland by a deeply unpopular party dominant at Westminster. In the end, an apparently cordial alliance of Labour, SNP and Liberal Democrats ensured that the 'settled will of the Scottish people' (a phrase used by the beloved early-dead Labour leader, John Smith) prevailed in the 1997 Referendum that gave Scotland, by 1999, a Parliament possessed of the power to vary taxes 3% up or down on UK levels. But it would still have no authority over defence, foreign policy or social security and I am sure that Alasdair does not think that its powers now (2001) are strong enough. Nevertheless, his 1992 formulation anticipates the multi-party alliance of 1997 while evoking the idea of a Popular Front against Fascism/Nazism common on the left in his Thirties childhood.

Alasdair's case for 'independence' is based primarily on the view that the people who live in the territory called 'Scotland' should have a democratic forum through which their 'will' can be expressed. But why Scotland, in particular? His chief effort in the pamphlet is to explore Scotland's distinctive history. There seems to be no other way of explaining why Scotland, with a population much smaller than that of Greater London, and exceeded by several regions of England, should be independent with its own Parliament.

He commences with a debatable point distinguishing 'Upland' cultures, characterised by a prevalence of 'peasants' with small holdings, and 'Farmer' cultures – the Scots, like the Swiss, are prone to set up banks and insurance companies and to emigrate to make their way in the world, well-equipped by upbringing 'at once strenuous, frugal and provident'.[6] He moves on to less questionable ground when he spots the difference between 'clannish' Scotland and England, which after the Norman Conquest was ruled by a 'self-perpetuating class of military landowners'. Bruce's victory at Bannockburn in 1314 was 'the victory of an ancient system over one more modern'.[7] After Bannockburn, the Norman-Scots who had previously held estates also in England, turned inward and 'owed their power, and knew they owed it, to the will of the commoners'.[8] He rejoices to quote Froissart's fourteenth-century astonishment at the bad manners of the Scottish 'peasants'. The Frenchman noted that 'if a nobleman rode over a field the man who worked it screamed and yelled at him to get off'. After 1314, Scotland became, Alasdair avers, 'the first European nation state – the first to have territorial unity under one king'.[9] This statement raises numerous problems. Historians see the 'nation-state' as a post-medieval, early modern invention. 'Nationalism' as we now know it originates no earlier than the late eighteenth century. Anyway, could Scotland's ancient priority as a 'nation state', if somehow conceded, be sound grounds for twenty-first century 'independence' (in or outside Europe)? Many such priorities have been superseded. The Swedish Government would be unwise to claim the State of Delaware on the basis that the original white settlers there were planted in the seventeenth century by the Kingdom of Sweden (and I understand that they were mostly Finns).

Yet Alasdair's ensuing arguments about culture are compelling. 'English Literature' was kickstarted by the Black Death of the 1340s, which made labour scarce and gave the common toiler power: 1360-1400 sees the achievements of the Gawain Poet, Chaucer and Langland, and Wyclif's Bible. Then the ruling class clamp down and literature in English languishes. But in Scotland, with a total of perhaps only 5,000 or 6,000 readers of 'Inglis' – that is, 'Scots' – the Makars flourish mightily. I think Alasdair must be right that Kings, landlords and clergy in Scotland, in a poor and 'clannit' country, without the buffer of a secure middle class between themselves and the common speech, were in touch with the language and songs of their people. And to the present day it is demonstrably true that Scottish writers and musicians typically connect themselves to 'folk tradition' and 'popular culture' in ways not characteristic of their English counterparts. Such points meld the case for 'democracy in Scotland' with the case for an independently democratic Scotland. We have something distinctive to offer.

Alasdair is in more trouble, though, with his discussion of John Knox – 'a man of admirable courage and honesty, horrible single-mindedness and cruelty'.[10] He likes Knox's idea of a school in every parish, shudders away from what he conceives to be puritanical harshness – as exemplified, in his view, by actual Scottish schoolteachers down the centuries. Knox, to state the obvious, had no power single-handed to turn the Scots into a people who commonly internalised Calvinism (and, in actual fact, Lutheranism predominated amongst those who supported 'his' Reformation of the 1550s). The peculiar hardness of the Scottish puritan conscience (as compared with those of Swiss, Danes, Dutch), Alasdair attributes to 'the absence of a firm government, law-abiding landlords and a comfortable clergy', which 'made the Scottish soul a bleaker, less social thing'.[11] This is hard to square with the famous emphasis placed on society by the thinkers of the Enlightenment and by Robert Burns, it is easier to place (as Alasdair doesn't) in relation to the peasant bloodymindnedness that struck Froissart. But in a brilliant passage he does seem to me to 'fix' something in common between Paterson, stubborn progenitor of the doomed Darien colony, Livingstone, roaming Central Africa as a lone obsessed white man, and John Maclean, almost as solitary in his dying fight for a Scottish Workers' Republic:

> It is as if we had a small god in our brain who may sometimes sound like John Knox or a local schoolteacher but has nothing to do with landlords, kings, and such gentry. The demands of this little god are sometimes so severe that whenever he has been supported by clergymen of his own kind he has destroyed the happiness of whole communities, delighted in smashing church organs and sculptures, and revelled in the burning of poor old women; but Scots with radical new ideas who get their deity to co-operate with them have acted with courage and independence – the opposition or indifference of clergy, kings, bosses and nations has seemed trivial compared with their staunch self-approval.[12]

Put that together with the Burnsian idea of 'social union' and you have Burns' 'man of independent mind' who will 'bear the gree an a'that' in the great song chosen by Sheena Wellington, and delivered by her, to focus the return of democracy to Scotland at the State Opening of the new Parliament in 1999.

I will skip over Alasdair's contentious chapters, in this 1992 pamphlet, dealing with Scottish history from the sixteenth through to the twentieth century, and arrive at Chapter 9, called 'The Scottish Archipelago – Some Light Relief'. This introduces facts about Scotland that Unionists sometimes deploy to undermine those calling for independence and with characteristic candour exhibits Alasdair himself in an interesting light. A French writer who visited Alasdair in 1983 told him that Scotland was an archipelago of different cultures. Whereas France was overdependent on the metropolis of Paris, Scotland was an example of a decentralised nation 'in good working order, though without a government of its own'. Alasdair's reaction was that the archipelago idea was 'hideously true', although Scotland, with health, housing, wages and employment indices so much worse than those of South Britain, was 'not a nation in good working order'.[13]

The archipelago idea is certainly worth much thought. The Gaelic of the outer isles and the Norse-inflected dialect of Shetland are not only mutually incomprehensible, both also baffle Scots from other areas. A Glaswegian alighting in Aberdeen station will find the local Doric speech as penetrable as a dry stone dyke. The SNP's main problem in recent years has been to escape from its position as effectually a regional party of the North-East of Scotland, while Lib Dem enclaves in Borders and Orkney represent further particularisms.

Like Alasdair's Frenchman, I love this.

But as someone brought up by Scottish parents in exile, and thus equally an outsider in the first instance everywhere in Scotland, I have not had Alasdair's problem, shared with other Glaswegian writers, of rootedness in the West of Scotland. The great poet MacCaig lived in Edinburgh, despite his deep attachment to ancestral Highlands. He wrote exclusively in English – however, in readings his Edinburgh accent made his poems colourfully Scottish for many listeners. Alasdair, though, was incensed at a conference when MacCaig, at some Festival, joked about the 'Glasgow literary mafia'. In 1985, the two men met at a series of events supporting the Miners' Strike. 'Since MacCaig was from Edinburgh and his accent struck my ears as upper class I had thought MacCaig would be against the miners – I give that as an example of the stupid prejudice which develops in a split-apart land'.[14] But the great cultural achievement of the eighteen years between 1979 and 1997 was to unite the Scottish archipelago in support for the idea of a Parliament.

Alasdair's last chapter in 1992 was prophetic in one detail. He envisaged, rightly, that Scotland's last steelworks at Ravenscraig would be closed and that British Steel would centre its operations in Wales. 'Good for the Welsh! But [...] the Welsh steel industry may be a halfway house in shifting all British industrial investment to Germany'.[15] As I write, 'Corus', the successor company to British Steel, is in the process of closing down steel in Wales in favour of (as it happens) Holland. Alasdair's vision of a future independent Scotland was dourly puritanical. Scottish poverty would get worse with or without home rule. A new Scottish Parliament would be 'squabbling and disunited'. The London government would be vindictive and strip Scotland of even more assets. But Alasdair believed that 'an independent country run by a government not much richer than the People has more hope than one governed by a big rich neighbour'.[16] He aspired towards a Scotland 'where Scots mainly live by making and growing and doing things for each other. It should be possible. We have the room to do it'.[17]

One crucial change in Alasdair's next pamphlet, *Why Scots Should Rule Scotland 1997*, is boldly signalled on its cover. Front and back, this bears the flags of 21 nations, 20 of which are independent, ranging in population from Iceland's 260,000 upwards towards Scotland's 5.1 million, exactly equally to Denmark's, a smidgen larger than Finland's. Six of these countries have more people than Scotland, but the Netherlands, with 15 million, would still be classed as 'small'. Some of these countries (Jordan, Malta, Cyprus) are quite poor. The Scandinavian ones are more prosperous, for ordinary people, than England, with 'a basis of social welfare which Britain has abandoned or perhaps never reached'.[18] So it is clear that 'little' Scotland need not be 'poor little Scotland'. This reinforces Alasdair's two previous arguments for independence – democracy and distinctiveness – with a third, attractive to voters, that Scotland might emulate other small but economically successful countries.

The 1997 pamphlet is longer – so much longer that it might be considered a short book. The device of interruptions by 'Publisher' is retained, but manifestly as a literary gadget – the sense of immediacy is lost. Alasdair tells us that this pamphlet is not a revised version of the 1992 item, but 'completely rewritten, though it retains some of the old lucid passages', which he had found, on re-reading, amidst 'a muddle of unconnected historical details and personal anecdotes'.[19] His first chapter now gives us a fourth, overwhelming (as he sees it) ground for Scottish independence – geology. 'Landscape is what defines the most lasting nations'.[20] Yet he rapidly reverts to the cultural-historical case. The English (Angles, Norman-English, etc) who settled north of the Tweed were driven to 'become Scottish' by an oppressive new government centred on London. Malcolm Canmore, raiding into England, was just as nasty as any English king – but 'his power to hurt was limited by the [smaller] number of people he ruled and by Scottish geology'.[21] Thinly dispersed and gathered in clans and chiefdoms, the Scots created 'a new kind of European nation'. Bruce 'only ruled because he had proved his fitness to the Scottish commoners – despite the fact that he was a greedy murderer who began by betraying the Scots to their enemies'.[22]

Alasdair's chapter on the Wars of Independence ends comparing Scotland's 72 Westminster MPs to the Scottish noblemen with estates in England who swore allegiance to Edward I. 'Their problem is now to keep their seats in the best club in Europe without losing ground in Scotland. For nearly twenty years Scottish barons hung around Edward's court at Westminster with a similar problem, and Bruce was one of these hangers-on'.[23] Later, he compares the 'Heads of local Labour Parties who control our town councils', and who promoted the policies of Thatcher and Major with zeal, to Henry Dundas, 'King Harry the Ninth', who 'managed' Scotland for the Tory London government in the late eighteenth century. This polemical outburst is part of an otherwise quite urbane survey of Scottish history, much less questionable than that uttered by Gray in 1992 – and so, perhaps, less interesting. But as we enter the period after the Great War, the survey becomes avowedly personal, intercut with Alasdair's own biography and special passions.

It is not true, *pace* Alasdair, that the 1922 General Election 'returned the first Labour Party majority in history'. In 1923 Labour formed its first, short-lived *minority* government. But the jubilation in Glasgow in the earlier year when suddenly Clydeside elected ten 'Red' MPs was indeed as rapturous as his father reported to the child Alasdair:

> The millennial mood came partly from socialists like my father whose educations made them think the election of a people's government was foretold by Christ when he said the lowly would be lifted up, the meek would inherit the earth. [...] This unity of political and religious faith may seem ridiculous to some readers. I cannot think of it without tears.[24]

Alasdair goes on to pick out three figures from the twenties who saw that left-wing Scots MPs going to Westminster could not make Britain socialist – Guy Aldred, an English anarchist based in Glasgow, the recalcitrant Marxist John Maclean, and Hugh MacDiarmid. But he adds that he cannot share their contempt for the 'Red Clydeside' MPs and the old parliamentary Labour Party. 'They did me and my family and our neighbours and nearly all my friends so much good that I am as grateful to them as any Etonian or Oxonian to the founders of *his* institutions'.[25] John Wheatley, Catholic Clydesider and housing minister in the first Labour Government, pushed through legislation giving state support to municipal house-building that 'quickly changed the appearance of towns throughout Britain'.[26] And so human civilisation culminated in Riddrie, 'one of the first housing estates' built under the Wheatley dispensation – 'and I am sure it was one of the best designed'.[27] Through the fifties and sixties, Alasdair tells us, he took the Welfare State introduced by Labour post-1945, and 'the future of British socialism' for granted, though dread of atomic war propelled him into the Campaign for Nuclear Disarmament and he could not and cannot forgive the Labour Party leadership, then as now, for siding with the Tories on the matter of the 'nuclear deterrent'.

Alasdair therefore stands before us as a reluctant ex-Labourite, to whom the party had once seemed to promise Socialism, whereas now it flagrantly favours the interests of rich people. In his anger and disillusionment he speaks for many writers in his generation and the next one. Younger people may share his contempt for New Blairism, but cannot know the pain of hope betrayed. However, the small-n 'nationalism' of the Scottish intelligentsia incorporates a tradition of small-s socialism. It is attracted by the models of public provision offered by small Scandinavian countries (not least because these find ways of saving estimable authors from poverty). It is *not* – and this must be shouted – *anti-English*.

3

At the outset of his 1997 pamphlet Alasdair repeats an announcement already made five years earlier:

> Readers who live in Scotland but were born elsewhere may feel threatened by the title of this pamphlet; I must therefore explain that by *Scots* I mean everyone in Scotland who is able to vote. This definition excludes a multitude who live and vote abroad yet are Scottish by birth or ancestry, yet includes many who feel thoroughly English yet manage Scottish farms, hotels, businesses, industries and national institutions. It includes second or third generation half-breeds like me whose parents or parents' parents were English, Irish, Chinese, Indian, Polish, Italian and Russian Jewish.[28]

So there is no self-contradiction, let alone treachery, in Alasdair's years of dedication to the cause of English literature. Alasdair is pro-Scottish, not anti-English. And his early years gave him privileged access to the mighty tradition of literature in English. While Wordsworth's writing was overarched by memories of the hills and fields of Cumbria, Alasdair's early intimations of immortality, as he tells us in his introduction to Withers' book, occurred in Riddrie:

> Like most middle-class offspring of working-class parents I am a creature of the Welfare State. My birth-place was Riddrie, a Glasgow housing scheme built under the Wheatley Acts, and so posh that I had a feeling of superiority to people who lived elsewhere. A postman, nurse, printer and tobacconist lived up our close. My father worked a machine which cut cardboard boxes in Lairds, at Bridgeton. He did unpaid work for the Scottish Youth Hostel Association and the Camping Club of Great Britain. He knew Glasgow's Deputy Town Clerk, who lived in a semi-detached nearby on the Cumbernauld Road. My mother had been a shop girl who sang in the Glasgow Orpheus Choir. Besides going to the local cinema we went to the Citizens Theatre, the Doyle Carte Opera Company and any visiting repertory theatre showing the plays of Bernard Shaw.
>
> I therefore *knew* that Glasgow culture, industry and art were maintained by folk like us in Riddrie. When the National Health Service gave me a course of anti-asthma injections my mother could hardly have afforded – *when I discovered that through Glasgow Public Libraries I could order and read any great books I heard of without paying a penny* – when the taxpayers (of whom my father was one) paid my Art School fees and an allowance which he could not, singly, have paid – I did not take this exactly for granted. I knew these good things had been won by hard social struggle and was proud that Glasgow folk had been part of this struggle.[29]

The words I have italicised explain in their context how a book collecting prefaces to great books in English, mostly by English people, can be seen, as clearly as *Lanark*, as the passionate testament of a Scottish Socialist. Alasdair believes in the right of every Glaswegian, every Scot, and everybody anywhere, to access – not exactly 'free', since taxes pay for it, but free at the point of delivery to spotty schoolboys and retired jannies – to the best books that have been written. And those great books written in English by English people are especially important to us in Scotland because we share with England at least as much language as is distinctly our own. There are more great books in English by English people than by Scots because historically England has had five, and in recent centuries ten times our population. We need feel no diffidence or grudge about our relationship with English, since it was a Scot who animated the great King James Bible, and from the eighteenth century onwards Scottish writers have had disproportionate influence on southern writers.

One cannot imagine Wordsworth without 'Ossian' and Burns, the Brontës' and Hardy's novels without Scott, mature Dickens without Carlyle, Housman without R. L. S. The English now have a problem, with which we must in decency sympathise very sincerely, of coming to terms with the fact that 'English identity', as crystallised in beautiful, definitive writing, from *Lyrical Ballads* to *The Shropshire Lad*, owes so much to Scottish precedents. I nearly phoned up the BBC recently when a presenter on Radio Three shocked me by describing Vaughan Williams' wonderful settings of Stevenson's *Songs of Travel* as expressing 'English love of wandering'. But I let the matter rest. We must sympathise with the English in their muddle because we must in honesty admit that Dunbar was proud to follow in the footsteps of Chaucer, that Scott idolised Dryden, Burns worshipped Pope, and we all owe as much as the English to those two compulsory Desert Island companions, Shakespeare and the Authorised Version. Alasdair's subtitle to *The Book of Prefaces – A Short History of Literate Thought in Words By Great Writers of Four Nations from the 7th to the 20th Century –* suggests that Irish and American authors have also made free use of the language that the English are liable to regard as their most special gift to civilisation. Tough tittie.

When Jefferson deployed English against British rule in North America and Wilde used it to satirise the English upper classes, they demonstrated that unlike other languages it could not be the basis of an exclusive nationalism. It remains the most important of Scotland's 'three leids' in so far as most writing by Scots is in English.

The Book of Prefaces is explicitly based on what historians have confusingly styled a 'Whig' interpretation of history. (The original Whigs were Galloway cattlekeepers who urged their beasts on, 'Whiggam, Whiggam', and marched on Edinburgh in support of the

Covenant, but the term came to apply to the dominant oligarchy in British politics after the allegedly 'Glorious' Revolution of 1688-9. It has latterly been used as shorthand to denote a view of history that posits the upward ascent of Britain through revolutions, as distinct from older cyclical and pessimistic concepts.) In a 'Postscript', Alasdair tells us how when a literary agent early in the eighties suggested that he might try 'non-fiction' he responded at once with an idea derived from William Smellie, the remarkable autodidact who created *Encyclopaedia Britannica* in Edinburgh in 1768 – a collection of prefaces. What could be more useful? And easy? To give the agent something to show to publishers, 'I quickly wrote [...] glosses on prefaces to *The Cloud of Unknowing*, Hobbes' *Leviathan* and *The Lyrical Ballads* [...]. Each gloss began with the sentence *This was written in an age of great revolutions [...]'.*[30] Though already fifty, Alasdair 'still believed in the progressive view of history – believed that each generation had added good new social and scientific and artistic works to those of the past, thus giving more people comfort, security and freedom for the future'.[31] He goes on to expand on that Riddrie upbringing. 'Like many others in those days I believed Britain had attained a high new state of civilisation from which it would never descend'.[32] Attlee's Government seemed to be realising, with the creation of a Welfare State (somewhat behind Sweden and New Zealand) the aims of the British Labour Movement, which was saturated in an optimistic view of cultural history. In Edwardian times, when Imperialist propagandists had been appropriating the history and literature of Britain for their own purposes, the new 'Labour' culture based on trade unions and the co-operative wholesale movement enthusiastically embraced all the British tradition which it believed that working people inherited as of right. Even Imperialists sought admiration for Wallace because he stood for British Liberty and for Burns because he wrote beautiful royalist songs. But just as Glasgow's great Orpheus Choir represented the right of everybody to the finest music, and the Ramblers' Association would assert a kind of universal right of Britons to roam their own land freely, so public libraries and cheap reprints were seen as giving everyone access to mighty canons of literature and thought. Since the upshot of the British struggles for liberty was the soon-to-be-triumphant Labour Movement, almost everything in British history, from Alfred the Great to Charles Darwin, could be co-opted for socialism. Everyman's Library was not an explicitly 'socialist' venture, but its dissemination of poetry and novels, ancient classics and quite recent scientific treatises, in accordance with a grand plan of marshalling all great books behind uniform, colour-coded covers, was perfectly attuned to the autodidactic fervour of Welsh miners and Clydeside rivetters. From this and from other series of cheap reprints (two came from Scotland – Nelson and Collins) Alasdair's generation, and my own (not much later), inherited that thing now questioned when it is not execrated, a 'canon'. If Calderon and Edward Gibbon were in Everyman, there was no doubt at all that some day one should read them.

This was in days when most people never thought of going to university. As recently as 1990, I am told, there were only some fifty final honours year students of English Literature at Edinburgh University – now there are nearly five times as many. They are confronted with 'literary theory' as it has burgeoned in the last twenty years, which is pitched as intrinsically hostile to canons (though logically much of it need not be so). Canons are now notorious for having left out many significant female writers and all non-white users of English – not to speak of most Scots. Canons won't go away, of course. Since each of us has only a limited amount of time on this earth for reading, we all need mental checklists of things we should get round to, and if Stevie Smith and Equiano supersede Thackeray and Matthew Arnold, new canons are being created. But meanwhile, current students may feel exempted from all canons. If you can make a pretence of grasping the theories of Derrida and Homi Bhaba, there is no need to read any particular 'classics' whatsoever before you compose your essay on post-colonialism in the fiction of Nick Hornby.

The Book of Prefaces explores – 'glosses' – a canon of Alasdair's, which he does not claim to be all-inclusive. He has interpreted the word 'Preface' very flexibly, so that opening passages in long poems and prologues spoken in plays may be included. This being so it may seem odd to captious persons (amongst whom I must be numbered) that he includes Donne and Vaughan, but not Herbert and Marvell, leaves out Goldsmith and Crabbe and Thoreau, and fails to acknowledge Elizabeth

Barrett Browning's *Aurora Leigh* – not just a brilliant verse narrative but a big bestseller. Granted that the expense of copyright prohibited him from getting further into the twentieth century than Wilfred Owen's unfinished preface to his poems, published in 1920 after his death, there is still some sense of tailing off and thinning out before that.

D. H. Lawrence would provide an especially good endpoint for Alasdair's canon because his work depends, to an extent that his worse-read Leavisite admirers never noticed, on his early immersion into the language and imagery of the King James Bible and nonconformist Protestantism. Alasdair rightly perceives the extreme importance of religious writings in general, and of translations of the Bible in particular, in the development of English – and of course of Scottish uses of English and Scots. In his Introduction, he sets a translation of Christ's prayer, c.650, against the Tudor English version penned about 900 years later. 'Faeder ure,/Thu the eart on heofonum' – 'Our father/ Whyche art in heaven' and adds 'Spoken in northern accents Christ's prayer in Anglo-Saxon sounds oddly familiar. Some Scottish and Northumbrian folk still say "oor faither" and "thoo art" '.[33] Taking the beginning of Genesis and the opening of St John's Gospel to be 'prefaces', Alasdair gives us excerpts from Aelfric's version, c.990, the Lollard Bible of c.1395 (already remarkably familiar – 'In the bigynning god made of nought: hevene and erthe') – Tyndal's of 1530 and 'King Jamie's' great work of 1611. This in itself amply fulfils his original hope, echoing Smellie, that a book of prefaces would be useful. One has not thought of Alasdair as a 'religiously' inclined writer. His father broke with the Congregationalist church, itself almost the plainest and most freethinking variant of Christianity on offer. But religion was deeply inscribed within what we might call the 'Riddrie Canon', and Alasdair does not grudge it full presence. It is a rather attractive near-inconsistency that he should claim that Bunyan ('To be a Pilgrim') and Blake ('Jerusalem') were the only 'great' English writers to produce hymns, then rightly acknowledge what might well be called the 'greatness' of Isaac Watts, whose hymns, as he observes, adopted by most denominations, continued to compel the imaginations of Hardy and D. H. Lawrence even after these men had lost their faith.

Explosion or reconstruction of the canon might have saved Alasdair from what a sincere friend must frankly deplore as Arminian deviations. By the era of Everyman's Library, the really fierce Calvinist and post-Calvinist religious writing of the seventeenth century had fallen into disrepute. Folk were infatuated with the absurd Evangelical heresy that all men may be saved and with Victorian faith in gradual, not drastic, reform as the British way. Alasdair admits, from the snakepit of pamphlets thus covered decorously over, the eloquent Digger, Gerard Winstanley, and gives full due to Bunyan's wonderful prose, but otherwise is so curiously cordial towards the arch-Arminian Archbishop Laud that one begins to wonder if there is an agenda behind his omission of that supreme, though Anglican, Calvinist George Herbert. I think, though, that the way Alasdair's Riddrie (as opposed to original Galloway) whiggism works here is to approve Anglicans who were relatively tolerant, like Donne, mystical, like Vaughan and Traherne, or somewhat soppy, like Herrick, as against puritans and wild post-Calvinist extremists, though many of both sorts happened to be serious social revolutionaries. His implication (or, it may be, his collaborator Stephen Mulrine's – I will come back to this matter) that the Arminian cavalier Urquhart is the only Scottish writer of his era still worth reading means that a chance is missed to acknowledge certain long-influential, and unpleasantly powerful writings by Covenanters. For that matter, Patrick Walker's chapbook lives of the Covenanting preachers, loved by Walter Scott and most others who have read them, might aptly have been canonised here for the first time, with the effect of encouraging a monstrously-overdue reprint.

Now I must, as if in Parliament, declare an interest. Because I am one of some thirty fellow authors conscripted, at a late stage when Alasdair had long since realised that compiling a book of prefaces was very far from easy, to help him out with glosses on texts which he hadn't got round to, I have some inner knowledge of those final processes of composition, which a PhD student from Yale, or Rattlesnake College, Indiana, will surely inspect closely pretty soon. To be blunt, I must say, without the least rancour, that my glosses ain't here as I wrote 'em. In his postscript, Alasdair observes that 'Janice Galloway says her commentaries on Brontë and George Eliot have Gray fingermarks all over them'.[34] So do mine on Pope's *Iliad* and Tennyson's *Princess*, the latter in particularly being greatly and valuably extended. My impression is that Alasdair used some, if not all, such contributions to kickstart his own interpretations of certain authors and their place in history. A further factor must have been the exigencies of layout. Those who have not yet handled this very beautiful book must realise that a salient reason for Alasdair taking so many years to produce it is the fact that its design is his down to the last detail. For a mere £35 to the emptor, Bloomsbury have allowed him a book that would seem a bargain (if only to wealthy connoisseurs) at twice the price. In this rather sordid, though exciting, era of cheap desktop publishing and print set up from floppy disk, lo! and behold! Besides lots of illustrations by Gray, including portraits of all those whom he considers to have helped him – except, oddly, Phillip Hobsbaum, to whom the book is dedicated – we have a cover such as Victorians produced cheaply and our age does not normally afford at all – embossed outside, with rich designs on coloured paper inside – and we have two-colour printing throughout. A few glosses are within main-text, capitalised, but the preponderance are printed in red down the margins. Not to labour an obvious point – length of gloss became a factor in design. Hence, perhaps, compressions – Coleridge becomes 'C' and 'one', in whatever sense, becomes 'I' throughout – and expansions of what others have written. Other Alasdairisations included the use of 'dad' throughout for 'father' and 'folk' for people. Where 'dads' are well-disposed to their offspring, as many are, the effect is charmingly intimate. When we are told that Adam Smith's dad died before his birth, this is subtly poignant. The fact that Patrick Brontë is described as 'father' becomes curiously sinister.

Is it safe, then, for readers to assume that the whole of this noble work is essentially Alasdair's, down, for instance, to the terse and cogent gloss on one unexpected item, John Clare's unpublished manuscript of 'The Midsummer Cushion', offered by Tom Leonard? A point made here is wholly in tune with what Alasdair, indisputably in his own person, writes elsewhere about language and class: 'Clare saw the link between enclosure of land & language. Both allowed efficient administracy of each, at the cost of people who lost their right to roam without toll'.[35] With one very obvious exception – we must assume that the philosopher

Roger Scruton's impeccably Tory gloss on Burke is left more or less as contributed – I think we may safely assume that contributions have in general been led by Alasdair – without distortion of their originators' views – into the main flow of his own re-examination of the canon, which is overarched by his own view of history.

The dust jacket carries a warning: 'Do not let smart children handle this book. It will help them pass examinations without reading anything else.' This seems justified, with one qualification. Kids who digest the Alasdairian view of British and American history will startle competent script markers with their precocious command of a cogent neo-Marxist interpretation of history and literature. They may miss top marks, however, by getting facts wrong, or stating speculations as facts. It suits Alasdair to believe that Shakespeare in youth 'served catholic nobles with a private theatre in Lancashire'. This idea is, so far, more persuasive with the Lancastrian Heritage Industry than with many respected scholars. Regarding straight errors, I am minded to mention just one, because innumerable other books and articles have cocked this matter up, so Alasdair is not egregiously culpable. You will learn from many 'authorities' that Lindsay's *Satire of the Thrie Estaitis* was first performed at Linlithgow Palace before James V in 1540. This notion derives from one document which mentions a play that is clearly not the Satire as we have it and does not refer to Lindsay at all. I think a sort of snobbery has persuaded reputable scholars that it was appropriate that the greatest play in Scots should have been first performed indoors before a king rather than, as actually, indisputably, happened, outdoors, in the writer's home town, Cupar, Fife, in 1552, in what must have been a 'community theatre' production. James V died in 1543, which has not prevented one broadsheet journalist recently from placing him in the Cupar audience. Royalty, in the person of the Queen Regent Mary of Guise, certainly attended a production in Edinburgh in 1554. The latest selection of Lindsay's poems, edited by Janet Hadley Williams, promotes further confusion by dating this event in 1555, I believe wrongly.[36] Anyway, the text heard in Edinburgh must have differed from the only one we have, which is clearly, with its local references, the playscript from Cupar. Alasdair redates the Cupar production to 1540, when James V and his court could have attended, as he says they did. But it wasn't performed then, and they didn't.

Such blips, and certain incautious generalisations, will have scholars specialised in most of the very numerous topics on which Alasdair ventures firm opinions gnashing their dentures. Unpleasant right-wing people may attempt to use them to discredit the entire venture. Worse still, persons of post-modernist and post-colonial theoretical persuasions may actually extol what might be misconstrued as an arbitrary indifference to fact. Watch this space. Some steroid-powered theorist in Yale (or Rattlesnake) is no doubt already deep into the argument that *The Book of Prefaces* is actually a work of post-modernist fiction. The worst thing about this kind of rubbish is that its perpetrators think they are on to something new. As Alasdair's book says *à propos de Tristram Shandy*, Laurence Sterne, in 1760, used 'every device that late 20th-century critics label post-modernist'. Many prefaces are fairly straightforward utterances by authors explaining how books came to be written, outlining general arguments, etc. But some are splendidly devious – a lovely example here, which her publishers refused to print, is Charlotte Brontë's knockdown, in a preface to her next novel, *Shirley*, of an anonymous reviewer of *Jane Eyre*, presumed to be *female*, by her own pseudonymous *male* alter-ego, 'Currer Bell'. Compared to numerous guileful predecessors, Gray has always been a remarkably candid writer. He presents his *Book of Prefaces* as a large work of, in effect, pedagogy, and that, m'lud, is what, I submit, it is.

What Alasdair will teach teenagers whose parents fail to prevent them from seeing this book is that language and free thought have made their way, over thirteen hundred years, stubbornly, sometimes bloodily, against the forces of ruling class self-interest. Some master-steerers have been nasty people or base trimmers – Francis Bacon and Edward Coke are not flattered in these pages. Some have lapsed from early grace. The brilliant gloss on Wordsworth's *Prelude*, here stemming from Edwin Morgan, cannot fail to note how conservative and boring the poet became. Many have been, to a greater or lesser extent, mad. But despite human frailties and eccentricities, Alasdair asks us to believe that these 'great' writers (what a naughty word to use in these post-modernist times!) have cumulatively contributed to the welfare of humankind. There is a jubilant vision here of Shakespeare at work in 1596:

> Better audiences than attend later theatres inspire him. Courtiers, workmen, merchants, tradesmen and wives of these mix in a theatre he manages and partly owns, all keen to hear splendidly convincing words from splendidly daring, evil or absurd figures. [...] All talk the language of a Bible whose grand diction is excitingly modern, not staled by centuries of being chanted in the increasingly separate dialect of England's rulers.[37]

Later, we have fighting talk on behalf of Johnny Keats, from Iain Crichton Smith: The 'melancholy, sensual music' of his poems 'hypnotised most British readers into thinking them unearthly, and that poetry should be like that. K's intellectual vigour would have shocked them awake if he had lived to write more'.[38] And then this, from James Kelman, on Dickens' *Bleak House*:

> Dickens is such a bold artist! – heightening the drama by working in the present tense. A fine amateur actor & director of stage plays, his sense of performance is crucial. In a superb interplay of oral and literary techniques, he sets scenes and issues instructions like a cinema director, using his readers' imaginations as his technicians and actors to make the whole story.[39]

The author is not dead, but alive and kicking in Glasgow. He has enlisted other authors who are, or have been, momentarily alive, to assist in a mighty project that celebrates authorship by women and men always propelled by the wonderful language handed on to them by dead authors. The seismic transformations of human thought by Newton, Hume, Marx, Darwin, have been effected because such people could set out ideas in language that all literate people could understand. Beside thinkers have marched prophets and visionaries, authors inspired, however distantly, by the rages of exalted Greeks and ancient Hebrews as passed on through contemporaneous translations into a language that will be profoundly affected by translations. (In parenthesis, I think that the notable new Scottish fashion for translating plays from French and Greek into our vernaculars is actually steadying our sense of what 'Scots language' is, with its own peculiar and precious resources.)

'Poetry', as Auden wisely wrote, 'makes nothing happen'. Not directly, that is – but language itself, as *The Book of Prefaces* impresses on us, has always been happening, as a precondition for other happenings. Two especially memorable points are made near the end of the book. 'Kipling was [...] the 1st important Victorian writer not to be scared of the working class.' The ballads voiced in cockney slang show the voice of the common soldier 'booming throughout the imperial universe'.[40] And then, in the note on Wilfred Owen from Adam Piette of Glasgow University, we are told that what survived the Great War, in Owen's verse, 'was a new rhythm & language, close to the talk of common soldiery. This war had stripped elegy of its heroes, of its panoply of consolations, dominions & powers, leaving a poetry of true feeling, without the bullshit of a bankrupt officer class'.[41]

Unfortunately, what has now 'happened' is that Owen's poetry, for several decades, has been taught in most British secondary schools to the point where it is received as benchmark-'poetical'. Its plangencies and defiances have become impersonal. Owen is how 'poetry' sounds, which in the first instance, he strikingly wasn't. What we may relish in *The Book of Prefaces* most of all is that, sometimes movingly, sometimes hilariously, but always pointedly, it serves to restore our immediate sense of real people actually writing, when and where they were at. It is a kind of epic of authorship in English, with its cardinal hero – its Achilles or Red Cross Knight – the nimble and sinewy language itself, sometimes ensorcelled by effete or corrupt, or merely bureaucratic, ruling classes, but always likely to spring free and stride on. As a footsoldier in the army of Language, I salute its Bard or Praise-Singer, Alasdair.

Notes

The author would like it acknowledged that parts of this essay are adapted from his review of *The Book of Prefaces* written for the literary journal *Chapman.*

1. Jack Withers, *A Real Glasgow Archipelago* (Glendaruel: Argyll, 1993).
2. Ibid., p. 18.
3. Ibid., p. 19.
4. Peter Ackroyd, 'Precious words as they appeared in the beginning', *The Times,* 11 May 2000.
5. Alasdair Gray, *Why Scots Should Rule Scotland: Independence* (Edinburgh: Canongate, 1992), p. 9.
6. Ibid., p. 12.
7. Ibid., p. 13.
8. Ibid., p. 15.
9. Ibid., p. 17.
10. Ibid., p. 25.
11. Ibid., p. 26, 28.
12. Ibid., p. 28.
13. Ibid., p. 56.
14. Ibid., p. 57.
15. Ibid., p. 62.
16. Ibid., p. 63.
17. Ibid., p. 64.
18. Alasdair Gray, *Why Scots Should Rule Scotland 1997* (Edinburgh: Canongate, 1997), p. 108.
19. Ibid., p. ix.
20. Ibid., p. 1.
21. Ibid., p. 11.
22. Ibid., p. 12.
23. Ibid., p. 20.
24. Ibid., pp. 85-6.
25. Ibid., p. 89.
26. Ibid., p. 90.
27. Ibid., p. 96.

28. Ibid., p. 1.
29. Withers, *A Real Glasgow Archipelago*, p. 13.
30. Alasdair Gray, *The Book of Prefaces* (London: Bloomsbury, 2000), p. 627.
31. Ibid., p. 627.
32. Ibid., p. 629.
33. Ibid., p. 40.
34. Ibid., p. 630.
35. Ibid., p. 496.
36. David Lyndsay, *Selected Poems*, ed. by Janet Hadley Williams (Glasgow: Association for Scottish Literary Studies, 2000), p. xii. But see Roderick Lyall, ed., *Ane Satyre of the Thrie Estaitis* (Edinburgh: Canongate, 1989), p. xii.
37. Gray, *The Book of Prefaces*, p. 233.
38. Ibid., p. 472.
39. Ibid., p. 541.
40. Ibid., p. 596.
41. Ibid., p. 625.

DOING AS THINGS DO WITH YOU
Alasdair Gray's Minor Novels

STEPHEN BERNSTEIN

IN CHARLES KINGSLEY'S *THE WATER BABIES*, THE nineteenth-century fantasy novel beloved by Alasdair Gray and cited by him as one of *Lanark's* key 'Difplags', the protagonist Tom meets two fairy matriarchs in his underwater vale of soul-making.[1] The gentle Mrs Doasyouwouldbedoneby slowly inculcates the Golden Rule, while Tom lives in fear of her counterpart, Mrs Bedonebyasyoudid, who metes out justice for his transgressions. At the tale's conclusion, Tom learns that the women are merely two aspects of the same universal force of goodness, and all turns to truth and light since Tom 'has done the thing he did not like'.[2] Doing and being done by turn out to be identical once such spiritual perfection is reached.

The quartet of short novels that Alasdair Gray published between 1985 and 1996 – *The Fall of Kelvin Walker, McGrotty and Ludmilla, A History Maker*, and *Mavis Belfrage* – feature protagonists (Kelvin Walker, Mungo McGrotty, Wat Dryhope, Mavis Belfrage and Colin Kerr) who are not so different from those of the major novels, and worlds that operate on them equally aggressively. People in these books are to a great extent forced to, as Kerr says, 'do as things do with them' so that the Golden Rule dissipates into a system of self-reproducing domination.³ Despite this dire common denominator, the novels remain true to their origin as plays. Each is farcical in one way or another, as Gray sweetens the possibly bitter pill of political pessimism with a compassionately humorous coating. In the essay that follows, I will discuss each of these works in the terms I have described above, as a way of demonstrating one more facet of Gray's remarkable versatility as a writer. Politics are never far from centre stage in these four works, but politics writ large so that they involve couples, families, cities, and nations. Despite the range of situations these narratives feature, from the twentieth to the twenty-third century, from a small house on Edinburgh's St Leonard's Bank to the Houses of Parliament in London, politics at all levels link them in theme and purpose as Gray demonstrates the small, fleeting pleasures and enormous, lingering costs of doing as you've been done by.

Subtitled *A Fable of the Sixties*, *The Fall of Kelvin Walker* sets its eponymous ingenue down in the heart of Swinging London, lampooning his stereotypical provincial Scottish seriousness against the casual bohemianism of his first acquaintances, an art student named Jake Whittington and his girlfriend Jill. With names that suggest nursery rhyme simplicity, these characters serve as a collective springboard for Kelvin on his way to media fame and eventual ignominy. He needs a place to stay so that he can mount his assault on the established bases of power, and Jake and Jill willingly and pityingly provide it, Jill gently mocking as she calls him 'a wee Scotch laddie just arrived in London to take us all over'.⁴

Kelvin's audacious job-hunting methods (pretending to be a well-known BBC television producer from his home town of Glaik) eventually land him on television, working for that very producer. This is where, though his meteoric rise will continue for some time, his plan starts to go wrong. Fame is Kelvin's undoing, though he becomes drunk with what it can do for him. Early in the novel, he tells Jill that 'famous people aren't important', since 'important people own and control things, but the public hardly ever know who they are'.⁵ Not for Kelvin are the illusory riches of the worlds of entertainment, science, or religion; his goal is to secure power as a disciple of Nietzsche, 'the new and effective Nietzsche who will triumph through me!'[6]

Gray allows no such triumph to occur, and in thwarting it provides an object lesson in what might happen to any enthusiast's best-laid plans. Kelvin believes whole-heartedly the words of Dylan Jones, the novel's Prime Minister, who tells him after a television interview that in the past 'men rose to fame by their employment of power, but in a television democracy it can work the other way round'.[7] Jones gains credibility with Kelvin by taking his reading seriously and Kelvin perseveres in his way. Though he has earlier claimed to see through grand notions of co-operation into the truth that people are simply 'tools, just tools', he lets himself be seduced by Jones' words: 'I am serving an apprenticeship,' he tells Jill.[8]

In 'The Fall', the novel's climactic eleventh chapter, Kelvin learns that things may indeed do back to you as they've been done by or, as Jake puts it, 'the bastards gave you a job because you were useful to them, then when they found you were working for yourself they screwed you up'.[9] His television style has been a matter of casting upon his guests the inquisitorial gaze that he once felt cast upon himself by the God of his father's Scottish religion and prayers, a God who feels to him like 'the headmaster of the universe'.[10] One can do as things do with one for only so long, though. Kelvin becomes the subject of his program when his father arrives from Scotland and humiliates him on the nationwide broadcast. In this reversal he is reduced to something like infancy, squeezing himself into a foetal position before 'the only power in the world he had ever really dreaded'.[11]

Infants, lacking the language, size, and muscle control necessary to do as things do with them, can accomplish little. But by the time Kelvin resumes his adulthood in Scotland he has remade himself into the image of his father, pursuing religious power and making his children miserable. The son who calls love 'an unnatural emotion' and cries out of only one eye replicates the father who has destroyed him out of his own version of love.[12] Thus the cycle is revived. The future in Scotland shows no promise but that of an eternal, miserable repetition, but the novel's final words are for Jake and Jill's children, 'often happy' because 'they are English'.[13] With its diagnosis for future generations, this comparison is dismal enough, but it also shows that even if Jake might 'fall down and break his crown' (he goes from aspiring artist to bus conductor) Jill will come 'tumbling after', while Kelvin's fall is a kind of banishment back into a world where he must remake himself into what he once despised. Happiness is a matter of landing in the right place, something that nationality and class alone seem to determine.

The chances of larger political change are likewise slim. Jake claims that 'most people are so afraid of running their own lives that they feel frightened when there's no-one to bully them', while an earlier producer of Kelvin's program observes in frustration that the British political parties 'don't really disagree' about the issues, 'they just pretend to', a diagnosis proven only too well by the politicians with whom Kelvin hobnobs.[14] It would be too much to expect readers to accept this dark vision were it not accompanied with the novel's abundant humour. Kelvin is seldom less than absurd from the moment he arrives in London with a 'blank, nearly characterless face' that quickly turns 'grimly purposeful'.[15] The energy with which he dedicates himself to his conquest combines with his nearly complete lack of understanding of other people to render him laughable even at his moments of greatest success: when he temporarily 'wins' Jill away from Jake, he shouts at the ceiling, 'God, I approve of you', and later charges her to decorate their apartment since he is convinced of 'fun being an essential ingredient of modern interior design' but 'will never be able to furnish a fashionably funny room'.[16] As a result of this unintentional clownishness, readers are likely to feel little pity indeed over Kelvin's fall and might read the novel's pessimism as attaching only to the fate of a cartoonishly arrogant *naïf*. As the final line of *A History Maker* has it: 'We prefer the comic to the tragic mode'.[17] That may be, but taken together the minor novels forestall any optimism that only fools suffer in the network of retributive sadism that constitutes society. Reality 'keeps hurting me' says Jake in a complaint that, over the course of these novels, swells into a universal chorus.[18]

Still, the laughter continues. Though he becomes a Prime Minister, *McGrotty and Ludmilla*'s Mungo McGrotty is also a prime contender for the most comical of Gray's protagonists, a character who rises in the world of the Civil Service because he is such unpleasant company. Sir

Arthur Shots, senior official in the Ministry of Social Stability, immediately recognises McGrotty's promise during a chance meeting and quickly has him installed in his office. Instrumentalism is again the order of the day, as Shots has already been planning a power play in the government through manipulation of a forthcoming document known as the Harbinger Report. Shots, depicted in the novel's iconography as a spider, works with his secretary Miss Panther as a weaver of webs 'invisible to the human flies trapped therein'.[19] The novel is modelled on the tale of Aladdin and his lamp; accordingly, McGrotty outdoes Shots in wiliness and turns the Report, the novel's magic lamp, to his own benefit. The upshot is that McGrotty eventually becomes Prime Minister, in a conclusion that states the complexities of British political manoeuvring in notably blunt terms. McGrotty suits so many cynical constituencies that it would be a wonder had he not risen to the top.

The control of the Harbinger Report may be central to McGrotty's success, but by itself it stands as a compendium of the ills paraded through the novel's larger plot. Its author, a bland functionary named Geoffrey Harbinger, is chosen by Shots months before he is actually appointed by the Prime Minister to write a report on malfeasance at the highest political levels. Shots singles out Harbinger – as he does McGrotty – for his ordinariness, expecting it will make him another complaisant link in the 'strong chain' he has forged 'to bind a nation'.[20] It is only much later, on the brink of a suicide brought on by the horrific knowledge of his Report's contents, that Harbinger will recall that the Prime Minister 'had spoken as if he had manoeuvred her into giving him the job'.[21]

The manoeuvring behind the writing of the Report is only the start. Its contents outline a complicated system of global control so extensive that Shots, reading it, 'discovered that he had not known a hundredthpart' of it.[22] Beginning with the image of 'a horrible huge, living-but-disembodied hand which gripped the throat of all Britain', Harbinger had outlined 'the body of which this hand was only part, the body of a beast which pressed on the world. [...] The beast was too huge to be opposed and in the near future would grow insupportably vaster'.[23] The Leviathan Harbinger has recognised represents one of Gray's most complete images of global domination. It has something in common with the pastiche of Hobbes' frontispiece that he places before *Lanark*'s fourth book as well as with the pervasive system of social control in that novel's Unthank, a system called simply and bleakly 'the Creature'. In *McGrotty and Ludmilla*'s comic mode, however, the image inspires Shots to a travesty of Marx, as he sees that 'the world was everywhere in chains: the Report was potentially a chain to bind the chainers'.[24]

Things get better. McGrotty reports to Ludmilla (the Minister's daughter, with whom he has fallen in love) that this beast goes beyond any conventional notion of conspiracy. Virtually no one involved 'knows all the organisations that are part of it. The few who understand most of it are so widely scattered that they never meet on a personal level', but they share the gift of eternal life.[25] When Shots reads the Report in an earlier chapter, he notes 'new and disturbing uses of human blood'; the phrase echoes over the scene with Ludmilla as she pronounces that eternal life for a few political leaders is 'bloody unfair' but also decides 'that politics could be fun if treated like a blood sport'.[26]

Shots, with a new 'chubby, boyish look', enjoys a brief, energetic parliamentary career at the novel's end. He is rumoured to be using 'a new and inadequately tested drug', dies of a stroke, and then decomposes 'at a rate which struck the undertakers as supernatural'.[27] The images recall those in countless vampire movies and give still more weight to the novel's strong suggestion that the mysterious term 'Pantocratoraphorbia', a word cried out 'in a kind of howling whisper' by Harbinger moments before his suicide and one that Shots cannot stand to hear after he loses control of the document, is a global vampirism conferring immortality on its users.[28] Thus at the core of the novel is the Report ('The Harbinger Report' is the book's subtitle), and at the core of the report is Pantocratoraphorbia. The levels of control and manipulation multiply exponentially as the net extends over the surface of the earth, while what powers it all is the consumption of human blood. 'The beast was too huge to be opposed', as Shots recognises; 'No sane man would wish to share the world with it – unless he was riding on top of it'.[29] Is *Lanark*'s Institute, with its 'softs pit', or Unthank, with its Creature, any bleaker than this?

As with *Kelvin Walker*, however, the darkness of this vision is diminished through comedy. McGrotty's ascent to power is no less absurd than Kelvin's but, if anything, more so. He moves through a world of farcically misleading appearances: Shots fabricates a story of having known McGrotty's father in the war, the globe in Shots' office houses a small bar, the Ministry's most powerful secretaries' surnames are Panther and Bee, McGrotty seldom understands when he is being used nor even always how he is using others. Even the novel's core exists only in replica. McGrotty's memory is so good that he can reproduce the Harbinger Report verbatim, but by the novel's close only this second version exists. The original, in keeping with the narrative's emphasis on the misleading and the inauthentic, is burned in an electric fire 'not designed to burn things' with 'purely decorative' fire tools.[30]

Kelvin, ground down by authority as a child and young man, learns how to grind others down and enjoy it. McGrotty, manipulated in the self-aggrandising schemes of others, learns to fashion his own schemes and to exploit his exploiters. What consistently happens in Gray's shorter novels, in fact, is an interesting variation on the strategy of the longer works. In *Lanark*, Gray dramatises the difficulties his protagonist faces by splitting the character into a double: the near co-existence of Duncan Thaw and Lanark allows the author to investigate a personality in its nuances by emphasising different tendencies in each character. In *1982, Janine*, Jock McLeish's anxieties are projected onto his creation Janine, another double that lets Gray exemplify the emotional damage his protagonist has suffered. Similarly, the multiple narratives in *Poor Things* dramatise the contingency of truth and perspective, while the protagonist, Bella or Victoria, is once again divided, doubled.

Such doubles do not appear in the shorter novels, but the nearly obsessive emphasis on manipulation, on instrumentalism, on doing as you have been done by, takes their place. In Forsterian terms, their protagonists tend to be flatter characters than those of the major novels, but this very flatness allows Gray more room to focus on the networks of control that move them, pawn-like, through their stories. Some of these pawns might reach the board's other side and transform themselves into something more powerful, but in doing so they are even more likely to be consumed by the stronger bishops and knights, the freely deployed power of church and state in all its multifarious manifestation. As if to provide more forceful punctuation to this account of social interaction as gamesmanship, Gray begins *A History Maker*'s central narrative with an account of a game in progress, a lethal war game of the twenty-third century.

As day dawns over the Scottish battlefield, the doomed General Craig Douglas rallies his troops by acknowledging 'Mibby I'm a waster, but I'm not feckless when it comes to strategy'.[31] The strategy he speaks of will cost most of these men and boys their lives within hours but, as television broadcasters note, 'Clan Ettrick has drawn on a technicality so even if the entire Ettrick army is exterminated it retires unbeaten'.[32] The carnage Craig Douglas has guaranteed serves pyrrhically to memorialise his Clan nearly at the expense of the Clan's existence. Thus the story of Wat Dryhope begins with his manipulation at the hands of his father (a manipulation to which he quickly enough accedes), and continues for several days until he can be ensnared in the conspiratorial meshes of Meg Mountbenger and the K20 plotters.

It is in Wat that Gray creates the most complex character in these four novels. Readers are given detailed descriptions of his childhood experience, background concerning his travels into space, direct narration of his thoughts (since the central narrative is ostensibly written by Wat in the third person), and accounts of his desires for the future. Frustrated with the role of men in the matriarchal society of the future, Wat finds release in the war games but ultimately becomes disgusted with the waste and meaninglessness of the sport. He longs for a return to history, to the time before the novel's powerplants that, since they supply all material human needs, have obviated the capitalist manufacturing cultures of earlier centuries. Gone are what Wat's brother Joe calls the 'dark ages when men fought wars without rules, and burned bombed looted peaceful houses, and killed raped enslaved whole families of women children and old ones', but nothing has appeared to receive the heroic sacrifices of strength and energy that the cause of good in such dark ages once required.[33] War is the only game in town, but Wat glumly notes that 'modern wars are nae great affairs'.[34] He fantasises about a pioneer's life with his young lover Annie, but after a lengthy catechism she finds his ideas so unworkable that she too teases him as Joe has, apologising that the society in which they live has 'no plagues, poverty or governments to escape from'.[35]

In these passages, Gray suggests that life without some sense of struggle is virtually meaningless, and that that struggle must be for Good, not merely the immoral gamesmanship of the novel's wars. Wat wants to read about history as a 'period of excitement when folk thought they were making a better world' and envisions raising a family in the wilderness, overcoming all the challenges of frontier life through sheer determination.[36] In his own society, nothing worth having takes that much devotion; once the better world exists, there is nothing left to make. Annie's mockery, though, and Wat's own awareness of the futility of such dreaming, embitters him and drives him from her presence. For much of the remainder of the novel, he is like an actor in search of a script, briefly trying on the role of General before finding himself written into Meg Mountbenger's 'Puddock Plot'.

In the first verbal skirmishes of this encounter, Wat is surprised by Meg's effrontery, grabbing broadcast and recording frequencies at will, making personal use of large amounts of communal energy. She has broken 'the first rule in the bill of human rights: NOBODY WILL BE USED BY ANOTHER WITHOUT KNOWING AND WILLING IT'.[37] This is a new wrinkle on the manipulative dystopias of *Kelvin Walker* or *McGrotty and Ludmilla*, but it is the twenty-third century, after all. And by violating this society's fundamental rule against manipulation, Meg's actions promise Wat an experience where history might, indeed, return. As Meg tells him, 'we are about to give birth to the future'.[38]

In 'La Belle Dame Sans Merci', John Keats demonstrated the conjunction of sexuality and mortality by showing a knight shaken from his experience with the Belle Dame, awakening from his dream-like night of pleasure to find himself:

> Alone and palely loitering,
> Though the sedge has withered from the lake,
> And no birds sing.

Gray easily transfers this chivalric image into the future, having Wat awaken from *his* dream-like night of pleasure to find himself 'on the shore of Saint Mary's Loch on a cold grey morning'.[39] What ails this knight-at-arms, however, is not the stark awareness that pleasure and the ephemeral world of mortality are inextricably linked, but rather that pain, humiliation, and the entree to old fashioned history are part and parcel of one another.

This is because the future that Wat and Meg's sexual encounter actually gives birth to is a viral epidemic with Wat at its centre. The powerplants are infected and quickly wiped out. The conspirators' plan is to return the world to barbarism, but instead humans band together and turn themselves back to the simple work that the powerplants have enabled them to forego and forget. The novel's closing notes delineate a new future where men and women will create small communities based on their mutual work and benefit. Plague-resistant powerplants might be used in an auxiliary capacity, but the human need for work, work as an ennobling physical pursuit of communal good, will be acknowledged as paramount.

It is important to recognise, though, that this will not be Wat's world. He is powerfully attracted to Meg's verbally and physically abusive manner; his sexuality has gradually been moulded into a kind of sadism where he enjoys fantasising 'about excluding women who loved him', and he appears equally aroused by a woman who threatens to take the reins and reject him.[40] None of the women he has known have held the appeal that Meg does, with her 'absolute contempt'.[41] 'She needs me like I need her', he exclaims; though admitting 'there was hatred in what she did with me', he is unable to see in her behaviour anything calculating or political, and can only happily conclude that 'It's a miracle that she's needed me all these years. I'll go to her.'[42] The blend of sadism and masochism that these quotations reveal helps explain Wat's willingness throughout the novel to be used by others. At *A History Maker*'s start, General Craig Douglas, Wat's father, knows that Wat will serve well in his dangerous gambit even though he openly opposes it, just as at the novel's close Meg knows that Wat will come back to her despite all the rational argument that Wat's mother Kittock can urge in opposition.

Characteristically, Gray tempers some of the bleakness of this ending as well. Wat's reunion with Meg will take place, she assures him, at the circus, so the novel's formal chapters end with the absurd image of the great fighter Wat Dryhope defying his mother's orders and literally running off to join the circus. And throughout the novel, there has been an absurdist comic energy at work in Gray's futuristic creations. The bizarre, media-saturated pastiches through which Meg communicates with Wat are only some of the most obvious examples of the verbal and visual inventiveness of the narrative. The book's true closing lines, too, add to this atmosphere of playfulness. 'So Wat went to the circus after all', closes the main narrative, but much is done in the novel's 'Notes & Glossary' (penned, like the 'Prologue', by Kittock) and 'Postscript' (by an unidentified hand) to fill out the book's larger goals.[43]

These sections, fully one third of the book, contain Gray's familiar forays over history, literature, economics, and politics. Here too we find the sentence I quoted above, which can stand for the vision that informs all of these novels: 'We prefer the comic to the tragic mode'.[44] In their context, they apply to the various interpretations, through folk songs, of what may have happened to Wat and Meg. The last substantiated account is that after the powerplant plague a broken and beleaguered Wat leaves his community to 'track down' Meg; 'I'll kill her for what she did to me, then I'll kill myself', he vows.[45] The apocryphal story of their continued unhappy relationship becomes the stuff of folk song, with one version ending with one of the pair dying of a broken neck sustained in a fall while the other 'Starved to death in the very same ditch'.[46] There we have it: the tragic mode is a murder/suicide, the comic a pair of fatal, 'Jack and Jill'-like accidents. Readers are presumably left to take their pick, but either way must witness the pathetic ends of those who would try to control others (or crave that control) without taking sufficient account of how history, in whatever form, already controls them.

History does not vanish as a form of control in *Mavis Belfrage*, though it takes a back seat to the inter-manipulations of the characters. Like *Kelvin Walker*, the novel is set in the mid- to late-1960s (as a reference to Enoch Powell attests).[47] This is a time when, as a prefatory paragraph tells us, 'Folk who would have missed university courses in other decades' were now helped to attend by the government. Thus Colin Kerr, a shopkeeper's son, can get a Cambridge philosophy degree, become a university teacher, and cross paths with the students who become the novel's other major characters, Mavis Belfrage and Clive Evans.

If history in *Mavis Belfrage* has made a small step in freeing up class divisions, it has left other forms of control untouched. Colin has a brief, mostly unpleasant, relationship with Mavis, but thanks her for what she has done. 'Before we met my life was almost wholly shaped by my father,' he says, '[...] Going to Cambridge changed nothing because Cambridge was a cosy patriarchy too. That's why I needed you who hated everything that cramped me. So you drove Dad out and started shaping my life yourself.'[48] Kerr, in other words, lives the same trajectory of manipulation that Kelvin and Wat do, going from the early moulding of the father to later moulding at the hands of some other force. Kerr is further like Wat in that this later moulding comes from a woman to whom he is almost masochistically attracted. Though Wat lives in the twenty-third century and Kerr in the twentieth, and though the other facets of their narratives must thus bear a less than identical relationship to one another, there are enough similarities for us to see that *Mavis Belfrage* too fits into the minor novel model of narratives about characters who, as Colin himself says, 'do as things do with them'.[49]

This statement's context is important. It comes during the novel's opening scene as Colin, recently out of Cambridge and enamoured of a teaching style that depends on repetition, is confronted by Mavis and Evans. Asked if he cannot give them at least an inkling of whether he prefers classic to romantic theories of education, he claims to have 'no opinion' and is further accused by Evans of a failure to 'admit that choice is *necessary*'.[50] Thus Colin's pedagogy is framed as an existential imperative, but one that he sidesteps through his claim that 'even educators do as things do with them'.[51] This denial of existential freedom is the start of Colin's narrative and is a condition not significantly relieved by the narrative's end.

In his relationship with Mavis, Colin again mirrors Wat. He gives her tacit permission to have an affair with Evans and hates himself for doing it. He and Mavis continue to live and sleep together, though in a style that Gray describes as 'mutual rape'.[52] He finally faces the fact that 'he could not sleep without her and could not join her in bed without loathing himself'.[53] The violence, reflexive cruelty, and self-disgust are all reminiscent of Wat; like Wat, as well, Colin relieves some of the pressure of the present by projecting a society based on the past, in his case the Lego-city of Glonda (its name, suggested by Mavis's son Bill, is a play on Anne and Emily Brontë's fantasy world of Gondal).

Initially, Glonda is a way for Colin to imagine a better place than where he is, one significantly rooted in nineteenth-century technology. But as his relationship with Mavis wears on him, Glonda comes to take on characteristics Colin attributes to her ('weakened by a night of debauchery, she writhes in uneasy slumber').[54] Finally, Colin and Bill destroy the model. Handel's 'Hallelujah Chorus' plays as the two unleash a *blitzkrieg* of books, the very books from which Colin teaches in the opening chapter. When the city, to Colin's eventual grief, is destroyed, he tells Mavis that he and Bill have been playing 'war games'. During this scene, Mavis has the look of 'a disapproving schoolmistress', so that now everything has come full circle.[55]

The debate in the opening chapter suggests that Plato's educational philosophy promotes 'obedience' while Rousseau's suggests 'a variety of choices'.[56] By denying, in Chapter One's classroom conversation with Evans, the validity of choice, Colin tacitly aligns himself with the Platonic model. He continues to show a kind of obedience in the destruction of Glonda, indulging in the same kind of destructive behaviour he feels Mavis the schoolmistress is. But if, at some deep level, Colin longs to throw away the books and symbolically destroy civilisation, all in the name of 'war games', he is also not very different from the Wat Dryhope of *A History Maker*'s opening chapter. That chapter, though, is the beginning of Wat's exploration of alternatives; Colin's analogous act comes close to the end of his story. My goal here is not to show that *Mavis Belfrage* is some sort of transformed *History Maker*, only to suggest that these similarities work powerfully to delineate the shape of Gray's persistent concern with masculinity, femininity, and the desire for control in both narratives. Mavis ultimately wins the battle with a monumental act of passive aggression, not appearing at a dinner party that she persuaded Colin to throw.

This social disaster sets up the key difference in the narratives. Unlike Wat and Meg, Colin and Mavis eventually part ways. He hits her (is this his Rousseauian-cum-existentialist act of choice?), she leaves, she begins an unhappy live-in relationship with Evans, Colin falls apart and puts himself back together. Though Gray is concerned to show that a great deal of Mavis' behaviour can be explained by the fact that as a woman she does not enjoy the freedoms Colin and Evans do, he also makes clear that in her treatment of men she is not innocent and perhaps sadistically enjoys doing as she is done with by the larger society. The newly confident and 'independent' Colin of a later, final meeting disgusts her; he has become one of the 'damnably sure' men who control the world.[57] And thus we find him going out into that world, not, as after his graduation from Cambridge, returning to the world of his father and home. He takes a job in Zambia, but Gray is careful to let us know by the story's end that all will not go well there either. Bidding Mavis farewell, he puts his hand on his stomach 'where twelve years later an ulcer would develop after his African wife left him'.[58]

There is less comedy in *Mavis Belfrage* than in the other minor novels. It hews closer to the naturalistic mode David Hutchison attributes to Gray's stage plays and is intended, as the dustjacket has it, for 'readers who do not find the world comfortable and don't expect to escape from it alive'.[59] The novel is devoid of the outright lampooning that fills the pages of the other three works under discussion, largely because it has, by far, the most reticent narrator of all. Mavis adds to the sobriety of the proceedings, as she remains an opaque character, one whose actions are comprehensible but suggest, simultaneously, a personal history filled with pain and self-doubt. Though Gray is happy to render these qualities absurd in characters from the other novels, he leaves Mavis ultimately unknowable. Though this seriousness may mark a key difference between *Mavis Belfrage* and the rest of these narratives, it does nothing to obscure the essential similarity, the way that it too emerges finally as a record of the forms of human manipulation.

'All of us over eighteen have been warped into deserving what happens to us', says Lanark at his most despondent.[60] Just the same, he lives to see the destruction of the dark forces in his world and the restoration of light. The last descriptive his narrative applies to him is 'glad'.[61] Similarly, Jock McLeish, though his story reflects a Kafkaesque conviction that his life has only progressed from cage to trap, emerges after a particularly dark night of the soul with the chastened but optimistic view that 'history is what we all make. [...] I will be gentle. I will be kind.'[62] *Poor Things* may be the darkest narrative of the three major novels, but there too the central character's final words (though undercut by historical irony) are full of a nearly millennial optimism.

Shortly before her death, Victoria writes to Hugh MacDiarmid that with the advent of the 1946 Labour government 'Britain is suddenly an exciting country. [...] I am going to die happy.'[63] None of the minor novels' protagonists finish up with such hope or happiness. The only possible exception is McGrotty, but his success comes at enormous cost and is shown through the preceding narrative to be highly unstable.

This is not to say, however, that the minor novels betray Gray's vision, revealing him as a closet pessimist and counteracting whatever hope his longer novels entertain. What might help us to see Gray's novels as all of a piece is to bear in mind the degree of irony involved in the depiction of Kelvin, McGrotty, Wat, or Colin. They persistently act in ways that we can see are misinformed, confused, or wrong. This may be true of Lanark, Jock, and Victoria, but in nothing like the same proportion. The farcical world of the minor novels allows Gray to examine society from another side, so that the protagonists' failures argue in favour of the values supported by the successes of the major novels' protagonists. If there is nevertheless a despondency behind this vision, one need not look far for the cause. Consider Gray's recent self-descriptions in *The Book of Prefaces*' 'Postscript', where he depicts himself as an erstwhile historical optimist, believing that 'each generation had added good new social and scientific and artistic works to those of the past, thus giving more people comfort, security and freedom for the future'.[64] By 1999, he is less convinced of such optimism, making the book 'a memorial to the kind of education British governments now think useless, especially for British working class children'.[65] *The Book of Prefaces*' covers still convey Gray's favourite motto, the exhortation to 'Work As If You Live In The Early Days of a Better Nation', so it may be premature to pronounce history a victim of the darkness. In the four cautionary tales examined here, at least, Gray shows the way not to work, the way not to give in to the darker forces of control.

In the end, this model is not so surprising. The worlds of the minor novels are moral laboratories where perfection does not yet obtain. With no Golden Rule in place, the protagonists have to learn the hard way. Rather than being rewarded by Mrs Doasyouwouldbedoneby, they must be punished by Mrs Bedonebyasyoudid, 'the ugliest fairy in the world

[…] till people behave themselves as they ought to do'.[66] In Kingsley's novel, the lesson is learned and Mrs Bedonebyasyoudid becomes one with her lovelier sister. In Gray's world, the lesson is always in progress, its completion, as with the example of Kingsley's Tom, attendant upon his characters doing the hardest thing, the thing they do not like.

Notes

1. Alasdair Gray, *Lanark: A Life in Four Books*, rev. edn (Edinburgh: Canongate, 1985), pp. 491–492.
2. Charles Kingsley, *The Water-Babies* (Stamford, Conn.: Longmeadow, 1994), p. 276.
3. Alasdair Gray, *Mavis Belfrage* (London: Bloomsbury, 1996), p. 13.
4. Alasdair Gray, *The Fall of Kelvin Walker* (Edinburgh: Canongate, 1985), p. 21.
5. Ibid., p. 12.
6. Ibid., p. 13.
7. Ibid., p. 93.
8. Ibid., pp. 12, 111.
9. Ibid., p. 135.
10. Ibid., p. 70.
11. Ibid., p. 131.
12. Ibid., pp. 42, 83.

13. Ibid., p. 141.

14. Ibid., pp. 57, 87.

15. Ibid., p. 1.

16. Ibid., pp. 101, 105-106.

17. Alasdair Gray, *A History Maker* (Edinburgh: Canongate, 1994), p. 222.

18. Gray, *The Fall of Kelvin Walker*, p. 64.

19. Alasdair Gray, *McGrotty and Ludmilla: or the Harbinger Report* (Glasgow: Dog and Bone, 1990), p. 16.

20. Ibid., p. 34.

21. Ibid., p. 40.

22. Ibid., p. 96.

23. Ibid., pp. 96-97.

24. Ibid., p. 97.

25. Ibid., p. 108.

26. Ibid., pp. 97, 109, 107.

27. Ibid., p. 121.

28. Ibid., p. 43, 113.

29. Ibid., p. 97.

30. Ibid., p. 116.

31. Gray, *A History Maker*, p. 12.

32. Ibid., p. 18.

33. Ibid., p. 33.

34. Ibid., p. 51.

35. Ibid., p. 55.

36. Ibid., p. 28.

37. Ibid., p. 108.

38. Ibid., p. 111.

39. Ibid., p. 121.

40. Ibid., p. 145.

41. Ibid., p. 146.

42. Ibid., p. 152.

43. Ibid., p. 156.

44. Ibid., p. 222.

45. Ibid., p. 220.

46. Ibid., p. 222.

47. Gray, *Mavis Belfrage*, p. 35.

48. Ibid., pp. 72-73.

49. Ibid., p. 13.

50. Ibid., p. 12.

51. Ibid., p. 13.

52. Ibid., p. 47.

53. Ibid., p. 62.

54. Ibid., p. 50.

55. Ibid., p. 52.

56. Ibid., p. 11.

57. Ibid., p. 73.

58. Ibid., p. 74.

59. David Hutchinson, 'Gray the Dramatist', in *The Arts of Alasdair Gray*, ed. by Robert Crawford and Thom Nairn (Edinburgh: Edinburgh University Press, 1991), p. 150.

60. Alasdair Gray, *Lanark*, p. 551.

61. Ibid., p. 560.

62. Alasdair Gray, *1982, Janine* (London: Cape, 1984), pp. 340-341.

63. Alasdair Gray, *Poor Things* (London: Bloomsbury, 1992), p. 316.

64. Alasdair Gray, *The Book of Prefaces* (London: Bloomsbury, 2000), p. 627.

65. Ibid., p. 631.

66. Kingsley, *The Water-Babies*, p. 168.

UNDER THE INFLUENCE

KEVIN WILLIAMSON

ALASDAIR GRAY WAS A MISTAKE.

My first copy of *Lanark* arrived in 1982, quietly, in an elegant monochrome paperback edition published by Granada, wrapped in green-and-yellow striped gift paper.

When she arrived with the book, which was a birthday present, at my dingy basement flat in Edinburgh, Aileen was her usual dash of colour, this time wearing a pair of green-and-yellow stripey trousers that matched the wrapping paper. I had to smile. When it came to the small details she thought of everything.

In her wardrobe Aileen had over fifty pairs of tight-fitting stripy trousers, mostly bright colours, and she had these short legs that were beautiful and soft, just like her personality, and I worried what would happen if stripy trousers went out of fashion.

She didn't seem that bothered. She liked them, she looked good in them, and when she walked the trousers made her legs move in a restricted turned-in-at-the-feet sort of way that swivelled her hips and was both graceful and hypnotic to watch.

I opened her card, laughed at what she had written, and tore apart the wrapping paper.

I gave her a big hug.

'Is it the right one?' she asked.

'I think so,' I said, turning over the book to read the blurb on the back. The sci-fi writer, Brian Aldiss, described the novel as 'a saga of a city where reality is about as reliable as a Salvador Dali watch'.

Right enough, it was the same book I had read about in a newspaper article, a futuristic sci-fi novel set in an unnamed Scottish city. It sounded pretty weird, well worth checking out.

The idea of Scottish science fiction tickled me back then. The Scotland I knew had hills and glens, fishermen and farms, dole queues a mile long, high rise slums, alcohol coming out of every pore, and football supporters who were aff their heids. Scotland didn't seem to be the raw material of science fiction. It was a place that seemed more preoccupied with the past than the future.

Since my days at Thurso High School, I had devoured sci-fi. At the age of sixteen, working at Dounreay as a trainee nuclear scientist, I spent a lot of time crawling into nuclear nooks and crannies where I would curl up undisturbed with an Asimov, a Moorcock or a Bradbury. Dounreay was a great place to read sci-fi. The ambience was just right for immersing oneself in sagas of intergalactic wars and life-threatening viruses, totalitarian police forces and science gone out of control.

Like crime fiction, for reasons that I don't really understand, there's a prejudice against science fiction in some quarters. Literary snobs look down their noses at it. It rarely gets reviewed in the broadsheets and never wins the big literary prizes. The very best of popular sci-fi writers like J. G. Ballard, Kurt Vonnegut, and Iain Banks tend to get recognition mainly for novels they write that are *not* exclusively sci-fi. It's as if the sci-fi part of them is just an aberration, something they do on the side, a hobby, not like *Empire of the Sun, Slaughterhouse Five,* or *The Wasp Factory,* which are great literary works about coming of age in a seemingly alien environment. Nuff said.

The best of sci-fi can be weird, wild and inspiring. But it can also be the perfect fictional vehicle for social satire. It is this aspect of sci-fi (although Gray himself considers *Lanark* to be a work of fantasy rather than sci-fi) that possibly attracted Gray to utilise the genre in the first place. In this respect, Gray has followed in the footsteps of many other leftist writers who, through their fiction, have felt impelled to explore what lies ahead for mankind.

Jack London was one such writer. A socialist revolutionary in his day who is mainly remembered now for his boys-own adventure stories like *White Fang* or *Call of the Wild*. Yet his political outlook drove him to write *The Iron Heel*, a tragically prophetic novel, dogmatic in parts, but that predicted *in great detail* the rise of fascism as far back as 1905. Despite its flaws, this sci-fi novel was a groundbreaking work of twentieth century fiction.

Many other lavish and visionary novels converge with the sci-fi genre: novels such as J. G. Ballard's *Crash*, a cold and futuristic work exploring the mechanisation of modern sexuality; or Olaf Stapledon's tripped-out classic from 1937, *Star Maker*, another allegorical warning about the dangers of fascism; or Kurt Vonnegut's early technophobic horror story, *Player Piano*; or indeed, Aldous Huxley and George Orwell's 'big two' of *Brave New World* and *Nineteen Eighty-Four*. Cautionary tales all.

Or take those old episodes of *Star Trek* – the original sixties ones that first got me into sci-fi – they may well have featured Kirk and Spock landing on weird planets, pitting their wits against all sorts of strange creatures, but underneath the shiny costumes and make-up they too were trying to deal with the burning issues of the day that were tearing apart America; a country that, like now, was in turmoil, at war with its neighbours, and at war with itself.

This is a long, drawn-out way of saying that I called it wrong with the birthday present and thought *Lanark* was just another sci-fi novel. If I hadn't got a copy of *Lanark* for that birthday, I would probably have moved onto a different sci-fi novel, possibly *Dune* – which is nice and weighty – or Robert Heinlein's *I Will Fear No Evil* (another weighty philosophical tome, which I'm convinced was the perverse inspiration for at least two Steve Martin comedy films).

But from beneath the colour co-ordinated wrapping paper emerged *Lanark*. A mistake, yes, but a pretty good one as it turned out.

I read *Lanark*, mesmerised, in a few massive all-night sittings. It had an impact not that different from being hit by a sledgehammer. No, that's not quite right. It was a bit more subtle and complex than that. It was like an alarm clock going off, a wake up call to another place, a place that was all around me, which I was part of, but that now seemed unfamiliar and exciting.

I didn't understand everything that was going on in the pages of *Lanark*. Some of it went right over my head. I had never heard of post-modernism, intertextuality, and all the other academic buzzwords I've since read in critical essays to describe *Lanark*. Before *Lanark*, I had never read anything that could be bracketed under the slippery and highly elitist term 'literary fiction' either. But the novel was weaving its spell.

The main response the book elicited was a personal one. *Lanark* opened my eyes to possibilities, and not just in the realm of fiction. *Lanark* was a revelation. What was written between the covers of that amazing book was enough to set cogs in motion. It got me thinking and questioning all sorts of things. Surely no writer could ask for more from their work?

Although *Lanark* was first published in 1981, I didn't read it until the paperback came out in 1982 so that's the year I tend to associate it with. In order to try and understand the effect *Lanark* had, and its influence, I'm going to have to go back in time to 1982 and put the book into its context.

(An aside: *Context* is a great tool for any reader to have in their critical armoury. It's a much more useful tool than, say, the concept of post-modernism. You don't need to be a university professor to know what context is all about. Context is a philosophy in and of itself. Putting things in context is useful to understand, well, anything really, whether it's literature, politics, history, ideas, big events, or even wee personal things. More often than not it becomes automatic, a subconscious act. But not always. We live in an increasingly sound-bite driven culture. Context is often rejected. There's *no time* to make sense of anything. The result can make a person feel like they're drowning in a sea of randomly generated information. Most of it seemingly useless or irrelevant.)

* * *

So the time is 1982 and the place is Edinburgh; the capital of Scotland, a country without a parliament or a government of its own, but with a stubborn and contrary population whose limits of endurance were being pushed to the limit by a foreign government whose values were more in tune with the young spivs in suits drinking champagne in the City of London and talking in loud braying voices about stocks and shares.

But I'm running ahead of myself here. Back in 1982, I wasn't *that* bothered whether Scotland had a government of its own. Girls, football, drinking, reading sci-fi, shooting pool, these were the important matters of the day.

Seen from twenty years later, 1982 seems as alien a place as any of those old episodes of *Star Trek*. Especially that long hot summer. I seem to remember spending most of it wearing a blue-and-white striped Argentina football shirt which, for some reason, seemed to provoke complete strangers to the point of violence. I remember standing at the top of the Mound in Edinburgh, beside the Reverend Ian Paisley as Pope John Paul II drove past in his Popemobile smiling and waving. I also remember vividly a Paolo Rossi hat-trick and a Dave Narey toe-poke.

I remember hitchhiking between Edinburgh and Thurso every fortnight for months. The three best spots for thumbing a lift north were at the Queensferry roundabout in Edinburgh; then at the start of the A9 outside the Caithness Glass factory in Perth; and then beside the turnoff onto the smart new Kessock Bridge opposite the Black Isle. This constant travelling in the company of strangers gave me plenty of time to listen to the stories of the drivers as well as a chance to create some fictional identities and spin a few stories of my own.

Once in Thurso, I'd make my way to the Scotscoup Bookmakers – then located above The Comm Bar, which is still the best pub anywhere in Scotland – take up my perch behind the glass screen, stick the race sheets up with strip magnets, and holding a red magic marker in one hand (for the favourites), and a blue magic marker in the other, I'd be all set to pontificate to the punters on which horses and riders would win which race. Few ever did.

Back in Edinburgh, money spent, I remember vividly the depressing stench of the grotty dole centre in Tollcross – now knocked down, thank Christ – which was nothing like the nice clean civilised employment centres of today. I remember getting shunted from dole office to dole office across Edinburgh and Leith in search of something known back then as Supplementary Benefit, presumably because it supplemented the illegal cash-in-hand work you needed to survive. I remember ending back at the dole office I first started out from, and first learning the meaning of the word 'bureaucracy'.

I remember scouring through the Friday job pages in *The Scotsman* and *Evening News*, but the only job vacancies were for bar staff and door-to-door salesmen. I remember walking the streets of Leith with a pool cue in my hand and not being bothered by anything. I remember cadging money off family and mates, always borrowing, getting by, smoking skinny joints that weren't rolled properly, and happily hoovering the half-empty glasses at closing time.

I remember being in Edinburgh during the Festival for the first time. I remember the streets were full of magic and colour and posh accents and everyone was ducking and diving and taking the piss and laughing and sleeping all day and trying to get off with each other or playing cards or shooting pool. And Margaret Thatcher ... what the fuck was she all about?

So the sun was shining, people were starving, and Scotland was being royally screwed by faceless bureaucrats, flag-waving warmongers, and arrogant rich assholes. Same as it ever was. People knew the score, but at the time there seemed to be a state of punch-drunk disbelief as unemployment more than trebled, in only a few short years, as the heart was being ripped out of Scotland's ancient ability to produce things.

That's the way it was back in the summer of '82, and *Lanark* connected with all of this. The dole queue regulations, then as now, were designed to grind you down, make you feel impotent, and at the mercy of forces you had no control over. You were systematically stripped of your dignity and identity and you were made to *feel* it. The social security system wasn't designed to help those 'between jobs', but was there to make sure that getting government assistance was as difficult and unpleasant an experience as possible.

In the sequentially-deranged first book of *Lanark*, Book Three, the character Lanark steps off a train into a surreal nightmare city, not unlike Glasgow, which seemed to be part of a post-apocalyptic landscape, where daylight was a distant memory, a flicker on the edge of existence, and where government handouts were regulated by a pedantic bureaucracy.

The threat of nuclear war was a very tangible and frightening one back then. The Cold War was at its iciest. A B-movie actor in America and a grocer's daughter in Britain were running the show, fanning the flames of paranoia and distrust. No faraway island was too small or insignificant for these pair to bully – as Grenada and the Falkland Islands found out. CND held huge protest marches, Greenham Common was encircled by vilified but courageous women, and one of the most popular student wall posters of the day had a picture of two starry-eyed political lovers in a parody of *Gone With The Wind*. If that wasn't bad enough, a madcap scheme to create a nuclear defence system in outer space – named after a George Lucas sci-fi movie – was being seriously touted as a logical answer to our illogical fears.

The timing of the publication of *Lanark* could not have been better. Scottish writing needed a *Lanark*. Scotland needed a *Lanark*. Hell, writing needed a *Lanark*. Somebody, somewhere, *had* to articulate some of the concerns, fears and aspirations of ordinary folk in Scotland. But do it in such an entertaining, interesting and unique way that it made people sit up and think. At that time, for me, Alasdair Gray filled that vacuum.

Reading *Lanark* for the first time, I remember being a bit disappointed when the 'first' book finished and that dark, shadowy world of The Elite Café, Dragonhide, and The Institute was exposed to the glaring sunshine of post-war Glasgow. I wanted to stay in Unthank rather than be dragged backwards to the everyday realities of Duncan Thaw's childhood. They seemed, at first, so ordinary in comparison.

But it wasn't quite like that. Gray was off on a different trajectory. With a passionate sense of injustice and bewilderment and painfully raw honesty, Gray describes the embarrassing rites of (male) adolescence through the sexual and emotional awakening of Thaw and his love-hate relationship with the grim authority figures of the Scottish education system.

These I could relate to. I was back in there. This wasn't the exclusive story of the young Duncan Thaw anymore, this was *my* childhood laid bare. Seriously. To use a darts analogy, a sport that was at the very peak of its popularity in 1981/82, Gray was hammering the treble twenty, arrow after arrow.

The dole queue resonance, the detached but very real fear of a nuclear holocaust, and the awkward coming-of-age embarrassments were what I initially connected with in *Lanark*. Unless you've been trained in the secret codes of literature, what makes a book stand out as special are often the parallels with your own life, or those round about you, where the author creates characters you can empathise with, and they write about situations you can understand from your own experiences. Or pure escapism. The coda comes later.

It wasn't just the mutual recognition of shared things or experiences that connected in *Lanark*, it was the way Gray evoked the feelings associated with them. The fact that the non-linear sequence of the four books of *Lanark*, as Gray writes in the novel's Epilogue, is 'an old device' and that 'Homer, Vergil, Milton and Scott Fitzgerald used it' doesn't mean anything ... unless you have entered the carefully guarded gates of literary codes and devices.[1] Until then, you are more likely to be moved and immensely reassured by the way Gray describes the surprise, horror and disgust of a schoolboy's first sexual ejaculation.

Reading *Lanark* for the first time I was aware that this was a book that was soaring way above any place fiction had taken me before. This virgin reader had no idea what was going to happen next. This was no man's land, uncharted territory, the part of the fictional map on which they used to write: HERE BE DRAGONS ...

The icing on the cake, the point of revelation, came towards the end. The Index of Plagiarisms. Surely this was just taking the piss. An author had the brass neck to not only nick bits from other writers but boldly list them for all to see?!? Eh? Gray even organised his thievery into what degree of theft had taken place. I mean, come on, ye cannae dae that.

This was hilarious. I loved this guy. I wanted to know more about him, what else he had written, what he had read, what had influenced these wild ideas. And whether he was a sci-fi buff. Seeing as how the author had so kindly and audaciously listed his influences in that amazing Index, it seemed the best place to start finding out.

Next stop was the public library on George IV Bridge, Edinburgh. It became a home from home. I tried to work out which books in the Index sounded the most interesting and accessible. The poetry, plays, classics, and non-fiction I skipped. Maybe later. I made a note to check out Kurt Vonnegut's *Breakfast of Champions*; Franz Kafka's *The Trial*; and James Joyce's *Portrait Of The Artist As A Young Man*. I liked the titles, the descriptions of the books, and the authors all had cool foreign sounding names. A few of the other books I knew already, like those by H. G. Wells and Orwell, as well as a book I'd been forced to read at school, *The House With The Green Shutters*.

In their different ways, these three books by Vonnegut, Kafka and Joyce further opened my eyes to the possibilities of fiction, and for that alone it was worth reading *Lanark*. After these newly discovered authors, I sampled a few of the others in the Index. Once started, there was no going back. Soon the sci-fi was being scaled down and from my mate Steve, who was also in the Balfour's Bar pool team, I borrowed Albert Camus' *The Outsider*, Luke Rhinehart's *The Dice Man*, Sylvia Plath's *The Bell Jar*, and, ach, there were too many to read now! But it was better than going to work.

I still reckon this is the best way to discover new writers and new books: by complete chance, without any fixed game plan. Bounce from one book into the next. Sometimes you borrow a book from a mate, sometimes you pick one up in a second-hand book store, sometimes you hear people talking about a book in a pub, or a writer you like mentions a book that he or she has been influenced by. Keep it as random as possible and you'll never stop being delighted by what you find.

There was one other writer among this plagiarised bunch whose work The Index had me seeking out. The ultra-short story, 'Acid', by James Kelman, was there in the Index margins, in full, less than 150 words long, but a masterpiece in miniature. Despite the brevity, Kelman still managed to tell an incredibly visual, memorable, horrific and moving tale of a father's stoical response to his son's accidental death in a vat of industrial acid. This was prose stripped to the very bones.

It seemed so easy to be able to write something like that. Nothing to it. It was so *ordinary* and so *short*. Of course, it was nothing of the sort. This was a master craftsman making it look easy.

I don't think I'm alone in saying that after reading Kelman and Gray, an attempt at writing fiction was the next logical step. Hell, if these Glaswegians could do it, locate it among us, then why not have a go as well? So what if the results were derivative and crap. That wasn't the point. Those first experiments in fiction were an enjoyable outpouring of jumbled-up thoughts, it was pure selfish pleasure, and meant something important to me, something hard to understand at the time, but that now makes complete sense: writing had become a participatory thing rather than a spectator sport. What I didn't realise at the time was that I wasn't the only person who now felt they had been given the keys to what had previously seemed like a closed and secret society.

Few realised it back then but the foundations were undoubtedly being laid for a reinvigorated literary and cultural renaissance in Scotland – although that sounds a bit too academic and grand for what was really happening on the ground. Fuses had been lit, and it wasn't long before we were marvelling at the explosive bangs, shifting patterns, and brilliant hues of what could easily be described as a very democratic fireworks display of self-expression. Now things were getting interesting.

* * *

The second, eagerly awaited, Alasdair Gray novel was published in 1984. Such were the reverberations caused by *Lanark*, I don't think anyone really anticipated what a hugely influential book *1982, Janine* would turn out to be.

I was chuffed to bits, partly because Janine was my sister's middle name and up to then I'd thought my dad had made the name up. (Except my dad had spelt it wrong on the birth certificate as Jeaneen, a fact that gets cast up on the occasional family Hogmanay, alcohol being mentioned as a possible excuse.) Partly, too, because the year 1982 had such a big effect on me. (I mean, Scotland scoring against Brazil in the World Cup Finals? It would be another sixteen years and seven Alasdair Gray novels before that happened again.)

I was also chuffed because Gray seemed to put absolutely everything he had to say about Scotland into this novel. This was more than just a story, it was a state of the nation address, an outpouring of our history and culture, our concerns and our aspirations, personified and refracted through the character of Jock McLeish, an alcoholic working for National Security Ltd. McLeish drinks and dreams his way through a night in a hotel room, alone with his fantasies and fears, his memories and hopes. It was also as near to a call to arms as any novel of recent times.

Jock McLeish is about as far from the macho Scottish male stereotype as you can get. Jock McLeish is in many ways more akin to so many real Scotsmen, who, beneath the bluff and bluster, are as confused and insecure as the next guy.

The women in McLeish's elaborate sexual fantasies, like the women in the lives of Thaw/Lanark and the 'real' McLeish, are often strong, confident and intimidating figures. Even in the comparative safety of his feverish fantasising, McLeish is never quite able to gain total control over these women's actions.

Through these psychological and sexual struggles is revealed one of the most endearing trademarks of Gray's writing: the way he tries to understand what his female characters are thinking, what these women want, and what makes these women so different from their male protagonists. His female characters are rarely peripheral. You get the impression that as a writer he really does care, not in some phoney new man sort of way, but as a fellow human being, and as an instinctive champion of all whose voices are marginalised or silenced.

Writers don't come any more explicitly political than Alasdair Gray. This political dimension to Gray's writing is fundamental, yet is often deliberately played down or misrepresented. Gray wittily commented on this in a way that very few leftfield writers would have the courage to risk stating quite so explicitly:

> My stories try to seduce the reader by disguising themselves as sensational entertainment, but are propaganda for democratic welfare-state Socialism and an independent Scottish parliament. My jacket designs and illustrations – especially the erotic ones – are designed with the same high purpose.[2]

Critics and academics, with their canons loaded, and their predictable compare-and-contrast literary techniques at the ready, had a hard job on their hands with *1982, Janine*. In some respects – perhaps because of their sharply contrasting social backgrounds from the author and his subject matter – some of the critics may be a little bit out of their depth as they try to play down the political aspects of the novel, and are left scratching their heids as they try in vain to pigeonhole this fantastically conceived and perfectly executed work.

(Another aside: One of the things that made me smile when reading *Lanark* was the two line rhymes at the top of each pair of facing pages of the Prologue. I like to imagine that there are all these academics in universities, poring over the nuances of *Lanark*, maybe wondering why these jaunty wee rhymes are there, maybe missing them completely, while childhood readers of a certain four pages of a certain Scottish Sunday newspaper wink at each other behind the academics' backs, not letting on.)

I was blown away by *1982, Janine.* For me, this was Scottish writing's equivalent to The Clash's first album. A cultural landmark and a political education in one. It just didn't seem possible that a writer could produce such a masterpiece as *Lanark* and then surpass it two years later.

Timing and context come into it again. When *1982, Janine* was first published, in 1984, the social backdrop was dominated by the year-long miners' strike. For the trade unions, for the labour movement, for mining communities, for the police, for the Thatcher government, and for millions of working class people at the time, this strike was a turning point in society. For Alasdair Gray, like the character in the novel, the timing was Superb.

* * *

Fast forward to 1992. April 9th, 1992 to be precise. The four nations of the United Kingdom have gone to the electoral polls. Thanks to the disastrous adoption of a mishmash of reheated Tory policies, the 'modernisers' of the Labour Party somehow allow a Tory government in disarray to arise from the ashes of the poll tax and be re-elected. Even Paul Daniels would have struggled with a conjuring trick of such magnitude.

This didn't go down too well in Scotland. The majority of Scots didn't vote for this Tory government, didn't want this Tory government, and had seriously thought – since the tyrant Thatcher had been unceremoniously dumped along with her daft poll tax – that they wouldn't have this Tory government re-imposed on them. Nae such luck. Like Schwarzenegger's robot anti-hero in the Terminator movies, they were back.

It was a bitter pill to swallow. Within weeks, tens of thousands had taken to demonstrating on the streets of Edinburgh demanding self-government. Outside the historic location of the Scottish parliament on Calton Hill, a vigil was set up and occupied 24/7 by self-sacrificing folk that had had enough. Pressure was mounting for some sort of home rule.

Alasdair Gray's response was to throw an incendiary pamphlet of democratic reason and historical perspective into the ring. It was called quite simply, *Why Scots Should Rule Scotland.* Now, if there's one thing conservatives of all colours detest it's lefties who go around spouting history. Especially when the last page of history is the present. History for the ruling classes has always been about a rudimentary knowledge of kings and queens, wars and battles, dates and places. There are few profitable uses for a detailed knowledge of social and political history in the world of commerce. But for anyone who cares about those hoary old chestnuts of equality, freedom, self-determination and justice, it's important to study history in order to work out why these things now seem more elusive than ever. Gray was doing what the esteemed Scottish education system had failed to do. He was helping us to educate ourselves in our own history and culture. This noble cause underpins so much of his writings.

Two years later, in 1994, Gray threw another fictional grenade into proceedings, appropriately titled, *A History Maker. A History Maker* was a return to sci-fi. (Cheers from the back row.) Scottish sci-fi. (More cheers.)

There's a line in *Lanark* when the young Duncan Thaw snorts his disapproval of sci-fi to his pal Coulter: 'I don't like science fiction much. It's pessimistic.' A quick mental check through some of the great sci-fi novels and Gray's comments ring true. So, maybe, with *A History Maker,* Gray sought to remedy this by writing optimistic science fiction!

Gray had the courage to bolt into the structure of this novel an optimistic harmonious vision of the way life could be. The way it could be even here, in the bear pit of macho, pugilistic, alcohol-swilling Scotland. Gray's bold vision of a possible future in *A History Maker* is socialistic and feminist and progressive. This is a courageous vision from a writer who shuns pigeon-holing but knows there are plenty who would like to pigeon hole him – either because of his socialist politics or despite them. In the hands of a writer as good as Gray, though, the politics are always subordinate to the writing.

One of the very, very few sci-fi novels to have attempted to paint an optimistic future for mankind was William Morris' *News From Nowhere*. This is interesting in itself. If there was one figure from the past whose life and work suggests that he was a worthy predecessor to Alasdair Gray it was William Morris. Morris, remembered by most for his wallpaper and fabric designs, was a writer, a poet, a painter, a pamphleteer, a Marxist thinker and political activist. A true renaissance man. His futuristic novel, *News From Nowhere*, published in 1890, was described by his contemporary H. G. Wells as 'a graceful impossible book' and 'a dream' where 'everyone worked for the joy of working and took what he needed'. This was in stark contrast to Wells' own pessimistic prophecies for the future of mankind.

There is probably much more that could be written about the possible influence of William Morris on Alasdair Gray, but as this essay is already based mostly on guesswork I'll leave it to someone better informed.

The Notes at the end of *A History Maker* contain a special treat for the reader who is less than enamoured by post-modernists and their conservative, metaphysical, dog's dinner of an approach to history. I could have kicked myself for wasting all those non-returnable hours trying to get my head round the complicated sophistry of its champions. Gray writes:

> Postmodernism happened when landlords, businessmen, brokers and bankers who owned the rest of the world had used new technologies to destroy the power of labour unions. Like owners of earlier empires they felt that history had ended because they and their sort could now dominate the world for ever. This indifference to most people's wellbeing and taste appeared in the fashionable art of the wealthy. Critics called their period *postmodern* to separate it from the modern world begun by the Renaissance when most

creative thinkers believed they could improve their community. Postmodernists had no interest in the future, which they expected to be an amusing rearrangement of things they already knew. Postmodernism did not survive disasters caused by 'competitive exploitation of human and natural resources' in the twenty-first century.[3]

It's probably as useful a definition of post-modernism as you're likely to read anywhere.

Unfortunately, from a commercial sense, *A History Maker* was published in the slipstream of another celebrated Scottish novel – Irvine Welsh's *Trainspotting*. *Trainspotting* was hogging all the media spotlights at this time. It became the cultural touchstone of the day and had a profound effect on the perception of Scottish writing. Gray's sci-fi novel slipped by almost unnoticed.

A History Maker was also handicapped by being published by a small Scottish publisher – which made it of little interest to reviewers and critics based in London. Worse, the publishers, Canongate Books, went into receivership just prior to the book's publication and copies ended up stuck in a warehouse somewhere in the Baltic states. None of this helped much. Which is a shame, because the novel is a wee gem.

A History Maker is set in a cunningly matriarchal society in the Scottish Borders – so cunning that most of the males don't even realise it's a matriarchal society – where war is a voluntary sport played by young males. Here tribal warfare is pure entertainment, is unconnected to commerce, and is mostly about glory and egos. 'Public eyes' are everywhere, floating around in the air, reporting back on whatever they see fit for the entertainment of the masses. In Gray's futuristic society, 'the open intelligence network' and 'organic powerplants' have 'made cities, nations, money and industrial power obsolete'.

In *A History Maker*, Gray takes up the historical cudgels once more and shows that when it comes to pushing the seemingly limitless boundaries of sci-fi, he can hold his own with the best of them.

The short period between 1992 and 1994 was an intensely exciting time for Scottish writing. The third of Gray's major novels, *Poor Things*, won the Whitbread Best Novel Award in 1992. Jeff Torrington's *Swing Hammer Swing* won the Whitbread Book of the Year award in 1992. James Kelman's *How Late It Was, How Late* won the Booker prize in

1994. A. L. Kennedy was cited as one of the 25 Best Young British Novelists by Granta magazine in 1992. Janice Galloway's *Foreign Parts* won the 1994 McVitie prize. And Irvine Welsh's *Trainspotting* was published in 1993. The prizes and plaudits might not mean much in themselves, but all of this taken together meant that people were sitting up and taking notice of what was happening up here.

On the ground, there was a real buzz and a sense that something important was happening. (In 1992 I started up *Rebel Inc* magazine, which initially intended to try and provide an East Coast outlet for some of the new Scottish writing of the time.)

Soon the fickle snouts of those who create literary fads snuffled around north Britain in search of 'new young Scottish writers' to shower with their fifteen minutes worth of praise and pesos. Literature's style police hauled their London-centric prejudices up over Hadrian's Wall in search of 'youth'. Ho hum. But, as Gray's fictional character Kelvin Walker would surely have appreciated, opportunities now manifested themselves for many of the assorted bright young things of Scottish fiction – as well as a few wily opportunists who were involved in the promotion of 'new young Scottish writers'.

If the electoral situation in Scotland from 1979 to 1997 had left millions feeling politically disenfranchised and unrepresented, and even imposed upon, it was inevitable that some of those disenfranchised voices would seek alternative ways of being heard.

One of the most interesting consequences of this was what writer Duncan McLean referred to as the emergence of 'a government of books'. Writers were using fiction to articulate the concerns of ordinary people in a way that politicians of all parties had thus far failed to achieve. The marginalised and the disaffected were having their voices heard.

In the early nineties, a seemingly endless conveyor belt of new writing talent appeared in Scotland, completely disproportionate to the country's size. But this was just an acceleration in a process started much earlier by the likes of Alasdair Gray and James Kelman. Now their influence was really kicking in.

* * *

Iain Banks' début novel, *The Wasp Factory*, was published in 1984, hot on the heels of Gray's *Lanark*. Like the young Duncan Thaw in the second book of *Lanark*, Frank, the main protagonist in *The Wasp Factory*, is an obsessive loner, a misfit, an awkward, contrary boy fascinated by the macabre. Banks generously makes no bones about the effect *Lanark* had on him. Blazoned across the front of the recent Picador edition of *Lanark* is the Banks quote: 'I was absolutely knocked out by *Lanark*. I think it's the best in Scottish literature this century.'

A few years later, in 1989, came the dazzling début novel *The Trick Is To Keep Breathing*, from another important and influential Scottish writer, Janice Galloway. *The Trick Is To Keep Breathing* is a wildly experimental *tour de force* of a novel, which chronicles the descent into grief and mental breakdown of a disturbed young woman following the death of her (married) lover. Like Gray's work, it pulls you relentlessly through the full spectrum of conflicting emotions, needle-sharpened to the point of pain by the devastated narrator's situation, and just like the book's title it leaves you gasping for air at the end.

Galloway has never been afraid to go on record to credit the huge influence Alasdair Gray has had on her writing. In one magazine interview, she writes passionately about her first encounter with *Lanark*:

> I had fallen in love – or something – with it. The mixture of clarity, exactness, and near-childlike sincerity; its high expectations of me as a reader, that I was somehow a partner in the enterprise, capable of creative insights and interaction with an author who was prepared to share his power had a profound effect.[4]

Again, it is just a guess on my part, but the experimental and playful structure of Gray's *Lanark*, and even more so with *1982, Janine*, must surely have influenced Galloway's courageous decision to structure her first novel the way she did. In this respect, as in others, the daring, groundbreaking, and liberating approach to fiction forged by Gray was sowing seeds that were landing on fertile ground and fertile imaginations. And, boy, was Scottish literature being enriched as a result.

Without wishing to downplay the influence of many of the other writers working in Scotland – especially the likes of William McIlvaney, Tom Leonard, Liz Lochhead, Carl MacDougall, Agnes Owens, and Alan

Spence – it would be true to say that thanks to the inspiration, encouragement, and the writing – both fictional and critical – of Gray and Kelman in particular, the floodgates had opened in the world of Scottish writing.

When you look at some of the new voices in Scottish fiction who were soon to make their mark in the 90s – such as A. L. Kennedy, James Meek, Duncan McLean, Brain McCabe, Irvine Welsh, Jeff Torrington, Gordon Legge, Dilys Rose, Laura Hird, James Robertson, Carl MacDougall, Ali Smith and Alan Warner, to name just a few, and there are plenty more – some common features of their writing come to light.

One common bond that these authors share with Gray, Kelman, Galloway, Spence, et al., is a real love and enthusiasm for the short story form. With the exception of Alan Warner, who has had short stories published in many anthologies and magazines, all of the above named writers have collections of short stories in print. This is worth thinking about and surely no coincidence. It hints at the driving force behind much of the explosion of new Scottish writing.

Short stories aren't just handy for reading on the toilet or on the bus or train. Through a collection of short stories, an author can often explore *a sense of location or community* in more depth than say a novel narrated by a single character. The sense of north Edinburgh and Leith portrayed in Welsh's *Trainspotting* for instance was best conveyed through the many varied voices of its different narrators. It is unlikely this aspect of the novel would have been so effective if the whole book had been seen through the eyes of its main protagonist, Mark Renton. In this sense, *Trainspotting* is in essence a collection of short stories rather than a novel, with the drug deal episode that figures so centrally in the movie added for narrative purposes. Comparisons with the objectives and structure of Joyce's *Dubliners* wouldn't be out of place.

For many of these writers – who choose to return again and again to the form of the short story – there is undoubtedly a desire to give voice and expression not just to marginalised (fictional) individuals but to those (fictional) characters who live within marginalised (but very real) communities.

(Yet another aside: If Scotland could have a government of writers, *à la* Duncan McLean, we could do worse than imagine Alasdair Gray as its

Minister of Education, James Kelman as its Cultural Ambassador, and Janice Galloway as its uncompromising Prime Minister. They'd get my vote before the Lib-Lab parcel of rogues currently with their noses in the Holyrood trough.)

Another common feature of much of the emerging Scottish fiction was the conscious or subconscious adaptation of what might be called 'social realism'. Many of these new writers were infusing their fiction with something that Alan Warner called – only half jokingly – 'social surrealism'.

Writers often have to react against what went before. It's like continually rearranging the furniture. In this instance, Scottish fiction was often perceived, unfairly, as being a tough uncompromising bastion of grim West Coast urban realism. The fictional output in the early '90s of East Coast-based writers such as James Meek, Duncan McLean, Alan Warner, Laura Hird and Irvine Welsh was often imaginatively surreal. Alexander Trocchi may have been the heroin-addicted existentialist outsider adopted and championed by many of the emerging East Coast writers who were looking beyond social realism, James Kelman was widely acknowledged an inspirational figure, but for my money, on the East Coast anyway, it was Alasdair Gray who was the major Scottish literary influence of the day.

To conjecture further on the influence of Alasdair Gray: the almost avant-garde experiments of Irvine Welsh in his third novel, *Filth*, seem to owe much to Gray and to *1982, Janine* in particular. The typographical way the tapeworm in *Filth* communicates to its host Bruce Robertson must surely have been influenced by the section in *1982, Janine* called 'The Ministry of Voices'. (Okay I'm only guessing but there's no law against that.) In this section of Gray's novel, his own typographical experiments create fragmentary sentences and shapes on the page, which descend into a single word chant of, funnily enough, 'filth, filth, filth, filth, filth, filth, filth, filth'.

More recently, in *Under The Skin*, the début novel of 'Scottish' writer Michel Faber (using Gray's own definition of Scots in *Why Scots Should Rule Scotland*) there seems to be more than a passing nod to the opening book of *Lanark*. Without wanting to spoil the revelation in Faber's horror story, I'll just say *scran* and leave it at that.

But it isn't in these iffy speculations about isolated specifics but in the totality of Gray's approach to imaginative fiction that his influence is seen to be most pervasive. We just wouldn't have got here in such good shape without him.

It would be easy to sign off this article here, and say the boy done good, but it is a measure of Gray's ambition and motivation that possibly his most influential work is destined to be his most recent undertaking, his mammoth *Book of Prefaces*.

The idea behind this project is so big that a writer would have to be mad to even attempt it. Gray sets out to try and provide a comprehensive history of the key texts of vernacular literature written in English from the earliest times to the turn of the twentieth century. He chooses to do this by including the introductions written by the respective authors at the time of publication alongside his own commentary on each text. (Plus additional commentaries from friends who helped Gray finish the project as the book's deadlines passed more often than rain clouds over Skye.) And as if that wasn't a big enough project, Gray also provides a series of illuminating essays in the book, which put the great works of English literature into their social, political, cultural and historical contexts.

Rarely have history, religion, politics and literature wrapped themselves around each other in such an accessible, erudite and informative way. This is a book that is as idiosyncratically playful as it is definitive. And so, so useful.

For instance, when reading a letter in a socialist newspaper, which denigrated the idea of a spoken Scots language, saying it was just a dialect of English, it was in Gray's *Book of Prefaces* that I found the ammunition for a counter-blast.[5] Gray presented a clear explanation of how spoken English consisted mainly of a guttural mixture of short Anglo-Saxon and Danish words up until the Norman Invasion of England in 1066. The subsequent incorporation of French words into the vernacular language over the following three centuries also made sense once the history of the period was laid bare. Far from having a 'proper' version or being a 'pure' language, Gray's work explains how English is as much a mongrel tongue as any other spoken language.

Once the ebbs and flows of history are patiently explained, the language of Bede and of the epic poem *Beowulf* become differentiated from the language of Chaucer and Mandeville, and all of these texts now have a historical context, which makes them easier to understand and also makes reading them a much more enjoyable experience. It is difficult not to read Gray's marginal commentaries on Chaucer's *Canterbury Tales*, for instance, and not think, possibly for the first time, hey, this sounds really good. This is the mark of a great teacher. The kind we all wish we had at school.

In his 'Editor's Postscript', Gray explains what drove him to create such a work:

> I consider this anthology a memorial to the kind of education British governments now think useless, especially for British working class children. But it has been my education, so I am bound to believe it one of the best in the world.[6]

The Book of Prefaces is a mighty achievement and is in itself the summation of a lifetime's rapacious study. In an ideal world, it would be only a matter of time before it elbowed its way into every educational curriculum in the country.

When you add together all the poetry, plays, shorter fiction, novels, critical work, non-fiction, and of course, his art and murals, it's some output. But here's hoping that Gray isn't finished yet by a long chalk and that he remains the driven author who keeps coming up with the goods.

How to end this article – which was supposed to be about the influence of Alasdair Gray but found itself detouring a bit along the way – is difficult. This is because the influence of Alasdair Gray shows no sign of ending and, indeed, will inevitably increase on an exponential basis as the years roll on. And as it is impossible to write exponentially…

An Optimistic Futuristic Epilogue

A boy and his mother enter a tenement in the city's west end, situated on the top of a hill, which has been converted on all floors into a museum and a gallery. Great murals and drawings and paintings and sketches hang on each of the walls. Manuscripts and extravagant book designs are scattered around in glass display cases. In the dark subterranean basement of the converted tenement, half-spoken sentences hang in the air and low guttural voices growl from behind panels in the floor and on the ceiling. In the lower of the building's two cafes, people argue passionately, but without rancour, and scraps of food are left on mouldy plates. No one is quite sure whether they should be cleaned away or not. Wrought iron staircases take the mother and her son up through many different levels where they stop and stare at the exhibits too numerous to be described here. Artists and academics wander around on the balconies, muttering to themselves, as children scribble in notebooks and splash bright primary colours onto provided sheets of canvas. A tall man with a clipped moustache and a poker-straight back takes visitors on tours and chats to them about the old days. On the roof garden, there are many fantastic plants and exotic birds and monstrous carvings and intricately constructed models that create a mosaic of evershifting shapes and colours when they are bathed in the bright Scottish sunshine. Occasionally, lovers emerge from the shadows to kiss and hold hands and gaze out over one of the most inspiring panoramic views imaginable. In the middle of the roof garden there is a life-size bronze statue of a short man who stands in a manner that suggests he means business except that his shoulders are hunched forwards and his arms hang stiffly by his sides. His stomach paunch rests majestically over the top of his belted trousers and a corner of his shirt hangs out over his right trouser pocket. His hair is dishevelled and a pair of square spectacles are balanced at a squint of an angle over his nose. His beady metal eyes are an explosion of wonder and incredulity as they peer out over the top of his thick spectacle frames. The statue has no pedestal and no words inscribed on it. 'Is that him?' asks the wee boy. 'Aye, that's him, son,' says his mother. The small boy looks into the statue's comical face and sticks his tongue out. The mother pulls him along. On their way out of the converted tenement, clutching handfuls of free souvenirs, they see above the door an entrance sign that has a single, neon-lit word emblazoned on it: the first two letters of which – a U and an N – have been deliberately removed, leaving a faint but clearly discernible shadow. The word above the door now says quite simply: THANKS.

Notes

1. Alasdair Gray, *Lanark: A Life in Four Books*, rev. edn. (Edinburgh: Canongate, 1985), p. 483.
2. *Contemporary Novelists*, 6th edn, ed. by Susan Windisch Brown (London: St James Press, 1996).
3. Alasdair Gray, *A History Maker* (Edinburgh: Canongate, 1994), pp. 202-203.
4. Janice Galloway, 'Reading Alasdair Gray', *Context: A Forum for Literary Arts and Culture*, 7 (2000).
5. Letter by A. Cannon and reply by K. Williamson, in *Scottish Socialist Voice*, 53 (22 June 2001) and 55 (6 July 2001).
6. Alasdair Gray, *The Book of Prefaces* (London: Bloomsbury, 2000), p. 631.

AN ALASDAIR GRAY
BIBLIOGRAPHY

PHIL MOORES

COMPILING THIS BIBLIOGRAPHY HAS BEEN A PLEASURE, IF
more arduous than expected. I have discovered works I had not known
existed and found new subtleties in those with which I was already
familiar. I believe the bibliography to be complete as far as Alasdair
Gray's major published work is concerned, though less so in the case of
material published in magazines and anthologies. The typographic and
graphic design of so many of Gray's books being an integral part of the
author's work, I have described this aspect of his work in more detail
than would normally be expected in such a compilation. Works I have
been unable to examine are marked with an asterisk (*).

I am obliged to Stephen Bernstein and Holly Hammontree for
information about certain American editions that I would otherwise
have had difficulty in locating. Alasdair himself offered far more help
than I had any right to expect. Despite this assistance, all mistakes are of
course entirely down to me.

A. *Short Story Collections*

1. **The Comedy of the White Dog**

a) Glasgow: Print Studio Press, 1979.

24p; £1.75 (signed), £0.75 (unsigned)

    ISBN: 0-906112-07-9 (signed); 0-906112-06-0 (unsigned)

Edition comprises 26 signed copies, lettered A-Z, and 574 unsigned copies. According to Rees (see Section N), '200 copies were returned to the author in 1984 and subsequently destroyed'.

CONTENTS: The Comedy of the White Dog; The Crank Who Made the Revolution.

White card cover with a black and white photograph (uncredited) of a featureless doll in Victorian dress perched upon a white china dog. The publication is not illustrated, though Gray's 'Independence' vignette, later used on the boards of *Mavis Belfrage*, is used as part of the publisher's logo on the title page.

2. **Unlikely Stories, Mostly**

a) Edinburgh: Canongate, 1983.

276p; ill; £7.50; hbk   ISBN: 0-86241-029-0

First edition. Dedication: To the good angel Mullane and Christopher Boyce and to their daughter Petra Davina. Copies were issued with an erratum slip (3" x 1") printed in red, 'ERRATUM: This slip has been inserted by mistake'.

CONTENTS: The Star; The Spread of Ian Nicol; The Problem; The Cause of Some Recent Changes; The Comedy of the White Dog; The Crank That Made the Revolution; The Great Bear Cult; The Start of the Axletree; Five Letters from an Eastern Empire; Logopandocy; Prometheus; The End of the Axletree; A Likely Story in a Nonmarital Setting; A Likely Story in a Domestic Setting.

Probably the most profusely illustrated of Gray's books. On the front endpaper the young Thomas Urquhart (from the tale 'Logopandocy') sails away. He is surrounded by the names in

archaic language of many of the author's contemporaries (mainly)
– 'Philip the Jew', 'Kelman, agnamed The Cool', 'Lochhead of
Motherwell', 'Master Morgan; agnamed Fast Eddie', and
'Mistress Owens of the Vale'. These are scripted in Alasdair
Gray's handwriting. On the rear endpaper the elderly Urquhart is
returning to Scotland, into the picture of the Leviathan State used
to introduce book four of *Lanark*.

The boards are dark blue blocked in gold with a repeating tall
thistle design, similar to that later used on the boards of *Poor
Things*. The 'Work as if you were living in the early days of a
better nation' motto runs along the top; 'SCOTLAND 1983' runs
along the bottom.

The dust jacket is white, red and gold with a 'foetal angel inside a
skull' motif repeated as a border round the title, and an 'improved
duck'. Below the border appears the boy-poet flying on the kite
used in *Five Letters*. The same layout is repeated on the back panel,
the title details being replaced with spoof quotes from a Col.
Sebastian Moran and Lady Nicola Stewart, Countess of
Dunfermline. The spine is decorated with two images of the
White Dog doing what he does best. The front flap gives a
fulsome and lengthy review by Fiona Fullerton from *The
Bookseller*. The back flap has a pencil portrait of Gray by James
Bliss with, under the heading 'About the Author', the poem
'Awaiting' from *Old Negatives*.

b) Harmondsworth: Penguin Books, 1984.
   276p; ill; £4.95; pbk   ISBN: 0-14-006925-9

   First paperback edition.

The internal illustrations have been altered slightly and the
mottoes from the boards have been added to the drawing of the
half-naked buxom mermaid on the first and last pages. The
hardcover jacket, including the flaps, is reproduced almost exactly
on the cover. The flaps were removed from later printings, an
additional image of the White Dog was added to the spine and a
barcode was incorporated.

c) Edinburgh: Canongate, 1997.
294p; ill; £5.99; pbk (Canongate classics; no. 81)

ISBN: 0-86241-737-6

Revised edition.

CONTENTS: As the first edition with two additional stories, 'A Unique Case' and 'Inches in a Column'. Four stories are retitled: 'Logopandocy' as 'Sir Thomas's Logopandocy', 'Prometheus' as 'M. Pollard's Prometheus', 'A Likely Story in a Nonmarital Setting' as 'A Likely Story Outside a Domestic Setting' and 'A Likely Story in a Domestic Setting' as 'A Likely Story Within a Domestic Setting'. A lengthy postscript, by the author and Douglas Gifford, has been added.

The illustrations appear in a slightly different order. A new mock erratum slip is printed on the opening page: 'ERRATUM: The Publishers apologise for the loss of the erratum slip'.
The slightly redesigned cover is printed in blue, yellow and white. The white dog on the spine is replaced with the 'improved duck' and the Emperor, from *Five Letters*, is added to the front cover.

3. Lean Tales (with James Kelman and Agnes Owens)

a) London: Jonathan Cape, 1985.
292p; ill; £8.95; hbk   ISBN: 0-224-02262-8

First edition.

CONTENTS: **James Kelman**: Busted Scotch; The Same Is Here Again; The Glenchecked Effort; The Witness; Are You Drinking Sir?; In a Betting Shop to the Rear of Shaftesbury Avenue; Where I Was; Extra Cup; Learning the Story; Getting There; The Paperbag; Old Holborn; O Jesus, Here Come the Dwarfs; Manufactured In Paris; The Place!; A Nightboilerman's Notes; The City Slicker and the Barmaid; An Enquiry Concerning Human Understanding. **Agnes Owens**: Arabella; Bus Queue; Getting Sent For; Commemoration Day; The Silver Cup; Fellow Travellers; McIntyre; We Don't Shoot Prisoners on a Sunday; A Change of Face. **Alasdair Gray**: A Report to the Trustees; The Answer; The Story of a Recluse; Portrait of a Playwright; Portrait of a Painter; The Grumbler; I Own Nothing, I Owe Nothing; Decision; Authority; Translation; Humanity; Ending; Postscript.

Each section is introduced with a pen and ink portrait of the author, drawn by Gray, and a facsimile author signature. The Postscript gives a detailed memoir of Philip Hobsbaum's writing group in the 1970s and of Gray and Kelman's friendship with Agnes Owens.

Jade green endpapers. Dark blue boards with gold blocking of interlocking shapes infilled partly with small stars round the publisher's logo. The colour jacket has a thistle design with line drawings of the authors looking out from each corner (Owens appears twice).

b) London: Abacus, 1987.
   288p; ill; £3.99; pbk   ISBN: 0-349-11542-7

First paperback edition.

CONTENTS: As first edition with three additional short tales in Gray's section: A Small Thistle; The Domino Game; Money.

The hardcover jacket image is reproduced on the front cover. Quotes from four reviews of the collection are added to the back cover.

c) London: Vintage, 1995.
   287p; ill; £5.99; pbk   ISBN: 0-09-958541-3

Second paperback edition.

CONTENTS: As the Abacus edition.

Compared to the first paperback edition, the reproduction of the internal portraits has improved but the cover is poorer in quality. The layout of the title and author details has been altered. The back cover carries quotes from two reviews of the first edition and a new blurb.

4. Ten Tales Tall & True: Social Realism, Sexual Comedy, Science Fiction and Satire

a) London: Bloomsbury, 1993.

   176p; ill; £15.99; hbk   ISBN: 0-7475-1427-7

First edition. Dedication: To the onelie begetters of these stories: Tom Maschler and Xandra Hardie and Morag McAlpine. Some copies were issued with an erratum slip (4" x 1½") explaining that the story 'Time Travel' should be dedicated to James Kelman.

CONTENTS: Getting Started – a Prologue; Houses & Small Labour Parties; Homeward Bound; Loss of the Golden Silence; You; Internal Memorandum; Are You a Lesbian?; The Marriage Feast; Fictional Exits; A New World; The Trendelenburg Position; Time Travel; Near the Driver; Mr Meikle – An Epilogue; Notes, Thanks and Critic Fuel.

The internal line drawings are mostly of animals and their tails. Each story, apart from the last, opens with a pictorial drop initial. A rubric is given in the right margin of each recto.

Turquoise-blue endpapers and emerald green ribbon bookmark. Navy blue boards blocked in silver with a design featuring a lattice background, a (Scots?) pine stump putting forth a healthy new shoot with the motto 'TRY AGAIN', and a spider dangling by a thread from the lattice. This design was also used on the hardcover edition of *A History Maker*.

The colour jacket uses the tails of ten animals to border the title information. The blurb on the front flap is printed in a spectrum of colours, from red to green:

> This book contains more tales than ten so the title is a tall tale too.
> I would spoil my book if I shortened it, spoil the title if I made it true.

There is a new pencil portrait of Gray by James Bliss on the back flap and the first promise of *The Anthology of Prefaces*, which he 'plans to complete [...] before the 21st century'.

*b) New York: Harcourt Brace, 1993.

171p; ill; $19.95; hbk   ISBN: 0-15-100090-5

First US edition.

c) Harmondsworth: Penguin Books, 1994.

176p; ill; £5.99; pbk   ISBN: 0-14-017579-2

First paperback edition.

A reprint of the Bloomsbury edition. The illustration of Mr Meikle at the end of the last story is embellished with the portraits of eleven other people. The list of works by Gray drops *The State We Are In* which was never published, but adds *Occasional Essays*, which has also not yet appeared, and *A History Maker*, which has.

d) San Diego: Harcourt Brace, 1995.

171p; ill; $11.00; pbk   ISBN: 0-15-600196-9

First US paperback edition.

A reprint of the UK paperback edition. The blurb on the back cover has been edited for the American market.

5. Five Letters From An Eastern Empire: Describing Etiquette, Government, Irrigation, Education, Clogs, Kites, Rumour, Poetry, Justice, Massage, Town-planning, Sex and Ventriloquism in an Obsolete Nation

a) London: Penguin Books, 1995.

58p; £0.60; pbk (Penguin 60s)   ISBN: 0-14-600044-7

Originally collected in: Unlikely Stories, Mostly.

One of a series of sixty small books selling at 60p each to celebrate the sixtieth birthday of Penguin Books in 1995. The title page verso incorrectly gives the copyright date as 1951. The text is not illustrated.

The front cover features the wizened head of the emperor, printed in black and white in a red roundel.

6. **Mavis Belfrage: A Romantic Novel With Five Shorter Tales**

a) London: Bloomsbury, 1996.

224p; ill; £13.99; hbk   ISBN: 0-7475-2506-4

First edition. Dedication: For Alexandra Gray when she is much older.

CONTENTS: Mavis Belfrage; A Night Off; Mr Goodchild; Money; Edison's *Tractatus*; The Shortest Tale.

'Mavis Belfrage' is adapted from a play completed in 1968 and reworked several times until 1976. It has appeared under various titles, including 'Mavis Watson', 'Triangles', 'Colchis', 'Agnes Belfrage', 'Agnes Watson' and 'Mavis Belfrage'. The work was produced as a television play under the title 'Triangles' in 1973 and 1976, and was staged in 1975/76.

A rubric is given in the right margin of each recto. The shorter tales are introduced on a section title page as 'Five Other Sober Stories' and are illustrated with devilish drawings.

Bright red endpapers and red ribbon bookmark. Brick-red boards blocked in gold with a lattice framework with a roundel picture of a woman picking fruit from a tree that is also a tail, with the 'INDEPENDENCE' scroll below. The boards also carry the following comments on the book's contents:

> I call this book a novel since most readers prefer long stories to short. – Front board.

> Under the paper jacket I admit this book should be called ~ Teachers: 6 short tales. – Back board.

The main characters of the title story are illustrated on the colour jacket. The front flap claims:

> This is the least fanciful of Gray's fiction collections and will amuse readers who do not find the world comfortable and don't expect to escape from it alive.

The back flap lists Gray's publications.

b) London: Bloomsbury, 1997.
224p; ill; £5.99; pbk   ISBN: 0-7475-3089-0

First paperback edition.

Contents are as the hardcover edition. The original jacket image has been cropped to show just Mavis with the buildings of Glonda in the background. Three reviews are quoted on the back cover.

B. *Novels*

1. **Lanark: a Life in Four Books**

a) Edinburgh: Canongate Publishing, 1981.
572p; ill; £7.95; hbk   ISBN: 0-903937-74-3

First edition. Dedication: For Andrew Gray.

A main feature of the book is the five 'allegorical title pages' with pen and ink illustrations – a main title page and section title pages for each of the four books, which appear in the order 3, 1, 2, 4. The main title page is made up of several line drawings. Three images run along the top: 'Cowcaddens Landscape 1950' without the figures, the 'independence' motif of a woman eating fruit sprouting from her tail, and a hand reaching out of the sea towards the sun. In the centre, a couple (male dark, female pale) suckle upon the breast of a sea monster. On the right, a thin serious man uses a pencil and compass on a model of his own head laid upon an open book. On the left is a head and shoulders portrait of a lady. Along the bottom are three open books and two foetuses curled up in skulls. The title, author and dedication details are slotted in between the images.

The title page for Book 3 gives prominence to five female figures, Fama Bona, Fama Mala, Experientia, Veritas, and Magistra Vitæ, the latter holding aloft a beautifully detailed allegorical globe. Along the bottom lie the skeletal Mors (1614) and sleeping Oblivio (1979).

The title page for Book 1 shows a microcosm of Glasgow being engulfed by water, a galleon heading towards a whale and part of the Leviathan State figure. On each side are pillars engraved with the epigraph 'Let Glasgow Flourish by Telling the Truth'. Three faces appear in the bottom corners.

The title page for Book 2 depicts a dissection taking place before an audience. At the top of the page two cherubs hold aloft elements from the Glasgow city coat of arms.

The title page for Book 4 depicts Hobbes' allegorical Leviathan State overlooking Glasgow and its environs with oil rigs, tower blocks, nuclear submarines, cottages, power plants, boats and people. Illustrated at the bottom are the ways a state controls its citizens (army, police, education and law) around the words 'Or the Matter, Form and Power of a Commonwealth'. Along the top runs the text: 'Foremost of the Beasts of the Earth for Pride. Job c41 v34.' The verse referred to is 'He beholdeth all high things; he is a king over all the children of pride' (King James Bible).

Scarlet endpapers. The black boards are blocked in gilt on the spine with the title, author and publisher details. The wraparound jacket features a pen and ink composition meshing images of Glasgow (shipbuilding, bridges, the statue of Knox) with characters and episodes from the book. It is dominated by one of Gray's typically buxom nude women holding aloft the sun.

*b) New York: Harper & Row, 1981.

560p; ill; $8.95; pbk   ISBN: 0-06-090862-9

First US edition. Offset from the Canongate edition.

Originally scheduled for publication a few months after the Canongate edition, changes in the management of Harper & Row meant that it appeared simultaneously. It was marketed as a straight science fiction book and disappeared without trace.

c) St Albans: Granada, 1982.

572p; ill; £2.95; pbk   ISBN: 0-586-05549-5

First UK paperback edition.

Uses the text of the first Canongate edition. The main title page has been altered by the addition of a celestial background and a new arrangement of the author, title and publisher information.

All UK paperback editions to date have used the Leviathan State image from the title page to Book 4 as the cover image. The sky has been blocked in gold. Other images from the original jacket are used on the spine: a baby being born, a riot in Glasgow and an old man shoulder-to-shoulder with a young boy.
Reissued in 1987 under the Paladin imprint.

d) Edinburgh: Canongate Publishing, 1985.
560p; ill; £15.00; hbk   ISBN: 0-903937-74-3

The second hardcover edition, described as 'Definitive' comprising 1,000 signed and numbered copies.

The main title page illustration has been simplified. Book 4's title page motto has been altered to: 'By Arts is formed that great Mechanical Man called a State, foremost of the Beasts of the Earth for Pride', and the biblical reference has been dropped.
Scarlet endpapers. The motto 'ENDURE YOU ARE NOT ALONE' is blocked in gold across the black boards with the 'R' in 'ARE' forming an acrostic with 'LANARK' running vertically down the spine. Gray suggested to Canongate that he sign every copy in order to fund the gold blocking on the boards.
The newly designed jacket is mostly beige, with bronze metallic detailing. The front panel illustration is of the Earth-mother from 'Prometheus' in *Unlikely Stories, Mostly*. The back panel has a list of 'Praise for Lanark'.

e) New York: George Braziller, 1985.
561p; ill; $20.00; hbk   ISBN: 0-8076-1108-5

First US hardcover edition.

As the 1985 Canongate hardcover edition but unsigned.

f) London: Picador, 1991.
572p; ill; £6.99; pbk   ISBN: 0-330-31965-5

Second UK paperback edition.

Follows the text and illustrations for the 1985 Canongate hardcover edition. The front cover artwork is the same as that on the Granada paperback, but is set against a black background.

*g) San Diego: Harcourt Brace, 1996.
560p; ill; $16.00; pbk   ISBN: 0-15-600361-9

Second US paperback edition.

Follows the 1985 Canongate hardcover edition. The front cover illustration is 'Cowcaddens Landscape 1950', linking the gloomy world of Unthank and the Glasgow in which Thaw grows up.

h) Edinburgh: Canongate Books Ltd, 2001.
4 vols.: 572p; ill; £35.00; hbk (Canongate classics; no. 100)
                                                 ISBN: 1-84195-120-X

Third UK hardcover edition.

A special edition of 2,000 signed and numbered copies, issued as four hardcover volumes in a slipcase, produced for the twentieth anniversary of *Lanark*'s first publication. Gray signed each set on top of the slipcase and numbered each volume and the slipcase. The text follows the 1985 Canongate 'Definitive' text with a new Tailpiece added at the end of Book 4. The volumes are numbered 1-4, but follow the original order of books 3, 1, 2, 4.

The boards of each volume are blocked with a design of an angel breaking out of a skull with giant thistles on each side and a narrow scroll falling down the middle with the epigraph 'work as if you lived in the early days of a better nation'. The outer volumes, the Lanark books, have burgundy boards with gold blocking, navy blue endpapers and jackets with colour wraparound images. The inner volumes, the Thaw books, have navy blue boards with silver blocking, burgundy endpapers and colour jackets where the front panel images are reversed on the back panel. 'Other books by Alasdair Gray' are listed on the back flaps of each volume.

Volume One: The jacket image is 'Cowcaddens Landscape 1950'. This was previously used on the 1996 US edition of *Lanark*.

Volume Two: The jacket image is 'Two Hills', a naïve painting of terraced houses, schools and churches, populated by stick figures. On a page preceding the contents page is printed a poem beginning 'The angel said, "His house is burning"…', that purports to be from Mirandola's *Sybilene Apocrypha*, but which is in fact 'A Burning' from *Old Negatives*.

Volume Three: The jacket image is 'The Garden of Eden', depicting a dark-brown man and a white woman kneeling in an embrace against a landscape populated with animals, some real, some mythical, and God. On the horizon can be seen future events: the expulsion from Eden, the Flood, Moses and the tablets of the law, Sodom and Gomorrah, the Tower of Babel and Christ's crucifixion. The picture is reminiscent of the church mural described in the text. On a page preceding the contents page is printed a poem beginning, 'Who unpick their anatomy…', that purports to be from Clegthorpe's *Thus Spake Sam Clegthorpe*, but which is actually 'Two Gods' from *Old Negatives*.

Volume Four: The jacket image is 'The Triumph of Death', an apocalyptic scene of the city ablaze and under attack from giant, blind, long-limbed monsters, while the human inhabitants huddle scared in the foreground. On a page preceding the contents page is printed a poem beginning 'Who is all fire and wings and hearts and seed?', that purports to be anonymous but which is in fact 'Lyrical' from *Old Negatives*. After the final 'Goodbye', Gray pops up again with a cheery 'Hullo again' and explains the background to the writing and gestation of the book in the 'Tailpiece: How *Lanark* Grew'.

Slipcase: The illustration from the 1981 Canongate jacket is reproduced on the paper-covered slipcase with gold and black lettering on a white ground. The top of the case pictures a hand holding a pen and is signed and numbered by the author.

*i) Edinburgh: Canongate Books Ltd, 2002.
   592p; ill; £8.99; pbk (Canongate classics; no. 100

ISBN: 1-84195-183-8

Third UK paperback edition.
Includes a new introduction by Janice Galloway and the tailpiece from the Canongate hardcover. The jacket is an adaption of the 1981 Canongate first edition jacket.

2. **1982, Janine**

a) London: Jonathan Cape, 1984.

347p; £8.95; hbk   ISBN: 0-224-02094-3

First edition. Dedication: For Bethsy. Rees (see Section N) notes that copies were later price-clipped and re-issued at £9.95.

There is a rubric in the outside margin of all pages. The table of contents includes chapter summaries worth reading in their own right, for example –

> Chapter 7: On being an instrument. A friend with a mind like the mind of God reveals one weakness and introduces me to Helen and showbusiness. A sexual quartet for shrinkfit jeans and hairdryers. Yahoohay. A dream

On pages 177-190 Gray makes dramatic use of page layout and typographic design to present the text in complex patterns of font and form in perhaps the most radical use of typography in any popular novel since *Tristram Shandy*. Of all his novels, *1982, Janine* is Gray's favourite.

Scarlet endpapers. Black boards blocked all over in gold with a repeating pattern of 'Y's, alternately right-way-up and upside down. The pattern is interrupted by a large square (on front and back panels) containing the image of Prometheus, previously used on the opening page of the short story of that name in *Unlikely Stories, Mostly*, and a quote from a poem credited to Alan Jackson:

> Truly the remedy's inside the disease
> And the meaning of being ill is to bring the eye to the heart.

The jacket is white with red lettering. The Prometheus image is reversed out of a black background. Instead of the usual blurb and author biography, both flaps are almost completely filled with the repeated 'Y' motif – inverted on the front, right-way-up on the back.

*b) New York: Viking, 1984.

345p; $16.95; hbk   ISBN: 0-670-51387-3

First US hardcover edition.

As the UK hardcover edition.

c) Harmondsworth: Penguin, 1985.

353p; £3.95; pbk   ISBN: 0-14-007110-5

First UK paperback edition.

A five-page advertisement entitled 'Criticism of the Foregoing' is added at the end. It contains extracts from thirteen reviews, nine very positive –

> *1982, Janine* has a verbal energy, an intensity of vision that has mostly been missing from the English novel since D. H. Lawrence – *Jonathan Baumbach*

three decidedly negative –

> I recommend nobody to read this book.... It is sexually oppressive, the sentences are far too long and it is boring ... hogwash – *Peter Levi*

and one undecided. There is also a letter to the author from a reader in Denmark. The hardcover jacket image and layout is used on the cover. A strapline, 'By the author of the award-winning Poor Things', is added to later printings.

3. The Fall of Kelvin Walker: a Fable of the Sixties

a) Edinburgh: Canongate Publishing, 1985.

144p; £7.95; hbk   ISBN: 0-86241-072-X

First edition. Dedication: For MORA, at long last, a book by her brother which will not make her blush.

The text was adapted from a play of the same title written in 1964. The play was produced for television by the BBC in 1968 and staged in 1972.

Unusually, there are no internal illustrations.

Turquoise endpapers. Steel grey boards blocked in silver with an illustration of a male nude falling head first, a look of annoyance on his face, his hands holding his head. The title and author details run clockwise round the image forming a border. The entire design is mirrored on the back board.

The design is also repeated on the jacket with the image set against a turquoise background with black lettering. The front flap has a quote from the book and a short blurb. The back flap quotes from five reviews of Gray's earlier work.

*b) New York: George Braziller, 1986.
144p; $14.95; hbk   ISBN: 0-8076-1144-1
First US edition.

As the UK hardcover edition.

c) Harmondsworth: Penguin Books, 1986.
142p; £2.95; pbk   ISBN: 0-14-008424-X
Revised edition – 'This King Penguin incorporates the author's corrections to the text of the first edition of Kelvin Walker, published by Canongate of Edinburgh' – half-title.

Despite losing the blank pages between chapters, the contents page has not been amended and consequently gives incorrect pagination for chapter three onwards.
The original jacket artwork is replaced by a Mark Entwisle illustration of a besuited, nervous young man being kissed by a barefooted bohemian girl – it isn't bad, it just isn't Gray. The front cover carries a quote from Melvyn Bragg. The back cover has a black and white photograph of Gray, part of the blurb from the hardcover and three quotes from reviews.
Reissued in 1991 with amended artwork from the hardcover edition. The falling man wears a more devilish and tortured expression and is set into a red flame against a black background.

*d) New York: Grove Press (Evergreen), 1987.
141p; $7.95; pbk   ISBN: 0-8021-3004-6
First US paperback edition.

4. McGrotty and Ludmilla, or, The Harbinger Report

a) Glasgow: Dog and Bone, 1990.
133p; ill; £5.00; pbk   ISBN: 1-872536-00-X
First edition. Dedication: To the only begetter of this ensuing romance. Angel, all happiness and that eternity our bigheaded author wishes the

wellwishing publisher setting forth. Typeset by Donald Saunders, this was the first publication from the Dog and Bone Press.

Although originally written in 1973 as a television play for a series based on nursery tales in modern settings, *McGrotty and Ludmilla* was first produced for radio and broadcast on 18 July 1975. Gray says that he 'give[s] the date to show that, though a blatant plagiarist, I did not plagiarise the Whitehall comedy programme Yes Minister'. In February 1987, it was produced at the Tron Theatre, Glasgow: details from this stage version found their way into the book and McGrotty's portrait on the cover is based on Kevin McMonigle in the role.

The running head is used to give an ironic commentary on the plot development. Each chapter closes with a line drawing: lamps, thistles, spiders and skulls recur, reflecting the tone of events.

The cover, printed in blue, turquoise and gold, features a Gray illustration of the eponymous characters with Big Ben towering in the background. McGrotty's tartan tie and the clock face are highlighted in gold. The white lettering runs clockwise round the square image. The blurb claims that the book differs from Gray's other books 'by having a hero who gets everything he wants, marries and lives happily ever after'.

5. **Something Leather**

a) London: Jonathan Cape, 1990.

254p; ill; £12.95; hbk   ISBN: 0-224-02627-5

First edition. Dedication: for Flo Allan. Designed and typeset by Dog & Bone.

As explained in 'Critic Fuel: an Epilogue', various chapters were originally written as individual plays: 'The Proposal' as *Martin,* produced for BBC Schools in 1971; 'The Man Who Knew About Electricity', produced for BBC Television in 1973; 'Mr Lang and Ms Tain', written in 1973 as *Sam Lang and Miss Watson,* but never produced; 'In the Boiler Room', written in 1974 but never produced; 'Quiet People', produced for BBC Radio in 1968; 'A

Free Man with a Pipe', written and produced by the BBC as *Dialogue* and broadcast on radio in 1969 and on television in 1972. A wasp motif is used throughout the text. Each chapter opens with a drop initial embellished with a portrait of one of the lead characters.

Citrus-yellow endpapers. Blue boards blocked in gold with dozens of wasps (viewed from the side on the front and back, viewed from above on the spine). In gold vertical lettering on the front board is 'HELLO' and on the back board 'GOODBYE'. The white jacket has plum-coloured lettering and a monochrome illustration of a confident woman in a leather skirt, fishnet stockings and blouse. Her lips and fingernails are highlighted in pink. The same image is used on both the front and back panels. The front flap carries a long description of the novel. The back flap contains 'Chapter 14: The Sitting Room, 221B Baker Street', in which Dr Watson complains of the absence of the lighthouse keeper and trained cormorant promised on the front flap. It ends with the statement: 'I doubt if this book will be taken seriously south of the Tweed – or north of it either'.

*b) New York: Random House, 1990.
256p; ill; $19.00; hbk   ISBN: 0-394-58963-7
First US hardback edition.

The internal illustrations from the UK edition, including the dropped initials, have been omitted. The blue boards are blocked in silver on the front with a wasp and the author's initials. The jacket uses a colour photograph, credited to Michel DelSol, of a woman wearing a long black-blue leather dress, bent at a 45° angle and photographed from the middle of her back down. The text of the flaps are as on the UK edition.

c) London: Picador, 1991.
256p; ill; £5.99; pbk   ISBN: 0-330-31944-2
'Revised edition'. First paperback edition.

An additional paragraph in the Acknowledgements states:

> I finally acknowledge that it was a bad idea to call this book *Something Leather*. It directed the attention of half the critics who noticed the novel to Chapters 1 and 12, so they reviewed it as if it was mainly a sado-masochistic Lesbian adventure story. Had I called it *Glaswegians* they might have paid more attention to the chapters from 2 to 11[...]. However, for excellent publicity reasons this book will keep its bad name until it is forgotten.

The cover is black with a colour photograph of what looks like a prostitute. This is probably the worst cover to any of Gray's works. Subsequent printings restore Gray's original cover design, but without the touches of colour on the lips and fingernails. Most of the description from the UK hardcover jacket appears on the back panel along with a selection of 'What the Critics Say'. One column is headed VERY FOR –

> Brilliantly funny, beautifully observed, and shot through with irony – Anne Smith, *Literary Review*

and the other NOT VERY FOR –

> A confection of self-indulgent tripe – Victoria Glendinning, *The Times*.

According to the author biography, Gray's

> first novel LANARK [...] came out in 1981. *Something Leather* is his last. For this edition he has corrected a few mistakes in the original and redesigned the opening and end pages.

In response to Dr Watson's protestations in the hardcover edition, there is a lighthouse keeper and cormorant (presumably trained) on the penultimate page.

6. Poor Things: Episodes from the Early Life of Archibald McCandless M.D. Scottish Public Health Officer

a) London: Bloomsbury Publishing, 1992.
   xiv, 319p; ill; £14.99; hbk   ISBN: 0-7475-1246-9

First edition. Dedication: For my wife Morag. Some copies were issued with an errata slip (4" x 6" card, printed in dark red) listing six mistakes, one of which is that the illustration on p187 'does not portray

Professor Jean Martin Charcot, but Count Robert de Montesquiou-Fezensac'.

This is the only Gray book to date not to end with 'Goodbye', though this is the title given to the final chapter of the McCandless narrative.

Purple endpapers and yellow ribbon bookmark. Slate grey boards blocked in silver with a repeating tall thistle motif. The familiar Gray motto, 'Work as if you live in the early days of a better nation', here credited on the title page verso to Denis Leigh, runs along the top of the front and back boards.

The colour wraparound jacket portrays the main characters, Baxter, Bella and McCandless, in a richly coloured interior setting; purple lettering runs round the illustration. The front flap carries two blurbs – one 'for a high-class hardback' and one 'for a popular paperback'. The back flap carries spoof reviews from Auberon Quinn in *Private Nose* and Paul Tomlin in the *Times Literary Implement*.

*b) New York: Harcourt Brace Jovanovich, 1992.
    xiv, 317p; ill; $21.95; hbk   ISBN: 0-15-173076-8

First US edition. Some copies were issued with an errata slip (3" x 4", printed in red) listing eleven mistakes, all but one of which are different from those listed on the UK errata slip. The duplicated 'mistake' is that of the illustration on p187.

The boards and jacket are very similar to the UK hardcover edition. The blurbs on the front flap are replaced with a plot description and a quote from *The Spectator*. The back flap carries a straight-faced author biography.

c) Harmondsworth: Penguin Books, 1993.
    xiv, 318p; ill; £5.99; pbk   ISBN: 0-14-017554-7

First paperback edition.

A mock biography of McCandless on the opening page laments the fact that his 'once famous epic *The Testament of Sawney Bean*, has long been unfairly neglected'. A mock erratum slip is printed on the following page together with a wide selection of quotes from reviews, good and bad, real and fake. Otherwise, apart from correcting typographical errors, the contents are as the UK hardcover edition.

The original jacket image has been reduced in size for the front cover. The back cover carries an amended version of the original 'Blurb for a Popular Paperback'.

d) San Diego: Harcourt Brace (Harvest), 1994.
   xiv, 317p; ill; $10.95; pbk   ISBN: 0-15-600068-7

First US paperback edition.

The contents are as the UK paperback edition, but without the McCandless biography, mock erratum slip and page of reviews. The back cover has a selection of quotes from American reviews alongside the proclamation that it was a *New York Times* Notable Book of the Year.

7. A History Maker

a) Edinburgh: Canongate Press, 1994.
   xv, 224p; ill; £13.99; hbk   ISBN: 0-86241-495-4

First edition. Dedication: For Chris Boyce.

Adapted from Gray's play *The History Maker* written in 1965 but never produced.

A variety of vignettes are used at chapter openings and closings – swords and shields, mothers with babies, chickens and toads, amongst others.

Acid-orange endpapers. Dark blue boards with silver blocking front and back with a design featuring a lattice background with a Scots pine stump putting forth a healthy new shoot and the motto 'TRY AGAIN'. The design was previously used on the 1993 hardcover edition of *Ten Tales Tall & True*. 'SCOTLAND' is printed along the bottom and is split in the middle by a spider dangling from the lattice. The spider motif recurs on the spine.

The colour jacket portrays an unusual amount of nudity. The author uses the front flap to apologise to the publisher that

> there is no porridge in this tale and Barrie's title is misquoted, but
> leave as given to distract reviewers from worse defects.

There is a portrait by Alasdair Taylor of the author on the back
flap with a list of Gray's works that, strangely, includes two books
yet to appear (as of 2001) and misses out *Lanark*.

Canongate had planned to publish a simultaneous paperback
edition and the assigned ISBN was included on the title page
verso of the hardcover. In the event the first paperback edition
was published by Penguin.

b) London: Penguin Books, 1995.
xv, 224p; ill; £5.99; pbk   ISBN: 0-14-024803-X

First paperback edition.

The text has been amended and corrected.

> This Penguin edition, published in 1995, has changes by the author
> which make it the text he wants reproduced in future editions. –
> t.p. verso.

According to Stephen Bernstein, these changes amount to a
rearrangement of the material at the end of the novel where the
details of the K20 plot and Meg Mountbenger's early life are
transferred from the Postscript to Kittock's notes.

The cover design is a simplified version of the hardcover jacket
design, whereby the main figures are placed against a less busy
background.

*c) San Diego: Harcourt Brace, 1996.
xv, 224p; ill; $25.00 (hbk), $14.00 (pbk)
                    ISBN: 0-15-100207-X (hbk); 0-15-600362-7 (pbk)

First US edition.

Issued simultaneously in hardcover and paperback.The text
follows the revised UK paperback edition.

The hardcover jacket uses a new version of the original artwork in
which the clouds are now swirls of blue and turquoise in a purple
night sky with moon and stars. The paperback cover uses the
same image but with an even darker night sky. It includes a quote
from the *Daily Telegraph*: 'Sir Walter Scott meets *Rollerball*'.

C. *Fiction First Published in Magazines or Anthologies*

1. **The Star**, in *Collins Magazine for Boys and Girls.* (May 1951), pp. 34-35.
   Later collected in *Unlikely Stories, Mostly.*

*2. **The Spread of Ian Nicol**, in *Ygorra* (Glasgow students' charity magazine) (1956).
   Later collected in *Unlikely Stories, Mostly.*

*3. **The Cause of Some Recent Changes**, in *Ygorra* (1957).
   Later collected in *Unlikely Stories, Mostly.*

4. **The Comedy of the White Dog** (first half only), in *Scottish International*, 8 (November 1969), pp. 18-21.
   Later collected in *The Comedy of the White Dog.*

5. **The Comedy of the White Dog**, in *GUM* (Glasgow University Magazine), vol. 81, number 3 (1970), pp. 3-9.
   Later collected in *The Comedy of the White Dog.*

6. **From the World of: Lanark**, in *Scottish International*, 12 (November 1970), pp. 30-40.
   Later collected as chapters 6 and 7 of *Lanark.*

*7. **The Crank that Made the Revolution**, in *The Scottish Field* (1971).
   Later collected in *Unlikely Stories, Mostly.*

8. **Alasdair Taylor**, in *Scottish International* (Oct-Nov 1973), pp. 18-21.
   Later published in *Cencrastus*, no. 18 (Autumn 1984), pp. 24-27 as 'Portrait of a Painter' and subsequently collected in *Lean Tales.*

*9. **A Small Thistle**, in *The Glasgow West End News* (1973).
   Later revised and collected in *Lean Tales.*

*10. **Prologue to Lanark**, in *GUM* (1974).
   Later published as part of *Lanark.*

*11. **From Lanark**, in *Words* (1978).
   Later collected as chapter 41 of *Lanark.*

*12. **Five Letters from an Eastern Empire**, in *Words* (1979).
Later collected in *Unlikely Stories, Mostly.*

*13. **From Lanark**, in *Words* (1979).
Later collected as chapter 35 of *Lanark.*

  14. **The Origin of the Axletree**, in *Scottish Short Stories 1979.* London:
Colllins, 1979, pp. 21-35.
Later collected in *Unlikely Stories, Mostly.*

*15. **The Answer**, in *Words* (1980).
Later collected in *Lean Tales.*

*16. **Joan Ure: 1919-1978**, in *Chapman,* 27/28 (1980/81), pp. 44-47.
Later collected as 'Portrait of a Playwright' in *Lean Tales.*

*17. **1982, Janine, Chapters 1-4**, in *The Short Story Monthly: Glasgow*
(October 1981, April 82, May 82 and June 82).
Later published in *1982, Janine.*

  18. **1982, Janine**, in *Cencrastus,* 6 (April 1983), pp. 25-26.
Later published in *1982, Janine.*

*19. **1982, Janine**, in *Firebird 3: New Writing from Britain and Ireland.*
Harmondsworth: Penguin Books, 1984.
Later published as the first 22 paragraphs of chapter 12 in *1982,
Janine.*

*20. **The Grumbler**, in *Fiction Magazine* (March 1985), pp. 11-12.
Later collected in *Lean Tales.*

  21. **The New World**, in *Fiction Magazine* (March 1987), pp. 12-13.
Later collected in *Ten Tales Tall and True.*

*22. **Near the Driver: A Play for Radio**, in *Chapman,* 50/51
(summer/winter 1987), pp. 87-99.
Later adapted as a short story in *Ten Tales Tall and True.*

*23. **The History Maker**, in *Chapman,* 50/51 (summer/winter 1987),
pp. 128-131.

*24. **The New World**, in *Landfall,* vol. 43, no. 2 (1989), pp. 151-153.
Later collected in *Ten Tales Tall and True.*

*25. **Lanark Storyboard**, in *Scottish Book Collector*, vol. 2, no. 2 (Oct-Nov 1989), pp. 16-17.

Storyboards for a projected film of *Lanark*, published irregularly between vol. 2, no. 2 (1989) and vol. 5, no. 10 (1997).

*26. **Jesus Christ**, in *The Sunday Independent* (17 March 1991).

Later collected as 'The Marriage Feast' in *Ten Tales Tall and True*.

27. **Homeward Bound**, in *New Writing* / edited by Malcolm Bradbury and Judy Cooke. London: Minerva in association with the British Council, 1992, pp. 22-32.

Later collected in *Ten Tales Tall and True*.

28. **The Loss of the Golden Silence**, in *Bête Noire* 12/13 (autumn 1991/spring 1992), pp. 233-252.

Later collected in *Ten Tales Tall and True*.

29. **You**, in *Casablanca* 4 (May-June 1993), pp. 32-35.

Later collected in *Ten Tales Tall and True*.

*30. **Houses and Small Labour Parties**, in *Living Issues* (August 1993).

Later collected in *Ten Tales Tall and True*.

*31. **Mr Meikle**, in *The Glasgow Herald* (summer 1993).

Later collected in *Ten Tales Tall and True*.

*32. **The Trendelenburg Position**, in *The Glasgow Herald* (summer 1993).

Later collected in *Ten Tales Tall and True*.

33. **Money**, in *Scotlands* 1 (1994), pp. 104-109.

Later collected in *Mavis Belfrage*.

34. **Edison's Tractatus**, in *The Printer's Devil*, issue D (1994), pp. 11-12.

Later collected in *Mavis Belfrage*.

35. **The Shortest Tale**, in *Madam X* 1 (spring 1996), p. 19.

Later collected in *Mavis Belfrage*.

36. **Big Pockets with Buttoned Flaps**, in *New Writing* 9 / edited by John Fowles and A. L. Kennedy. London: Vintage, 2000, pp 10-14.

D. *Poetry Collections & Anthologies*

1. **Old Negatives: Four Verse Sequences**

a) London: Jonathan Cape, 1989.
67p; ill; £15.00 (hbk), £5.95 (pbk)
ISBN: 0-224-02304-7 (hbk); 0-224-02656-9 (pbk)

First edition. Issued simultaneously in a hardcover printing of 500 signed and numbered copies and a paperback printing of 1,000 copies. Dedication: Amy Fleming 11-1-1902 24-5-1952. Most hardcover copies were issued with an errata sheet in Gray's facsimile handwriting dated 13 February 1989. It listed a series of errors that he asked 'the reader to correct for him' and requested the reader to ignore the poem 'Awaiting'.

CONTENTS: **In A Cold Room 1952-57:** Time And Place; Predicting; Loneliness; Mistaken; Split Unit Experiment; Cries Of Unceilinged Blood; Accept, Reject; Two; Gods; Reflecting Seashell. **Between Whiles 1957-61:** Unfit; Inside The Box; I Assume; Vacancy; Under The Water; Lamenting Alan Fletcher; Cowardly; Lost Absence; Announcement. **Inge Sørensen 1961-71:** Woundscape; Married; Mishap; Declaration; To Andrew, Before One; Both Perspectives; Awakening; Unlovely; Not Striving. **To Lyric Light 1977-83:** The Thinker; Wanting; Awaiting; Renewal; Cares; For Grass; Ripeness; Unlocks; A Burning; Lyrical; End.

The title page and table of contents are illustrated. Each sequence of verses is introduced by an illustrated section title page.
Pale grey endpapers. Black boards blocked in silver with an image of a fantastic creature – part woman, part gryphon – plunging a spear into a skull. The spear has roots at its point and a phoenix nests in branches sprouting from its hilt. A banner entwined in the branches proclaims 'Amy Fleming 1902-1952' (a tribute to Gray's mother).
The jacket, printed on linen wove paper, features black and white illustrations that run continuously from the front flap to the back flap. These are credited as 'from a set made in 1969-71 with help

from a Scottish Arts Council grant'. They depict male and female winged nudes dwarfing public buildings that fly flags emblazoned with either the word NO or YES (the NOs outnumber the YESes, perhaps reflecting the title). The front flap says that:

> Alasdair Gray's fiction is about modern states of love, faith, language and politics. The verses [...] deal with the same things, omitting politics. They have been written at different times since 1952 and are arranged chronologically to suggest growth. They are negative because they describe love mainly by its absences and reverses.

The paperback cover features the angel-in-a-skull motif that has become Gray's mark.

2. Vier + Four / Wolfgang Heyder, Joe Davie, Liz Lochhead, Christian Rothmann, Ernest Wichner, Murray Robertson, Alasdair Gray, Toni Wirthmèuller

*a) Glasgow, Berlin: Glasgow Print Studio, Edition Mariannenpresse, 1990.
54p (unnumbered); ill; £500.00; hbk

Limited edition of 150 copies in slipcase plus 30 copies signed by the contributors.

Comprises prints by four artists and texts by four writers, two of each from Glasgow and Berlin. Gray's contribution is the poem 'First of March 1990', later to appear as the opening poem in *Sixteen Occasional Poems*. The poem appears over eight pages, a verse to each page with a statement on the ninth page. Each verse is printed in a different position on the page to indicate the plane to Berlin taking off and landing. The texts in translation are included in a loosely inserted pamphlet.

Black cloth boards impressed with the title. The slipcase has the title printed in red.

3. **Eight Poems Written from 2 to 5 August 1998 on Eight Series of Prints by Ian McCulloch.** In: The Artist in His World: Prints 1986-1997 / Ian McCulloch with descriptive poems by Alasdair Gray

a) Glendaruel: Argyll Publishing, 1998.

112p; ill; £20.00; hbk   ISBN: 1-874640-14-9

First edition.

CONTENTS: Adam and Eve; Six Variations on a Still Life; Biblical Themes (Shuffled Like Dreams); Tales from the Polish Woods; Bosnian Heads; Agamemnon's Return; No Way Out; Alba.

Gray and McCulloch first met at Glasgow's Eastbank Academy in June 1952 and they both went on to the Glasgow School of Art. McCulloch and Gray visited Gibraltar and Andalucia in 1958, a trip which Gray later recounted in the story 'A Report to the Trustees', collected in *Lean Tales*. Gray's poems complement McCulloch's woodcuts. In his preface McCulloch writes:

> I still remember the shock of discovering at that time [the 1950s]
> Alasdair Gray's drawings made with biro – I still have one of the
> drawings on a fragment of newspaper from this period. It is a head
> – perhaps a self-portrait – which I took great delight in
> paraphrasing when developing the head of Adam for the
> 'Hyperborean Adam' print.

4. **Sixteen Occasional Poems: 1990-2000**

a) Glasgow: Morag McAlpine, 2000.

34p; £40.00 (hbk), £5.00 (pbk)

ISBN: 0-9538359-1-X (hbk); 0-9538359-0-1 (pbk)

First edition. Dedication: For my wife. Issued simultaneously in a hardcover printing of 200 signed and numbered copies and a paperback printing.

CONTENTS: First of March 1990; Winter Housekeeping; Waiting in Galway; South Africa April 1994; Postmodernism; Genesis; Dear Colleague; Epitaph 1998; Eden; Biblical Themes (Shuffled Like Dreams); Agamemnon's Return; Tales from the

Polish Woods; Bosnian Heads; No Way; Alba; To Tom Leonard; Postscript on What Occasioned the Foregoing Verses.

The poems are printed on blue paper in the hardcover with toning endpapers, and on grey paper with blue endpapers in the paperback. The blurb on the back cover of the paperback explains that the poems:

> were written when Gray was mainly working on his BOOK OF PREFACES, and reflects some themes in that book: self-government, love, god, legends, language and some national states.

The blue leather-covered boards of the hardcover are blocked in silver, front and back, with an image of an angel stepping out of a skull, the rising sun in the background. It was issued without a jacket. The same image, printed in red and black, appears on the front cover of the paperback and is also used on the title page of both editions.

E. *Poetry First Published in Magazines*

*1. **Terrible Structures Have Been Erected Upon the Skyline**, in *Lines Review*, 19 (winter 1962-63), p. 36.
   Later collected as 'Unfit' in *Old Negatives*.

*2. **For Two Or Three Weeks She Walked As If She Was Protecting Something**, in *Lines Review*, 20 (summer 1963), p. 36.
   Later collected as 'Vacancy' in *Old Negatives*.

*3. **Most Hearts Grow by Love**, in *Lines Review*, 22 (winter 1966), p. 25.
   Later collected as 'Lost Absence' in *Old Negatives*.

4. **On a Small Boy, at 8 Months**, in *GUM*, vol. 82, no. 3 (May 1971), p. 27
   Later collected as 'To Andrew, Before One' in *Old Negatives*.

*5. **Not Striving**, in *The Glasgow Review* (summer 1972).
   Later collected in *Old Negatives*.

*6. **Cowardly, Lost Absence, The Thinker,** in *Strata* (1984).
Later collected in *Old Negatives.*

7. **Inside the Box,** in *Clanjamfrie,* 1 (January 1984).
Later collected in *Old Negatives.*

8. **Loneliness,** in *Clanjamfrie,* 2 (September 1984).
Later collected in *Old Negatives.*

*9. **Old Negatives,** in *Chapman* 50/51 (summer/winter 1987),
pp. 118-127.
Later collected as the sequence 'In a Cold Room' in *Old Negatives.*

*10. **Between Whiles: 1957-61,** in *Prospice* (summer 1988).
Later collected in *Old Negatives.*

11. **Poems: 1962-71,** in *Bête Noire* 5 (spring 1988), pp. 45-53.
Later collected as the sequence 'Inge Sørensen: 1961-71' in *Old Negatives.* This issue also included an interview with Gray by Sean Figgis and Andrew McAllister.

12. **A Postmodern Hymn to Obscurity,** in *Times Literary Supplement* (11 August 1995), p. 10.
Later collected as 'Postmodernism' in *Sixteen Occasional Poems.*

13. **Winter Housekeeping, Waiting in Galway, South Africa April 1996,** in *New Writing 5* / edited by Christopher Hope and Peter Porter. London: Vintage, 1996, pp. 439-440.
Later collected in *Sixteen Occasional Poems.*

*14. **First of March 1990,** in *West Coast Magazine* (1997).
Later collected in *Sixteen Occasional Poems.*

*15. **Dear Colleague,** in *West Coast Magazine* (1998).
Later collected in *Sixteen Occasional Poems.*

16. **The Dictators,** in *Times Literary Supplement* (5 October 2001),
p. 36.

F. *Plays*

1. **Dialogue**

*a) Kirknewton: Scottish Theatre, 1971.

26p; unpriced; pbk (Play of the month; no. 3)

First UK edition.

Broadcast by BBC radio in 1969 and produced for television in 1972. More recently used as the basis for the chapter 'A Free Man with a Pipe' in *Something Leather*.

Produced in plain green covers without illustrations.

2. **Working Legs: a Two-Act Play for People Without Them**

a) Glasgow: Dog & Bone, 1997.

144p; ill; £5.00; pbk (Dog & Bone playbook; no. 1)

ISBN: 1-872536-17-4

First edition. Dedication: To Baroness Thatcher and all the Right Honourable Humpty Dipsies who have made our new, lean, fit, efficient Britain.

In 1996, Gray was asked to write a play for Birds of Paradise, a professional theatre company providing drama training for people with physical disabilities. He had not written a play since 1978, but enthusiastically threw himself into the project. It was premiered at the Traverse Theatre in Edinburgh on 20 June 1998. The performing rights remain the property of Birds of Paradise.

The text is illustrated with pen and ink portraits of members of the original production cast. There is a five-page description at the end of 'How This Play Got Written'.

The blue, red and black cover features pen and ink portraits of six members of the original production cast. The back panel carries a brief description of the play with a new Dog & Bone logo of a dog, similar to the White Dog, enjoying a bone.

Scenes 8 and 9 were first published in *West Coast Magazine* 23 (1996); scenes 2 and 10 in *The Glasgow Herald* (15 November 1997).

G. *Non-Fiction*

1. **Alasdair Gray**

a) Edinburgh: The Saltire Society, 1988.
   19p; £2.00; pbk (Saltire self-portraits; 4)   ISBN: 0-85411-043-7

The booklet consists of a short essay in two parts, either side of a 7-page history by Gray's father, Alexander Gray, about his own father and other early memories. It ends with the transcript of a 1982 BBC interview with Alasdair Gray by Christopher Swan and Frank Delaney.
The blue card cover is illustrated with a pen and ink self-portrait of Gray.

2. **Why Scots Should Rule Scotland: Independence**

a) Edinburgh: Canongate, 1992.
   64p; £3.00; pbk   ISBN: 0-86241-391-5
   First edition.

Written as a political tract for the United Kingdom's 1992 General Election, the text explains 'why so many Scots have wanted independence; haven't got it; should get it soon; and why life in a self-governed Scotland will be better but not easier'.
The text is not illustrated. The cover, designed by James Hutcheson, features a yellow lion rampant placed behind the title information. Royalities from the sale of the book went to Clydeside Action Against Asbestos.

3. **Why Scots Should Rule Scotland, 1997: a Carnaptious History of Britain from Roman Times Until Now**

a) Edinburgh: Canongate Books, 1997.

118p; £4.99; pbk   ISBN: 0-86241-671-X

Dedication: To Scott Pearson with thanks for all his help with this and many other books.

In his introduction Gray writes:

> With a view to reprinting [*Why Scots Should Rule Scotland*] I read it carefully three months ago and found it a muddle of unconnected historical details and personal anecdotes with a few lucid passages and at least one piece of nonsense [...]. The reviewers' kindness had been the condescension instinctively given to the art of children or half-wits.

Flags, predominantly the Scottish lion and the cross of St Andrew, are used throughout the text. The grey cover displays in colour the flags, names and populations of twenty independent nations of smaller or comparable size to Scotland.

4. **The Book of Prefaces: a Short History of Literate Thought in Words by Great Writers of Four Nations from the 7th to the 20th Century / edited & glossed by Alasdair Gray mainly**

a) London and New York: Bloomsbury Publishing, 2000.

640p; ill; £35.00; hbk   ISBN: 0-7475-4443-3

First edition. Dedication: To Philip Hobsbaum: Poet, Critic and Servant of Servants of Art. Some copies were issued with two errata slips.

Gray's ambitious anthology finally came into the world after sixteen years and a change of title from *Anthology of Prefaces*. The work had been so confidently predicted for so long that several books on collecting modern first editions listed it as published in 1989 and gave suggested values for it. Fortunately, for a project so long in gestation, it was (on the whole) very well received by the critics.

The book is heavily illustrated and includes pen and ink portraits of forty-three of the key contributors. The text is printed in red and black throughout. Within the 176 prefaces small typeface in red ink climbs the margins, creating the look of a Bible. In his 'Advertisement', Gray gives four reasons for enjoying reading his prefaces, one of which is 'seeing great writers in a huff'.

Both errata slips, also printed in red and black, are introduced in rhyme. The first, An Appeal to the Buyer, reads:

> When this book was printed and bound
> Twenty-two errors were found.
> The volume is therefore defective
> Unless YOU supply a corrective.
> Please take a pen in your fist
> And mend these mistakes that we missed.

The second, Editor's Postscript to the First List of Errors, reads:

> I regret and deplore
> that I've found fourteen more
> and probably you
> will find several too.

The blue endpapers are printed with elements from *Lanark* and the jacket of *Old Negatives*. A man ponders his own head on a board and a woman gives birth, overseen by a crowned skeletal Death. Down both sides are a list of alternatives (Commonwealth v. Empire, Co-operate v. Compete, Freedom v. Force), whilst framing it all are the two giant nudes from *Old Negatives*. The blue boards are blocked in gold with the flags of England, Scotland, Ireland and the USA. The epigraph 'Work as if you live in the early days of a better nation' has been added to the front and back. The jacket is printed in red and black on a white background, with touches of gold. It is illustrated with thirty-two portraits of writers whose prefaces are featured in the book. The front flap has a self-portrait with a crown of thistle above the caption 'Our Editor Confronts Critics'. The Author's Blurb follows:

> Only the rich and illiterate can afford to ignore our anthology. With this in their lavatory everyone else can read nothing but newspaper supplements and still seem educated.

The self-portrait, this time viewed from the rear, reappears on the back flap above the caption 'Our Editor Evades the Critics'. The Publisher's Blurb follows:

> This book is NOT a monster created by a literary Baron Frankenstein.

*b) New York: Bloomsbury, 2000.

672p; ill; $49.95; hbk   ISBN: 1-58234-037-4

First US edition.

As the UK edition.

5. A Short Survey of Classic Scottish Writing

a) Edinburgh: Canongate, 2001.

xiv, 159p; £1.99; pbk (Canongate pocket classics; no. 7)

ISBN: 1-84195-167-6

First edition. Dedication: To Tom Leonard.

Originally the volume was only available as part of a boxed set of the first seven pocket classics, priced at £9.99.

The cover illustration, printed on a metallic silver background, is Gray's 'A Scottish Literary Lion' – a red heraldic Scottish lion, quill in one front paw, the other on a laptop computer and a hind paw on a mouse. A scroll of paper headed 'Nemo' spills from the laptop.

H. *Essays, Introductions & Postscripts*

1. Postscript to: **Gentlemen of the West** / Agnes Owens.

Harmondsworth: Penguin Books, 1986.

141p; £2.95; pbk   ISBN: 0-14-008610-2

Gray gives a fine, if unfocused, review of novels written by and about the working class. *Lucky Jim, Room at the Top* and *Look Back in Anger* are dismissed as unreflective of the true working classes. Instead Gray looks to books like *A Kestrel for a Knave, This*

Sporting Life, Billy Liar and *The Loneliness of the Long Distance Runner*:

> These stories demonstrate the Great British assumption, which is also the Great British lie, that any special talent, initiative or knowledge not advertised as *popular* is a property of the affluent, a luxury of the posh. This particular lie [...] lets Royalty, the government and most professional people raise their wages and keep themselves employed without drawing much attention, and ensures that coalminers who try to do the same are treated like greedy unpatriotic scoundrels and enemies of the state.

Gray's hardcover jacket design was not used on the paperback.

2. Essay in: **Pierre Lavalle: Paintings 1947-1975**. Glasgow: Lavalle Retrospective Group, 1990.
   8p; ill; unpriced; pbk   ISBN: 0-9515960-0-4

Produced to accompany an exhibition of Lavalle's paintings held at Govan's Pearce Institute from 4-31 August 1990, the pamphlet contains Gray's essay, two black and white reproductions of Lavalle's work and a black and white photograph of Lavalle. The three-page essay details Lavalle's career and focuses on his connections to Glasgow, especially on his faith that true art, produced wherever, is valuable:

> Pierre Lavalle was the only [artist] I met who understood that for all but a lucky few it is as hard to be a good artist in London as Glasgow, and that fine art was worth making, whoever ignored it.

3. Introduction to: **A Real Glasgow Archipelago** / Jack Withers. Glendaruel: Argyll Publishing, 1993.
   96p; ill; £4.95; pbk   ISBN: 1-874640-25-4

A collection of poetry by Jack Withers, illustrated with woodcuts by Ian McCulloch. In the eleven-page introduction, Gray writes about the state of Glasgow's art and the morale of its artists at the time Glasgow became European City of Culture in 1990. He also includes some autobiographical background.

4. Essay (The Wasting of Old English Speech and How a New Was Got) in: **Soho Square VII: New Scottish Writing** / edited by Harry Ritchie. London: Bloomsbury, 1996.
252p   ISBN: 0-7475-2824-1

Reissued in paperback as *Acid Plaid*. Later collected in *The Book of Prefaces*.

5. Introduction to: **The Books Of Jonah, Micah and Nahum: authorised King James version** / with an introduction by Alasdair Gray. Edinburgh: Canongate, 1999.
xiv, 34p; £1.50; pbk (Pocket canon)   ISBN: 0-86241-971-9

In his eight-page introduction Gray united certain Muslim and Jewish groups in their condemnation. The front cover is illustrated with a black and white photograph of a whale's tail.

6. Essays (The Home Rule Handbook) in: **What a State!: Is Devolution for Scotland the End of Britain** / edited by Alan Taylor. London: HarperCollins, 2000.
xvii, 282p; £8.99; pbk   ISBN: 0-00-653218-7

These six pieces were nominally by both Gray and Angus Calder, although they were mostly written by Calder. The essays were originally published in *The Scotsman* in February 1991.

7. Introduction to: **Sartor Resartus** / Thomas Carlyle. Edinburgh: Canongate, 2002.
384p; £7.99; pbk   ISBN: 1-84195-278-8

I.   *Non-Fiction First Published in Magazines*

*1. **Instead of an Apology**, in *Glasgow Herald* (18 April 1969).

*2. **Education**, in *Glasgow Magazine*, 1 (winter 1982/83), pp. 7-9.

*3. **A Modest Proposal for Bypassing a Predicament**, in *Chapman*, 35/36 (1983), pp. 43-46.

4. **Thoughts Suggested by Agnes Owens's 'Gentlemen of the West' – And an Appreciation of it**, in *Edinburgh Review*, 71 (1985), pp. 27-32.

   Later issued as a postscript to the paperback edition of Owens' book.

*5. **The Curse of Burrell**, in *Glasgow Herald*, Weekender (6 December 1986), pp. 1, 3.

6. **Everything Leading to the First English**, in *Chapman*, 63 (spring 1991), pp. 1-13.

   Later collected, as 'Essay on what led to English Literature', in *The Book of Prefaces*.

*7. **Elspeth King**, in *The Independent* (13 July 1991), p. 46.

*8. **Frankly Gray**, in *The List* (28 Aug-10 Sept 1992), p. 63.

9. **Light and Heat: Scottish Eccentrics**, in *Cencrastus*, 47 (spring 1994), pp. 38-41.

10. **Museum**, in *Scotlands* 1 (1994), pp. 110-116.

11. **Letter in response to essay 'Concplags and Totplag: Lanark Exposed' by MacDonald Daly** in *Edinburgh Review*, 93 (1995), p. 200.

12. **Galt**, in *Southfields* (1996), pp. 37-39.

13. **How Much Do You Think a Writer Needs To Live On?** in *How Much Do You Think A Writer Needs To Live On?* / edited by Andrew Holgate and Honor Wilson-Fletcher. London: Waterstones Booksellers Ltd, 1998, pp. 60-61.

   Gray, along with forty-one other contemporary writers, answered six questions on writers' income and employment.

14. **On Neglect of Burns by Schools and His Disparagement by Moralists and Whitewashers with Some Critical Remarks**, in *Studies in Scottish Literature*, vol. 30 (1998), pp. 175-180.

*15. **The Home Rule Handbook**, in *The Scotsman*, (12, 13, 15, 16, 17 & 19 February 1999).

   Later collected in *What a State!*

*16. **Three National Bodies Reject a Head,** in *Chapman* (autumn 1999).

Later collected in *The Book of Prefaces.*

J. *Catalogues*

1. Alasdair Gray: Retrospective Exhibition

a) Glasgow: Strathclyde University, 1974.
   24p

A descriptive catalogue to accompany an exhibition held in the Collins Exhibition Hall, Strathclyde University, Glasgow, 27 February-26 March 1974. The text is by Alasdair Gray with poems by Liz Lochhead.

The front cover image is of a male nude figure inset with a female nude figure, towering over public buildings. The image was later developed for the jacket of *Old Negatives.*

2. 5 Scottish Artists Retrospective Show: Five Colour Catalogues and an Introduction by Alasdair Gray / Carole Gibbons, John Connolly, Alan Fletcher, Alasdair Taylor, Alasdair Gray

a) Gartocharn: Famedram, 1986.
   5 folded sheets + 1 leaflet in plastic wallet; unpriced

CONTENTS: Full colour reproductions (except where stated) of: A Self Portrait (b&w); The Cowcaddens in the Fifties (1964); Eden and After (1966); Snakes and Ladders (1973); Dawn Firth (197?); Janet on Red Felt (1980)

The '5 Scottish Artists Show' was held at the MacLellan Gallery in Glasgow in December 1986, travelling to Edinburgh and Aberdeen the following year

The catalogue comprised five folded sheets (one for each artist) about 4' x 1' when unfolded, printed on one side only. Each artist's sheet gives a potted biography, lists their works in the exhibition and reproduces selected works. Gray's sheet records, in chronological order (as far as the artist could remember), 148 pictures, some with brief autobiographical notes about what occasioned them. Fletcher's sheet ends with Gray's poem 'Lamenting Alan Fletcher', later to appear (slightly revised) in *Old Negatives.*

The 8-page introduction leaflet was written by Gray. It places himself and his fellow artists within Scotland's twentieth-century art history, and includes some poignant comments:

> Alan Fletcher is the only artist I know who naturally looked like the Bohemian artist of legend. He was the free-est soul I ever met, and impressed me so mightily that a diminished version of him has been a main character in all the novels I ever wrote. He had to be diminished, or he would have stolen attention from my main characters, who were versions of me.

K. *Book Design & Illustration*

This list does not include occasional illustrations in magazines, and 16 cover designs for the magazine *Chapman*. Where not stated otherwise, Gray has only designed the cover of the following books and pamphlets.

1. **A Scent of Water** / Carl MacDougall. Glasgow: The Molendinar Press, 1975.
    112p; ill; £3.50 (hbk), £2.50 (pbk)
    ISBN: 0-904002-12-8 (hbk); 0-904002-10-1 (pbk)
    A collection of modern folk tales. Gray illustrated the stories and designed the jacket with motifs reminiscent of Greek epic tales (castles, rearing horses, armoured half-naked soldiers waving spears).

2. **The Illlustrated Gaelic-English Dictionary**: Containing Every Gaelic Word and Meaning Given In All Previously Published Dictionaries, and A Great Number Never In Print Before, To Which Is Prefixed A Concise Gaelic Grammar / compiled by Edward Dwelly. 9th ed. Glasgow: Gairm Publications, 1977.
    xiv, 1034p; ill; hbk   ISBN: 0-901771-92-9

3. **Imaginary Wounds** / Aonghas MacNeacail. Glasgow: Print
   Studio Press, 1980.
   28p; £0.95; pbk   ISBN: 0-906112-16-8

4. **Grafts; Takes** / Edwin Morgan. Glasgow: Mariscat, 1983.
   28,28p; £3.00; pbk   ISBN: 0-946588-00-7
   Cover artwork. Gray also designed the publisher's feline logo.

5. **A Bad Day for the Sung Dynasty** / Frank Kuppner. Manchester:
   Carcanet, 1984.
   144p; £4.95; pbk   ISBN: 0-856355-14-3
   The front cover features Gray's interpretation of a Sung Mona
   Lisa.

6. **Gentlemen of the West** / Agnes Owens. Edinburgh: Polygon
   Books, 1984.
   127p; £6.95; hbk   ISBN: 0-904919-79-X
   Gray designed the jacket and later wrote a Postscript to the
   paperback edition.

7. **The Glasgow Diary** / Donald Saunders, mainly. Edinburgh:
   Polygon Books, 1984.
   256p; ill; £8.95; hbk   ISBN: 0-904919-75-7
   A day-by-day collection of 365 true incidents culled from
   Glasgow's history. Gray contributed marginal symbols used to
   indicate the subject or moral tone of the entry. His illustrations
   also included two versions of Glasgow's coat of arms, a portrait of
   Bill Skinner, and a drawing of 'Glasgow Green in the late
   Carboniferous Era, viewed from the site of Glasgow High Court
   of Justice, Stockwell Street'. Gray also wrote the entries for 2
   April, 24 May, 19 September, and 14 October.

8. **Sonnets from Scotland** / Edwin Morgan. Glasgow:
   Mariscat, 1984.
   64p; £3.75; pbk   ISBN: 0-946588-06-6

9. **Shoestring Gourmet** / Wilma Paterson. Edinburgh: Canongate,
   1986.
   156p; ill; £3.95; pbk   ISBN: 0-86241-110-6
   The book is designed and copiously illustrated by Gray in a
   lighthearted style. The recurring motifs include fish-heads, elves

getting up to culinary mischief, and hares running off with the sausages. Instead of ending Goodbye (as Gray's books do), the text ends Fare Thee Well. A drawing of the author appears as a frontispiece.

The front cover depicts a couple tucking into a meal of fish; on the back cover the table, now deserted, has the remains of the meal alongside one shoe from each diner.

> The witty illustrations suggest that sensuality is another ingredient that cooking need not lack. – Back cover

10. **Anti-Foundationalism and Practical Reasoning**: Conversations Between Hermeneutics and Analysis / edited by Evan Simpson. Edmonton, Canada: Academic Printing, 1987.
    254p; hbk   ISBN: 0-920980-26-0

11. **Petronius – The Book** / Andrew Lothian. London & Edinburgh: Butterworth & Law Society of Scotland, 1988.
    x, 95p; pbk   ISBN: 0-406-10396-8

12. **Snakes and Ladders** / edited by H. T. Robertson. London: Unwin Hyman, 1988.
    160p; £2.95; pbk   ISBN: 0-04-448004-0

In 1990 Angela Mullane set up the publishing company Dog & Bone. Gray was responsible for the logo, typographical design and covers of the following Dog & Bone books.

13. **Blooding Mister Naylor** / Chris Boyce. Glasgow: Dog and Bone, 1990.
    254p; £5.00; pbk   ISBN: 1-872536-04-2

14. **The Canongate Strangler** / Angus McAllister. Glasgow: Dog and Bone, 1990.
    220p; £5.00; pbk   ISBN: 1-872536-10-7

15. **Findrinny**: Selected Poems / Donald Saunders. Glasgow: Dog and Bone, 1990.
    64p; £4.50; pbk   ISBN: 1-872536-08-5

16. **Lord Byron's Relish**: Regency Recipes with Notes Culinary &
Byronic / Wilma Paterson. Glasgow: Dog & Bone, 1990.
139p; ill; £7.50; pbk　　　　　　　　ISBN: 1-872536-02-6
The book is dedicated to Gray who was responsible for the
typographic design but not the cover artwork.

17. **A Sense of Something Strange**: Investigations into the
Paranormal / Archie E. Roy. Glasgow: Dog and Bone, 1990.
300p; ill; £7.50; pbk　　　　　　　　ISBN: 1-872536-06-9

18. **Tramontana** / Hugh McMillan. Glasgow: Dog and Bone, 1990.
72p; £4.50; pbk　　　　　　　　ISBN: 1-872536-11-5

19. **Up Wyster!** / David Morrison. Wick: Pulteney Press, 1990.
38p; £4.50; pbk　　　　　　　　ISBN: 0-947861-40-8

20. **Fighting For Survival**: The Steel Industry in Scotland / James
Kelman. Glasgow: Clydeside Press, 1990.
16p; pbk　　　　　　　　ISBN: 0-9512057-5-7

21. **The Child Within** / Catherine Munroe. London: The Children's
Society, 1993.
115p; £4.95; pbk　　　　　　　　ISBN: 0-907324-73-8

22. **Scotland's Relations With England**: A Survey to 1707 / William
Ferguson. London: The Saltire Society, 1994.
vii, 319p; £12.99; pbk　　　　　　　　ISBN: 0-85411-058-5

23. **Move up, John** / Fionn MacColla; edited and introduced by John
Herdman. Edinburgh: Canongate Press, 1994.
218p; ill; £8.99; pbk　　　　　　　　ISBN: 0-86241-381-8
Dog and Bone are credited with the book design and Gray has
contributed six austere line drawings used as chapter title pages.

24. **A Working Mother** / Agnes Owens. London: Bloomsbury, 1994.
187p; £9.99; hbk　　　　　　　　ISBN: 0-7475-1714-2

25. **People Like That** / Agnes Owens. London: Bloomsbury, 1996.
276p; £13.99; hbk　　　　　　　　ISBN: 0-7475-2522-6
Gray's cover artwork portrays the characters from the stories.

26. **The Songs of Scotland**: a hundred of the best / edited by Wilma Paterson. Edinburgh: Mainstream, 1996.
220p; ill; £25.00; hbk   ISBN: 1-85158-722-5
Designed and illustrated by Gray, the text is printed throughout in black and red. The cream endpapers are printed with a parade of kilted Highlanders in bare feet carrying giant thistles. The blue boards are blocked with a design using the cross of St Andrew, bagpipes, harps and fiddles with a central bird perched on a tree stump with the exhortation: 'Sing as if you live in the early days of a better nation'.
The colourful jacket portrays a lady singing to her friends accompanied by a fiddler. There are portraits of both the editor and the illustrator on the back flap.

27. **Studies in Scottish Literature**: volume 30 / edited by G. Ross Roy. South Carolina: Department of English, University of South Carolina, 1998.   ISSN: 0039-3770
In addition to contributing an essay on Burns, Gray illustrated this special issue. Most of the illustrations had originally appeared in *Songs of Scotland*. A postcard from Gray to the editor, apologising for his incorrect Latin on the cover design, was printed inside the book.

28. **The World of C.L.R. James**: The Unfragmented Vision / James D. Young. Glasgow: Clydeside Press, 1999.
vii, 392p; pbk   ISBN: 1-873586-26-4

29. **A Twentieth Century Life** / Paul Henderson Scott. Glendaruel: Argyll Publishing, 2002.   ISBN: 1-902831-36-5

L. *Audio Recordings*

1. **Some Unlikely Stories**. Edinburgh: Canongate Audio, 1994.
   2 audio cassettes (140 mins); £8.99   ISBN: 1-85968-085-2

   CONTENTS: The Star; The Spread of Ian Nicol; The Problem;
   The Cause of Some Recent Changes; The Crank That Made The
   Revolution; The Comedy of the White Dog; Five Letters from an
   Eastern Empire

   Read by the author.

   This is a 'personal selection' of stories from *Unlikely Stories, Mostly.*
   The cover design features the kite picture from *Five Letters from
   an Eastern Empire* together with the angel-in-a-skull motif.

2. **Scenes from Alasdair Gray's Lanark**: volume 1 – Lanark and
   Rima. Edinburgh: Canongate Audio, 1995.
   2 audio cassettes (180 mins); £7.99   ISBN: 1-85968-091-7

   Abridged and read by the author.

   Features the story of Lanark and Rima in Unthank and the
   Institute from Book Three of *Lanark*. The cover design,
   confusingly perhaps, is the title page for Book Four of the novel.
   The text on the packaging reads: 'This recording is the first part
   of a four-volume set', although as of 2002, only two volumes have
   appeared. (The wording was left off volume two).

3. **Scenes from Alasdair Gray's Lanark**: volume 2. Edinburgh:
   Canongate Audio, 1996.
   2 audio cassettes (180 mins.); £8.99   ISBN: 1-85968-091-7

   Abridged and read by the author.

   Features the story of Duncan Thaw, beginning with the Oracle's
   prologue, from Book One of *Lanark*. The cover design is the title
   page from Book Three of the novel.

M. *Critical Works*

Essays may be found scattered throughout journals (especially the admirable *Chapman*, *Cencrastus* and *Edinburgh Review*) and the odd doctoral thesis has been written, but otherwise, in addition to the book in hand, the main academic sources are listed here.

1. **The Arts of Alasdair Gray** / edited by Robert Crawford and Thom Nairn. Edinburgh: Edinburgh University Press, 1991.

   This is the best source book on all aspects of Gray's creative output though coverage only extends to 1990.

2. **Alasdair Gray** / Stephen Bernstein. Lewisburg: Bucknell University Press, 1999.

   An excellent work on Gray's novels with interesting notes and a useful bibliography.

3. **Review of Contemporary Fiction**, vol. 15, issue 2 (1995).

   This special issue covering Alasdair Gray and Stanley Elkin contains an interesting selection of essays written in a variety of styles from Professor Hobsbaum's Leavisite reading of Gray's 'voice' to Janice Galloway's warm description of Gray's influence upon her own writing.

N. *Bibliographies*

1. **Brian Moore, Alasdair Gray, John McGahern**: A Bibliography of their First Editions / David Rees. London: The Colophon Press, 1991.
   24p; £6.00; pbk (ColophonPress bibliography series; no. 1)
   ISBN: 1-874122-00-8 (numbered); 1-874122-01-6 (lettered)
   Limited edition of 600 numbered copies and 26 signed lettered copies

   This has useful information on print-runs and brief descriptions of the jackets and boards. Proof copies, not covered in this bibliography, are also listed.

2. **Checklists and Unpublished Materials by Alasdair Gray** / Bruce Charlton. In: *The Arts of Alasdair Gray* / edited by Robert Crawford and Thom Nairn. Edinburgh: Edinburgh University Press, 1991.

This is the published result of Charlton's doctoral thesis, for which he delved into the boxes of papers that Gray has deposited with the National Library of Scotland.

3. **Alasdair Gray: Critical Appreciations and a Bibliography** / edited by Phil Moores. Boston Spa: The British Library, 2002. xii, 241p; ill; £20.00 (hbk), £50.00 (limited)
ISBN: 0-7123-1129-7 (hbk); 0-7123-1134-3 (limited)

O. *Forthcoming Projects*

1. An illustrated anthology of British political songs covering ballads and folk songs up to the twentieth century, similar in style to *The Songs of Scotland.*

2. Illustrations for a collection of song lyrics by the Glasgow-based indie-pop band Belle and Sebastian.

3. A sequel to the *Book of Prefaces*, in which the twentieth-century prefaces that could not be included in the first book would be glossed and commented upon without necessarily printing the actual prefaces.

4. A collection of artwork to be published in 2003 to accompany a major travelling exhibition.

5. Dalkey Archive Press in the United States are planning to reprint some of Gray's out-of-print books, starting with *Poor Things*. Canongate are likely to do the same in the UK, beginning with a new paperback edition of *Lanark*.

P. *Internet Resources*

Alasdair Gray will launch his own website at www.alasdairgray.co.uk during 2002.

Although many of the books mentioned in this bibliography are out of print, some are still available to purchase from Morag McAlpine. For a list of available titles, email her at: morag@mcalpine44.freeserve.co.uk.

Q. *Phantoms*

1. **Tickly Mince and The Pie of Damocles**. Glasgow: Dog and Bone, 1990.

   160p; ill; £5.00; pbk   ISBN: 1-872536-12-3

   Despite the allocation of an ISBN and its appearance in various catalogues, this collection was never published. It was to contain the complete scripts of two stage reviews written by Gray, Liz Lochhead, Tom Leonard (all Mince and Pie) and James Kelman (just Pie). No plans exist to print it.

A SHORT TALE OF WOE!

JOE MURRAY

THE HEAT WAS BECOMING UNBEARABLE AS WE WALKED, SINGLE file, towards the *Jobs Allocation* window. The furnaces were running full blast giving off the only light in that dark, oppressive place. Up ahead as each poor soul approached, the iron window opened, items were handed out, then it closed again. All the while could be heard the overseer's monotonous: 'move along there, no holding up the queue.'

When I reached it, the window scraped back, a hand reached out and gave me a bucket, 'the *Clyde*', said a voice, 'empty it'. The window screeched shut.

The bucket was old, the handle was broken and the bottom had rusted through.

'But ... there's a hole in it,' I said, 'the job will be impossible.'

'Move along there, no holding up the queue,' said the overseer.

I held up the bucket for him to see, 'but this is impossible'.

'Move along there, no holding up the queue,' said the overseer.

The window eeyawrr'd open, 'problem?' asked the voice.

'There's a hole in the bucket,' I said meekly, 'the job will be impossible.'

'Hmm,' claw-like nails rattled a tattoo on the sill for a moment then the hand reached out and grabbed the bucket, dragging it back with a goattish laugh, 'okay, here, do this instead.'

A large pile of papers was pushed through as the voice shouted, 'right, big fella, you're on.'

The window closed with a clank that rang of finality.

An iron door at the side of the window opened and a big chap walked through with the first friendly smile I had seen since coming to this place. I recognised him immediately. I looked down at the pile of papers, the top sheet read: *The Book of Prefaces by Alasdair Gray: for typesetting within the next millennium.*

I banged on the window and cried, 'give me back my bucket! Please, please, give me back my fucking bucket!'

'Move along there, no holding up the queue,' said the overseer.

NOTES ON THE CONTRIBUTORS

Phil Moores grew up in Prescot, near Liverpool. In 1986 he moved to Yorkshire, where he studied sociology at Leeds University and met his wife-to-be. He now lives near Ripon, works for the British Library and writes fiction.

Will Self is the author of three collections of short stories: *The Quantity Theory of Insanity*, *Grey Area*, and *Tough Tough Toys for Tough Tough Boys*; three novellas *Cock & Bull* and *The Sweet Smell of Psychosis* (illustrated by Martin Rowson); three novels *My Idea of Fun, Great Apes* and *How the Dead Live*; three collections of journalism *Junk Mail, Sore Sites* and *Feeding Frenzy*; and together with David Gamble the photo-essay *Perfidious Man*. He contributes as a journalist to a plethora of publications and is a regular broadcaster on the BBC.

Philip Hobsbaum is Emeritus Professor, Research Fellow and Doctor of Letters of the University of Glasgow, where he taught literature for thirty-one years. A graduate of Cambridge and of Sheffield Universities, his publications include four books of poetry and seven critical books, including *Metre, Rhythm and Verse Form* (Routledge, 1996).

Alasdair Gray, author, artist, poet, playwright and scholar; the subject of this book.

Kathy Acker was born in New York in 1945 and died in 1997. She left behind a body of work both influential and controversial. Originally a poet, she turned to novel writing in the 1970s and is remembered for works such as *Blood and Guts in High School, Don Quixote, Kathy Goes to Haiti* and *Empire of the Senseless*.

Jonathan Coe is the author of six novels, including *What a Carve Up!*, *The House of Sleep* and *The Rotters' Club*.

S. B. Kelly is a poet and regular reviwer for *Scotland on Sunday*. He is curently working on a psychogeographical exploration of the Scottish Borders.

Elspeth King MA FMA was born in Fife, graduated in medieval history from the University of St Andrews and is a museum curator to trade. From 1974-1991 she was curator of the People's Palace in Glasgow. When Director of Dunfermline Heritage Trust, 1991-1994, she created Abbot House, now a main heritage and cultural centre in Fife. Since 1994, she has been Director of the Stirling Smith Art Gallery and Museum.

Angus Calder, born near London in 1942, is a poet and historian who lives in Edinburgh as a freelance writer after some years of 'teaching literature' in Africa, then for the Open University. His best known book is still *The People's War* (1969) but he has also written extensively on imperial history and on Scottish history and literature. His last collection of poems was *Horace in Tollcross* (2000), versions of the Roman poet set in present-day Edinburgh.

Stephen Bernstein is the author of *Alasdair Gray* (Bucknell UP, 1999) as well as articles on a variety of writers including James Kelman, Don DeLillo, Paul Auster, Samuel Beckett, Virginia Woolf, and Charles Dickens. He is an English professor at the University of Michigan-Flint, where he teaches courses on the Scottish novel, Victorian literature, literary theory, and Romanticism.

Kevin Williamson is a writer, editor and Alasdair Gray fan. In 1992 he founded Rebel Inc, going on to edit both Rebel Inc magazine (1992-95) and Rebel Inc book imprint (1996-2000). He is the author of *Drugs and the Party Line* (Rebel Inc, 1997) plus poetry, fiction and non-fiction in various magazines and newspapers. He is currently working on the third reincarnation of his ongoing Rebel Inc project (www.rebelinc.net) to be launched in 2002. Kevin lives and works in Edinburgh.

Joe Murray formerly worked as an engineer in the petro-chemical industries. He has since worked as a project co-ordinator and adult trainer mainly in computer information technology and media systems. He has been a typesetter and designer, a publisher, a founder editor of *West Coast Magazine*, co-founder of Taranis Books, and Mythic Horse Press, and co-produced almost all of the writers' events for Glasgow's

City of Culture bash in 1990. Joe's own works have appeared in various magazines, journals, anthologies and newspapers. He co-edited the short fiction anthology *Tales from the Coast* published by Taranis Books in 1991, and his short collection of poetry, *Ruchazie Moon and Some Other Poems*, was published by Neruda Press in 1998. Along with Alasdair Gray, he broadcast the programme *The Art of Making Books* for Radio Scotland in 1995. Joe is, at present, studying for an honours degree in Environmental Science and Ecology at Glasgow Caledonian University. The story related in this book was written after a difficult day working on Alasdair's *The Book of Prefaces* and was adapted from a joke once heard as a boy.

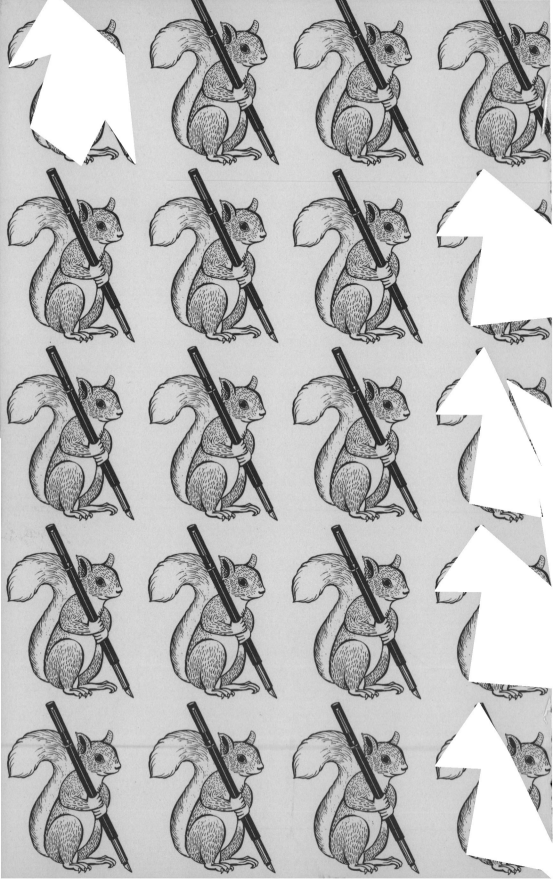